A SHORT HISTORY
OF OUR
TIMES

BY

J. A. SPENDER

GREENWOOD PRESS, PUBLISHERS
WESTPORT, CONNECTICUT

Originally published in 1934
by Cassell and Company, Ltd., London

First Greenwood Reprinting 1971

Library of Congress Catalogue Card Number 72-110865

SBN 8371-4538-4

Printed in the United States of America

PREFACE

I HAD been for some time at work on an extended history dealing in detail with the foreign and domestic events of our time when the need of a summarized version was strongly brought home to me by contact with teachers and students. Much of this period (1886 to 1932) is the "blind spot" of youth, in that it comprises events which have ceased to be politics but are not yet history, and are only known to the young by an oral tradition which grows dim and uncertain. To a previous generation this was relatively unimportant, but to the present generation some clear knowledge of the momentous events of the immediately preceding years is essential to any attempt to understand the present times.

I have therefore broken off my longer studies in order to make an effort to fill this gap by writing this book. There are of course special dangers and difficulties in any effort of this kind. The choice has to be made between leaving this history unwritten and bringing into it much that is still the subject of political controversy. My own impression is that the fear of politics has been carried to the point at which it threatens to deprive us of the history that is most serviceable at the time when it most needs to be written and taught. But it is quite impossible for anyone who has lived and worked through these times to write any account of them in which his own bias and personal opinions will not appear, and I will only say that I have endeavoured throughout this book to give the reader the facts which will enable him to form his own judgment, when he differs from mine.

Here and there I have borrowed a few phrases and sentences from previous books of my own, but I have not thought it necessary to trouble the reader with references.

J. A. SPENDER.

CONTENTS

CONTENTS

A SHORT HISTORY OF OUR TIMES

INTRODUCTION

As we look back on it, the period covered by this book has the appearance of a plunge into storm and strife after a long voyage in calm waters. A man born in England about the year 1820 might have lived to the end of a long life without having seen any great war or any serious challenge to the accepted principles of government. But if he had been born twenty years later and lived twenty years longer he would have seen greater and more sweeping changes than in any similar period of the world's history. He would have seen the map of Europe rolled up and redrawn after the greatest struggle of all time, old-established institutions everywhere challenged, and in his own country the polite competition of Whigs and Tories which he had known as politics in his youth, passing into the struggle of the great electorate to find safety and defend its standard of living in the economic confusion of the times. We are too near these events to do more than record them as facts, but there are certain clues which may help us to see their general tendency.

In foreign affairs Great Britain enjoyed a position of un-challenged authority for forty years after the Napoleonic wars. She was a little shaken by the Crimean War, which revealed the weakness of her military machine, and ten years later she received a sharp check in the affair of Schleswig-Holstein when her great Minister, Palmerston, was compelled by his Cabinet to beat a retreat in face of the rising power of Prussia under her formidable Minister, Bismarck. At the critical moment British Ministers, who had committed themselves deeply to support the Danes against Prussia, discovered that they would only have been able to put into the field 20,000 men armed with muzzle-loading rifles against 200,000 men armed with breech-loading rifles at the disposal of Prussia. Englishmen in these years thought of war as something to be waged by professional armies in remote regions without serious disturbance to the normal course of life at home, and they were taken aback by the sudden appearance of national armies, capable of indefinite expansion, on the European scene. The discovery of this new thing led to a rising demand for a policy of non-intervention in European affairs—the policy of "splendid isolation" as it came to be called—but it was at no time pursued with logic or consistency. British interests, or supposed interests, touched·those of other countries at too many points in Europe and the world, and the Palmerstonian tradition that the British voice should be heard whenever great affairs were being settled, proved too strong for the rôle of the disinterested spectator to be possible to any British Government.

Lord Beaconsfield in 1878 decided that Great Britain could not look on while Russia occupied Constantinople and dominated the Bosphorus and Dardanelles; Mr. Gladstone a little later became involved in European complications through the occupation of Egypt, and in the year 1885 decided that he must resist even to the point of war what seemed to be a Russian challenge on the Afghan frontier; Lord Rosebery in 1896 resigned the leadership of the Liberal party on the ground that a large number of its members, including the most pacifist, were pressing for a policy on behalf of the Christian subjects of the Sultan of Turkey which he thought would lead to war; Lord Salisbury at the end of his life found himself almost alone in his Cabinet in advocating isolation. Parties might differ as to the point which would justify intervention, but all parties had some point in mind which in their opinion would justify and even require it, and every British Foreign Minister had to bear in mind—though the British public might forget it— that the country was pledged to resist the violation of Belgian neutrality, which, as the years advanced, became a more and more probable incident of any war in Europe.

But the problem of British policy presented itself in a new aspect after the year 1894, when the conclusion of the Franco-Russian Alliance divided Europe into two camps and re-established the balance of power. The story from this time onwards is that of the effort to find security in the new conditions. The rôle most congenial to Great Britain and most in keeping with her past traditions was that of mediator between the European groups, and she endeavoured as long as possible to keep her hands free to play that part. During the greater part of the nineteenth century the idea persisted that France in Europe and Russia in Asia were the secular rivals, if not enemies, of Great Britain; and up to the end of the nineteenth century her preference was for a German alliance, if an alliance became necessary. The story of British foreign policy during the twenty years from 1894 to the Great War is that of the events which decided or compelled British Ministers to make common cause with their supposed traditional rivals and enemies against the rising power of Germany. As this story develops it will be found that the dominant fact was the construction of the great German fleet and the consequent threat to British sea-power. To prevent one Power dominating Europe and threatening the security and even the existence of the British Empire, was now, again, as in the eighteenth and early nineteenth centuries, the subconscious thought, if not the explicit aim, of British Ministers.

But if non-intervention was abandoned, the method of intervention was by no means decided. British Ministers and the greater part of the British public still cherished the idea that their Ententes with other Powers differed from " entangling alliances " in that the former left the decision for peace or war in the hands of the British Government and Parliament. Lord Salisbury had maintained this principle when Bismarck endeavoured to draw him into an alliance with Germany; his successors, Lord Lansdowne and Sir Edward Grey maintained it, when the French Entente was in question. " Military conversations " with their European friend they permitted as a necessary precaution when there was the possibility of war arising out of the promised " diplomatic support," but again and again it was repeated that these did not commit the country to an actual participation in war unless Parliament so decided. No question has been debated more in subsequent years than whether the acceptance of a binding alliance with France and Russia would have prevented war, or precipitated what is called a preventive war. Any conclusion on that matter requires the careful weighing of a vast number of complicated facts, both military and political, but it may be said that during these years the nations were more and more being bound together in a social, moral and economic interdependence which made it increasingly difficult for a great Power to stand outside the family of nations, or to be neutral in their struggles.

The immense and rapid development of applied science which characterized this period and produced this result must always be borne in mind by any student of history. It is likely enough that a future generation will judge that the art of government and the conduct of international affairs lagged far behind the advance of science in these years. Methods of statesmanship which served their purpose when nations were all but self-contained, when it took a fortnight to travel from Rome to London, and diplomatists waited on couriers, had suddenly to adapt themselves to a world vibrating with news and rumour, flashing its signals by day and by night over land and sea; provided with immense new facilities for travel and transport, tempting its merchant adventurers to race one another for places in the sun; a world in which the nations were developing an altogether new sense of contiguity and rivalry, which made it difficult for them to live together and impossible for them to live apart. Statesmen during these years continued to think of war as an inevitable and periodic clean-up of policy, which inflicted no irreparable or long-lasting injury upon the belligerents, and even in some ways advanced the common civilization, while science was preparing a kind of warfare which was all but wholesale slaughter, and came perilously near, on the first trial of it, to inflict a mortal wound on the common civilization. In these circumstances, the statesmen's specific of the balance of power was bound enormously to increase the scope and destructiveness of war when the peace was broken and the massed and evenly balanced forces of the great alliances came into collision.

In domestic affairs the education of the people and the extension of the franchise went hand in hand with a new awakening to the problem of poverty, which had been kept in the background or treated as an inevitable human condition by the industrial pioneers of the nineteenth century.

The world was moving more rapidly than those who lived in it realized, and the movement affected all classes.

It has been said that there were more changes in the outer aspects of life in the thirty middle years of the nineteenth century than in the thirty previous centuries, but the subsequent years surpassed even this period in the novelty and daring of its mechanical inventions. An enormous extension of steam-power, going hand in hand with the production of oil, added immensely to the output of industry, put a new type of great ship on the seas, and greatly extended the range of business and travel. The light oil engine made motor-car and aeroplane possible, all but abolished horse traffic and enabled privately owned vehicles to move at the speed of railway trains along roads specially designed to accommodate them (and many others to which they are extremely unsuitable). Rapid motion by land, sea and air became a fixed habit with vast numbers and the special demand of the rising generation. Electricity, meanwhile, seemed to be ushering in a new era of miracles with wireless telegraphy, cinema and broadcasting. The humblest listener now has his daily and nightly choice of great music, jazz, sermons, speeches, lectures, variety entertainments for a fee of ten shillings a year; and to speak across oceans from the telephone in his home or his office is the daily practice of the statesman, the man of business and the journalist. Accompanying these facilities and diversions there has been a world-wide development of sport, adding to the hours of leisure an excitement which is the counterpart of the increased pressure in hours of business. In the meantime the higher education of women, their enfranchisement, their entrance into many occupations and professions previously confined to men, their claim to equality in law and in daily life have greatly influenced the manners and customs as well as the thought and opinion of the country.

All through these years chemists and physicists were exploring both the infinitely great and the infinitely little, and discovering new principles and modes of action which profoundly changed the prevailing ideas about the universe and the nature of things. For the idea of a static universe governed by mechanical laws, most of which were supposed to have been discovered, there was now substituted the idea of a radio-active universe, vibrating with energy in the mass and in the atom, and inviting new and courageous speculations about its purpose and destiny.

The historian of morals may some day be able to trace the results on political and international affairs of the increased stimulus given to the human brain and other human faculties in these years. We are too near to generalize on that subject, but no one who was brought up in the nineteenth century and has lived into the twentieth can fail to be aware of the increased speed of modern life. We have still a vivid memory of the horrors of war, but events pass so rapidly that we scarcely realize the strain imposed on human brains and nerves by its aftermath, by the breathless chase of one emergency on the heels of another, by the accumulation in a few years of problems which in earlier times were spread over generations, even centuries, the enormous scale on which empires and institutions have crashed, and reconstructions have needed to be improvised. If it is possible with more or less accuracy to record the events of this period, the reader needs always to supply the background of passion and emotion against which they have gone forward.

CHAPTER I

IN 1871, when the Franco-German War ended, the great German Chancellor, Bismarck, saw the position of the new German Empire as one of great peril. France, he reflected, though defeated in war, was still the wealthier and more populous nation, and the wound inflicted on her by the German annexation of Alsace-Lorraine was one which she was unlikely to forgive or forget. He therefore wrote off the possibility of a reconciliation with her and sought security for Germany in an alliance of the monarchial Powers to keep her isolated and powerless for mischief. The Paris Commune and the establishment of a Republic in France gave him an opportunity of playing on the fears of the other European sovereigns for the stability of their thrones, and he used it to such effect that he induced the Austrian Emperor, upon whom only five years earlier he had inflicted a crushing defeat, to forget his grievances and join hands with his German and Russian brothers in the Three Emperors' League, the main purpose of which was to secure Germany against French revenge.

This League lasted nominally till the year 1887, but it was beset with difficulties from the beginning. In spite of their fear of France and its republican institutions, the other two Emperors were by no means inclined to devote themselves exclusively to German security or to accept a German ascendancy as the alternative to " the French peril." In 1875, when Bismarck was thought to be meditating another war with France, the Tsar actively intervened to keep the peace, and in the next two years developed a policy of his own which threatened to bring him into collision with Austria. During these years the Christian subjects of the Turks in Europe were in active rebellion against the oppression and misgovernment of their masters; and Russia, in virtue of race and religion, regarded herself as their natural patron and protector. In 1877 the world was ringing with the story of massacres and atrocities in Bulgaria; and after the other Powers had tried in vain to impose reforms on the Sultan, she resolved to act single-handed and declared war on Turkey.

This imposed a still greater strain upon the Three Emperors' League. Russia had previously obtained the consent of Austria, but when finally, after an exhausting struggle, she had the Turks at her mercy and proposed to wind up the war with the drastic Treaty of San Stefano, the Austrians declared the conditions proposed to be contrary to their agreement, and joined hands in threats and protests with Great Britain, which also saw a menace to her interests in the Mediterranean and the Near East in the "big Bulgaria" which Russia desired to create, and the occupation of Constantinople at which she was apparently aiming. The "integrity of the Ottoman Empire," in so far as it prevented the spread of Russian at the expense of Austrian or British interests in the Near East and ensured the closing of the Bosphorus and Dardanelles to Russian war-ships, was in those days supposed to be a common interest of Austria and Great Britain, the one being concerned to check Russian influence in the Balkans, the other to protect her road to India and her naval ascendancy in the Mediterranean from challenge by the Power which was thought to be her chief rival. Russia, therefore, found herself brought to a standstill at the gates of Constantinople.

The Berlin Congress and its Results

All through the spring of 1878 Europe was threatened with a war which, whatever other results it might have had, must have been fatal to the German policy of uniting the Three Emperors for the isolation of France. In England, Mr. Gladstone raised his powerful voice against the policy of bolstering up Turkey and perpetuating Turkish misrule for the convenience of Great Britain and Austria, and his agitation in the end proved fatal to the Government of Lord Beaconsfield which had adopted that policy. But this was two years after the event. Had Mr. Gladstone prevailed at the time and induced the Powers to co-operate in setting up a tolerable Government for the Christian subjects of the Turk, the whole subsequent history of Europe might have been different. But at that time, as later, the chief concern of the Powers was to prevent any of their rivals gaining at their expense in the dissolution of the Turkish Empire; and Bismarck, as he frankly said, cared nothing how their disputes were settled, so long as he could prevent Austria and Russia from fighting and keep the League of the Three Emperors in existence. When war threatened, he worked indefatigably for this purpose, and it was largely through his efforts that the peace was saved at the Congress of Berlin in 1878.

But at that Congress he was compelled to go beyond the part he had assigned to himself as " honest broker " between his allies, and to give his casting vote to Austria as against Russia. So at least the Russians said in their disappointment at being balked of the Treaty of San Stefano and at being compelled to concede the " Peace with Honour " which Lord Beaconsfield brought back from Berlin. The League of the Three Emperors still stood when the Congress ended and was formally renewed three years later, but it never recovered from the blow which it received in 1878. Being uncertain of his Russian ally, Bismarck now sought other ways of buttressing German security. In 1879 he concluded a secret treaty with Austria, in which the two Powers contracted to come to each other's assistance if either were attacked by Russia or by another Power with the support of Russia, an engagement which certainly was not in conformity with the spirit, even if it could be squared with the letter, of the Three Emperors' League. Two years later (1881) he brought Italy into the Triple Alliance with Austria and Germany, and shortly afterwards concluded a secret treaty with Rumania which made her to all intents and purposes a member of the same group.

Bismarck's Diplomacy

If statesmanship consists in skill and craft, the efforts of Bismarck in these years have never been surpassed. All over the field he worked with the one aim of promoting the interests and security of Germany. By encouraging France to seize Tunis he made sure that Italy, which had long cherished the dream of possessing that country, would be thrown back into the arms of Germany. By encouraging Great Britain to occupy

Egypt and inciting the French to protest against the occupation, he helped to drive a wedge between Britain and France. Wherever he saw a chance of dividing nations which might be formidable in combination, he was fertile in expedients of this kind, and he so worked that his hand should be as little seen as possible by those whom he was manipulating.

But as time went on the difficulty of keeping his friends united and his enemies divided steadily increased. In 1885 the chief part of the work done at the Berlin Congress was destroyed by the self-proclaimed union of the two Bulgarias, and sharp differences now developed between Russia and Austria about the government of the united province. The Tsar took strong objection to the efforts of his cousin, Prince Alexander of Battenberg, to establish himself as prince, and desired his own nominee to occupy that position. The Austrians objected to all the Russian nominees, and finally promoted the candidature of Duke Ferdinand of Coburg. The Serbians, meanwhile, demanded " compensation " for the aggrandizement of Bulgaria, and, failing to get it, attacked Bulgaria and were completely routed at the battle of Slivnitza. Prince Alexander greatly distinguished himself in this battle, but as the result incurred the wrath both of Austria, which intervened to save Serbia, and of Russia, which desired nothing less than that he should become a hero. In the end he was kidnapped by his own officers under Russian instigation, and after vainly endeavouring to appease the Tsar had to retire from the scene. For three years together, Russia and Austria glared at each other across their frontiers with mobilized or semi-mobilized armies, and it needed all the German Chancellor's ingenuity to keep the peace and play off the one against the other.

Britain, Germany and Russia

These events take us up to the year 1887 which has been called the zenith of Bismarck's diplomacy. That year is remarkable for two of his most skilful operations. First he persuaded the British Government to become a naval partner of the Triple Alliance, and by so doing was enabled to renew the Triple Alliance, which had all but foundered on Austria's objection to guarantee the Mediterranean interests and ambitions of Italy. Negotiations at the beginning of the year brought Britain and Italy together sufficiently to reassure Austria, and before the end of the year he had induced Lord Salisbury to enter into a formal agreement with Austria and Italy for joint action in the Mediterranean which could only be aimed at Russia. The British public and Parliament knew nothing of this agreement and its very existence remained for many years the most closely guarded secret of the Foreign Office.

In the course of the negotiations Bismarck had persuaded Lord Salisbury that by pledging her support to Austria and Italy, Great Britain would obtain a valuable guarantee against the designs of Russia, but that did not at all deter him from the second of his achievements of this year—the conclusion of the secret "Reinsurance Treaty" with Russia. The Tsar Alexander, who had been quarrelling with Austria, refused to renew the League of the Three Emperors, but he was willing to enter into a secret arrangement whereby Germany pledged herself to remain benevolently neutral if Austria attacked Russia, and Russia to do the same, if France attacked Germany. Austria, who had concluded a similar secret treaty with Germany behind the back of Russia in 1879 was now repaid in her own coin. Many attempts have been made to prove that the Austrian Secret Treaty, the Russian Reinsurance Treaty, the Triple Alliance, and the British-Austro-Italian-Mediterranean Agreement were in verbal conformity with one another, but there can at all events be no doubt that Bismarck's manœuvres with each of his partners in turn behind the backs of the others were contrary to the spirit of loyalty and candour to be expected between allies.

There was a brief period during the premiership of Jules Ferry when Bismarck endeavoured to make peace with France and induce her to accept the annexation of Alsace-Lorraine in return for German support of her colonial ambitions. But this ended abruptly in 1885, when Ferry was driven from power after the disaster which befell the French expedition in Tonquin. His successor, Freycinet, vetoed all flirtations with Germany, and appointed as his Minister for War the dashing Boulanger, who wrought the French public into a high state of military ardour by his bellicose speeches and fiery gestures. In the end Boulanger turned out to be only a flashy adventurer who lacked the nerve to seize power when opportunity offered, but for two years the ferment in France and the friction with Russia over the Bulgarian question left Bismarck in a constant state of apprehension lest these two Powers should join hands against Germany. In February, 1888, he came to the Reichstag demanding an increase in the German army by 700,000 men in order that it might be prepared for a war on two fronts. "We Germans," he said, "fear God but nothing else in the world." His speech on this occasion, nevertheless, made it evident that he feared a great many things and especially the "war on two fronts" which might result from a combination of France and Russia.

The Breakdown in Bismarck's Policy

Indeed by this time the original idea of winning security for Germany by the isolation of France was visibly breaking down, and looming ahead was the great divide which ranged the nations into two armed camps. In the months that remained to him Bismarck worked feverishly to patch and mend the cracking structure, or, failing this, to find substitutes for it in new combinations. Early in 1889 he approached Lord Salisbury with a positive proposal for a British-German Alliance, and after waiting three months for an answer, sent his son, Count Herbert Bismarck, to London to explore the ground. In spite of his Mediterranean agreement Lord Salisbury was still on the whole an upholder of splendid isolation for Great Britain, and pleading the unhappy nature of British parliamentary institutions which made it impossible for statesmen to act as they wished, he waved the proposal aside, " leaving it," in the diplomatic phrase, " on the table without saying yes or no."

This was Bismarck's final disappointment, for his sands were now rapidly running out. His old master, William I, had died in March, 1888, and after a few months of nominal reign as a hopeless invalid, his son, Frederick, had followed him to the grave. William II was now on the throne, and within a few months it became clear that there was no room in the German State for an old and illustrious statesman wielding a unique authority, and an impetuous young man claiming to be supreme and panting to take the direction of affairs into his own hands. March 10, 1890, the day of Bismarck's fall, is one of the decisive dates in European history. Germany from this time was embarked on what the young Kaiser called "the new course" which was to take her the whole way to her catastrophe in 1918.

The Great Divide

Within a few weeks the Kaiser and his new Chancellor had decided not to renew the "Reinsurance Treaty" with Russia which Bismarck had regarded as the corner-stone of his policy in the later years. Russia, thinking herself isolated in Europe, now began feeling her way toward France, which had abundant reasons for meeting her more than half-way. In the following year (1891) the two Powers came to the preliminary agreement which three years later led to the military Dual Alliance. There were many vicissitudes in the negotiations, and Alexander III had more than one cold fit about the propriety of allying himself with the "disreputable" French Republic. But the Germans in these years were again largely increasing their army with the openly expressed intention of guarding their Eastern frontier, and the Kaiser was claiming a position in the Near East, both as friend of the Sultan and protector of his Christian subjects, which was bound to bring him into collision with Russia. In 1894 the Tsar threw aside his doubts and scruples and entered into a formal alliance with France. From this time onwards the competition of Triple and Dual Alliance became the dominant factor in European politics.

. . . . .

Though the narratives of home and foreign affairs have generally to be told in separate chapters, it must always be remembered that they ran concurrently. Many of the transactions of these years were little, if at all, known to the public at the time, and it frequently happened that British Ministers were deeply involved in foreign crises of which the public knew nothing at a time when they seemed to be wholly occupied in domestic affairs.

CHAPTER II

FROM THE EIGHTIES TO THE NINETIES

THOUGH the reader of this book is assumed to be familiar with the general course of British domestic history up to the year 1886, a brief outline of the principal events in the immediately preceding years may help to the understanding of what follows. The classic Conservative Administration of Lord Beaconsfield had passed from the scene in 1880 when Mr. Gladstone returned to power to form his second Government. The life of that Government was a troubled one from beginning to end. South Africa, Egypt, India, Russia, and Ireland (the rise of Parnell, the Phœnix Park murders, the land question, Irish obstruction in Parliament) all presented it with problems of the greatest difficulty, and on some of them the group of able men composing the Cabinet held differing views, which led to dilatory or indecisive action. Its permanent legacy in foreign affairs was the occupation of Egypt, but that was marred at the time by the mishandling of the Sudan question, and the failure to relieve Gordon. In domestic affairs its chief achievement was the enfranchisement of the labourer, but on many other matters it was greatly divided between its Whig section under Lord Hartington (afterwards Duke of Devonshire) and its Radical section under Mr. Joseph Chamberlain; and in June, 1885, it came to an abrupt end, nominally on the defeat of an item in its Budget, but in reality through the dissensions of its members. Lord Salisbury succeeded as Prime Minister and Foreign Secretary, with a stop-gap Government which carried on until its defeat in the new Parliament in the following January, and the next few months were mainly occupied with the General Election which took place in November. The chief feature of this was Mr. Chamberlain's campaign with his " Unauthorized Programme " which seemed to open up a new era of advanced politics, and was joyfully welcomed both by the newly enfranchised labourer who was promised

" three acres and a cow " and by large numbers of town workmen.

The hopes raised at the election were doomed to disappointment. Under the new franchise Ireland for the first time returned a great majority of Parnellites and Home Rulers to the Imperial Parliament (85 out of a total of 103), and though the Liberals came back in a substantial majority, it was a little short of the number required to defeat a possible combination of Irish and Conservatives. Since it was quite certain that the Irish would vote with any Opposition against any Government which did not espouse their cause, it was now clear that a Liberal Government must either rely on Conservative support in resisting the Irish demand or be prepared to concede it. Mr. Gladstone was prepared. In the unceasing conflict between coercion and conciliation among his colleagues in the previous Parliament, he had more and more leant to conciliation, and he considered the return of a great Irish majority demanding Home Rule to be a decisive new fact which a Liberal and democratic party was bound to face.[1] Before Christmas, 1885, he had committed himself to Irish Home Rule, without, as appeared afterwards, consulting more than a few of his colleagues. He thereby caused a schism in the Liberal party which was profoundly to affect British politics for the next generation.

When the new Parliament assembled, the Liberals were united in turning the Conservative Government out of office, but deeply divided when Mr. Gladstone produced his Home Rule Bill. The defection of the Whigs under Lord Hartington was expected, but the final and crushing blow was the refusal of John Bright and Mr. Chamberlain to follow Mr. Gladstone's lead. This sealed the fate of his Home Rule Bill, which was rejected in the House of Commons by a majority of 30. In the election which followed the country endorsed this decision, and Lord Salisbury returned to power with a Conservative Government which, with the support of 74 Liberal Unionists, had a majority of 110 in the new House. To defend the Union and prevent the " disintegration of the Empire " were said

[1] Or indeed any party, for he offered his support to Conservative Ministers, if they would face it, and the Lord-Lieutenant of Ireland, Lord Carnarvon, who had had an interview with Mr Parnell before the election, seemed at one moment inclined to do so.

to be the main objects of the new Government, and Mr. Chamberlain, the former Radical leader, devoted himself to them with a whole-heartedness which was an unpleasant surprise to his former friends.

Mr. Gladstone had proposed to accompany his Home Rule Bill with a large scheme of land purchase, and in these days the land question was only less, if at all less, important than the question of Home Rule. Mr. Gladstone's policy having been rejected, the Irish retaliated with a violent agrarian agitation on a carefully organized " Plan of Campaign " for withholding all rents beyond the amount that they considered fair and applying the balance to an organized campaign for boycotting landlords and resisting evictions. To meet this the Government armed themselves with exceptional coercive powers which were drastically administered by the new Chief Secretary, Lord Salisbury's nephew, Mr. Arthur Balfour. For the next four years Government and Chief Secretary were engaged in perpetual struggles with the Irish members, many of whom were imprisoned under the " Crimes Act."

Feeling was greatly stirred on both sides of the Channel by various incidents in this conflict, and especially the determination of the Government to treat Irish political offenders as common criminals; and the new Chief Secretary, who till then had been regarded as little more than a clever amateur in politics, won himself the appellation of " bloody Balfour." " Remember Mitchelstown "—the scene of an eviction at which the Chief Secretary instructed the police " not to hesitate to shoot "—was for many years a battle-cry of the Irish. Mr. Balfour was fighting on difficult ground, for the Irish land system was admitted to be one of the worst in the world, and the grievances of the Irish tenants were very real. The Government endeavoured to allay them by extending the operation of judicial rents fixed by the land-courts set up under previous legislation, and by providing more money for land purchase, but experience was to prove that there was no remedy short of a complete buying-out of the landlords, and this was spread over many years. In the meantime Lord Salisbury prescribed " twenty years of resolute Government " as the right solution of the Irish problem.

The principal events in foreign policy during this Government—the conclusion of the Mediterranean Agreement of 1887, and the rejection of Prince Bismarck's overture for a British-German alliance—have been described in the previous chapter. In the tangled affairs of the Near East Lord Salisbury steered clear of the quarrel between Austria and Russia, and, to Bismarck's astonishment and annoyance, turned his back on the Treaty of Berlin, and refused to join the other Powers in re-establishing the *status quo* in Bulgaria and East Rumelia for which his former chief, Lord Beaconsfield, had been ready to go to war only eight years previously. He had never been a zealous supporter of this policy, and in these years he is seen gradually veering away from the pro-Turkish tradition of his party—the " backing of the wrong horse," as he called it at a later period. But he retained his suspicions of Russia and looked to the Triple Alliance to keep her in check.

The Death of Lord Iddesleigh

When he formed his second Government in July, 1886, Lord Salisbury made Lord Iddesleigh, better known as Sir Stafford Northcote, Foreign Secretary. There was no more respected member of the Tory party, and if long service, high character, gentle manners, and a well-earned reputation as the best of Conservative financiers were qualifications for this post, he was well chosen. But he was scarcely a match for Bismarck, who was using all his wiles to induce Great Britain to take the chestnuts out of the fire in Bulgaria and so save himself from the necessity of backing Austria against Russia. Lord Iddesleigh came perilously near to playing Bismarck's game in the month of September, thereby drawing a protest from Lord Randolph Churchill who gave the sound advice that Great Britain should do nothing unless she was sure of German as well as Austrian joint action. The British course was a wavering one during the next few weeks, and when Lord Salisbury reconstructed his Government after Lord Randolph's resignation he decided to take the Foreign Office himself. It was a painful decision for his old friend, Lord Iddesleigh, and the more so since he was left to learn of it for the first time in the newspapers. The same afternoon he called at Downing Street, and fell dead from heart disease in the presence of the Prime Minister. " As I looked upon the dead body stretched before

me I felt that politics was a cursed profession," wrote Lord
Salisbury in answer to a letter of condolence from Lord
Randolph. Mr. Gladstone had said that a Prime Minister in
forming a Government must act like a butcher, but he had
not seen any of his victims fall dead at his feet.

Lord Salisbury and Egypt

In 1887 Lord Salisbury's Government all but decided to
evacuate Egypt. In the eyes of Conservative Ministers the
occupation of that country was a legacy from the previous
Liberal Government which they had no great desire to take
up. It was associated with evil memories, like the death of
Gordon, and raised all manner of difficult questions for
the future. In 1885 Lord Randolph Churchill told Count
Herbert Bismarck that he was much more concerned about
Herat than about Egypt. It was, accordingly, one of Lord
Salisbury's first acts on becoming Prime Minister and Foreign
Secretary in 1885 to send Sir Henry Drummond Wolff to
Constantinople to negotiate with the Sultan for the evacuation
of the country. The negotiations resulted in the signing of
a Convention (May 22, 1887) whereby the British occupation
was to come to an end in three years, but Great Britain was to
have the right to prolong or renew it, if either internal peace
or external security were seriously threatened. France and
Russia, however, raised strong objection to this provision
and under pressure from the Sultan withdrew and declined
to ratify the Convention. The French afterwards bitterly
regretted their action, which, as it turned out, was to leave
the British occupation without serious challenge for an
indefinite number of years. During the next twenty years the
administration of Egypt under Lord Cromer was to be one of
the greatest and most beneficent achievements of British
imperialism. Having no nominal authority beyond that of
Agent or Consul-General, and living in great simplicity, he
yet to all intents and purposes governed the country, and with
the aid of an exceptionally able staff, set its finances in order,
banished corruption, and carried through great engineering
works which increased its water-supply and greatly added to
the prosperity of its peasantry.

The Partition of Africa

The struggle between the European Powers for possessions in Africa was a large part of foreign policy between 1886 and 1890. For the first ten years after the Franco-German War, Prince Bismarck had declared Germany to be a " sated Power," which not only had no ambition to obtain colonies herself, but actually desired her neighbours—and especially those who might give trouble to her in Europe—to be kept occupied in colonial expansion. But this was not an acceptable doctrine to German merchants and industrialists, who saw themselves being shut out from a lucrative trade by foreign competitors who raised tariff walls round their colonies as soon as they acquired them. The Germans watched jealously while King Leopold, the King of the Belgians, developed his scheme for a vast Congo State—notorious in later days for its cruel treatment of the natives—and when even little Portugal sought to acquire a great belt of territory, including the chief part of what is now called Rhodesia, stretching from Angola on the west coast to Mozambique on the east. Early in the eighties the cry went up from Germany that she too must have her place in the sun, and under this pressure Bismarck entered the field.

Thinking their position secure British Ministers had been slow to move, and were unpleasantly surprised when the German Chancellor started a vigorous diplomatic offensive and made himself extremely disagreeable to Lord Granville, then Foreign Minister, threatening to make trouble everywhere for Great Britain if she did not fall in with his plans for expansion in Africa. There was in those days no great enthusiasm in Downing Street for African colonies, and for the sake of a quiet life the Government conceded a good deal. Germany thus got her colony of South-West Africa (with the exception of Walfish Bay) and proclaimed Protectorates over Togoland and the Cameroons, having just got in front of the British Consul, who had been instructed to hoist the British flag over some part of the same region.

French and British, meanwhile, were racing each other for the control of the lower Niger, but here the British National African Company, afterwards the Royal Niger Company, under the spirited leadership of Sir Taubman Goldie, distanced their rivals and eventually bought them out. France in these years had acquired Tunisia, and was extending her influence in Morocco, but she had her eye also on Central Africa and cherished far-reaching ambitions for extending the French Congo to the head-waters of the Nile. These received their final check when Major Marchand encountered Kitchener at Fashoda in 1898, but by this time the French had made good their claim to a large part of the intervening territory, the Upper Nile, Senegal, Lake Chad, etc., and when the Great War came drew from it a large number of black and Senegalese troops. Italy too was in the field seeking to obtain a footing on the Red Sea coast in Somaliland and Eritrea, where she established herself after serious reverses at the hands of the Abyssinians; and Spain entered large and vague claims to parts of Morocco and the north-west coast. During the same years Great Britain and Germany were in perpetual conflict about the east coast, but after hard bargaining, in the course of which Lord Salisbury ceded Heligoland to Germany in return for a British Protectorate over the dominions of the Sultan of Zanzibar, the limits of German East Africa were laid down and Uganda definitely assigned to Great Britain.

These rivalries, and the perpetual claims and counter-claims to which they gave rise, as explorers and adventurers crossed each other's tracks and hoisted their respective flags on the same ground, had serious results upon the relations of the Powers. At a conference in Berlin in February, 1885, an effort had been made to lay down rules for the Congo and Niger basins, but these were very imperfectly observed even in that region, and elsewhere the scramble continued unabated until 1890-1, when a series of treaties was concluded between the Powers, which were in effect a partition of Africa. Under a British-German agreement, the two Powers defined their spheres of influence in East, West and South-West Africa; and under a similar agreement, France recognized British influence between the Niger and Lake Chad in return for British recognition of the French Protectorate over Madagascar, and French influence in the Sahara and the North-West. This was far from the end of the story. Even more exciting phases were to come when Cecil Rhodes appeared on the scene, and began working northwards from the south, and when Marchand appeared on the Nile after the British re-conquest of the Sudan. But the treaties of 1890-1 served to keep the peace and abate the more serious friction for the time being.

Domestic Affairs

Lord Salisbury's Government suffered a sharp blow a few months after it was formed from the impetuous resignation of its Chancellor of the Exchequer, Lord Randolph Churchill, as a protest against extravagant expenditure. That ended pre-maturely the career of one of the most brilliant Ruperts of politics, whose audacious speeches and advocacy of "Tory democracy" had been of great service to his party. Lord Randolph said afterwards that he had "forgotten Goschen," a former Liberal Minister and recognized authority on finance, who succeeded him at the Exchequer, and made his term of office memorable by the conversion of Consols to 2¾ per cent. As a starting-point in the unfolding story of national finance, it may be convenient for the reader to bear in mind that the Budget from which Lord Randolph Churchill recoiled in horror was a "ninety million Budget," and that in 1887 Mr. Goschen effectively dished his predecessor by bringing the national expenditure down to £87,000,000, and reducing the income-tax from sevenpence to sixpence.

Queen Victoria's Jubilee

The supreme moment in the year 1887 was the great ceremonial in Westminster Abbey on June 21 to celebrate the Jubilee of Queen Victoria. Surrounded by an imposing company of royal guests from Europe, Indian princes, British statesmen, officials and soldiers, and Ministers from the self-governing colonies, the Queen gave thanks for the fifty years of her reign. It was the first of the festivals of British Imperial-ism and everything conspired to lend lustre to the occasion. The Empire, which till then had taken itself for granted, seemed suddenly to have become self-conscious. It was the theme of eloquent perorations, and inspired writers and poets to their highest efforts. All the omens were said to be auspicious. The great conspiracy to disintegrate the United Kingdom had been defeated; India was loyal, the self-governing colonies offered their homage. The Queen's Ministers were men whom she trusted, and who could be trusted to uphold the dignity and prestige of Great Britain in Europe and over the seas.

The occasion marked the first effort to bring the self-governing dominions, or colonies as they were still called, into council with the Imperial Government. The Colonial Ministers who came as delegates to the Jubilee assembled in conference, discussed various legal and technical questions and were addressed by Lord Salisbury, who deprecated all ambitious constitutional schemes, and described the plans for Imperial Federation, which were already in the air, as "nebulous matter which in the course of ages would cool down into material and practical results." In the present age he was not for a general Union or a Zollverein—an Empire behind a tariff wall—but for a *Kriegsverein*—a combination for purposes of self-defence. He dwelt on the importance of the "shield thrown over the colonies by the Imperial connexion," and said that their unity rested on the "most solid and reasonable foundations of self-interest and security."

Local Government

In domestic politics the chief achievements of the Government were the reform of local government by the Act of 1888, which established elective Councils in the Counties and County Boroughs of Great Britain, and the abolition of fees in elementary schools (1891). The London County Council, which was established by a special Act, astonished and alarmed its parents by falling into the hands of a vigorous Progressive majority, largely influenced by Fabian Socialists, which did important and useful work for London during the next twenty years. Its first chairman was Lord Rosebery, who greatly added to his own reputation by the skill and energy with which he launched the new authority on its career. Eleven years later (1899) another Unionist Government passed another Act creating twenty-eight London Boroughs, each with its separate mayor and municipality—largely, it was thought at the time, to limit the activities and ambitions of the County Council.

From the year 1888 onwards the Government seemed to be losing ground in the country. Liberals, under Mr. Gladstone's indefatigable leadership, had been active in educating the public on the Irish question and in 1891 they launched their " Newcastle Programme " which opened up a long vista of social reform. They were greatly encouraged in the spring of 1890 by the exposure in the Parnell Commission of the Pigott forgeries, purporting to implicate the Irish leader in the Phœnix Park murders, to which Ministers and the Unionist party had rashly pinned their faith. Pigott, the forger, collapsed in the witness-box under the merciless cross-examination of Sir Charles Russell—afterwards Lord Chief Justice—and fled to Spain, where he committed suicide.

Everything now seemed to point to the return of Mr. Gladstone to power with a great majority. But in the autumn of 1890 there came the shattering blow of the Parnell Divorce, and—equally damaging—the schism in the Irish party to which it gave rise. Parnell's intrigue with Mrs. O'Shea had for long been a very open secret, but it was the kind of secret which would not bear exposure either to Catholic Ireland or to Protestant England, and in the confusion which followed, British fears of Irish Home Rule revived and the Unionist party recovered much of its lost ground. When the election came in July, 1892, the Liberals struggled back with a majority of no more than 40, including the Irish, and Mr. Gladstone's majority in his citadel at Midlothian had dwindled from 4000 to 690

Mr. Gladstone's Last Government

The Liberal leaders confided to one another that such a victory was worse than a defeat. Mr. Gladstone himself had declared it to be highly desirable that any party which propounded a solution of the Irish question should have a majority independent of the Irish party, and he now found himself dependent for even a bare majority on the Irish party which itself was deeply divided. But nothing daunted this old warrior, and when the new Parliament assembled, Liberals and Irish voted together to displace the Unionist Government, and decided to proceed as if they were entrenched in power with all the parliamentary forces behind them.

Mr. Gladstone thus formed his fourth and last Administration. It was a Government of all the talents with able and distinguished men in the chief departments. It contained three future Prime Ministers, Lord Rosebery as Foreign Secretary, Mr. Campbell-Bannerman as Secretary for War, and Mr. Asquith at the Home Office. Mr. John Morley, a famous man of letters who had rallied to Mr. Gladstone in 1886, was again Irish Chief Secretary. Within a week of his appointment he had suspended the Crimes Act, and in his own words " lifted Coercion off the back of Ireland." Ministers decided at once that, though Liberal legislation might be difficult, they would do their utmost to make administration progressive. Home Office, Education Office, Local Government Board, set to work to infuse a Liberal spirit into the departments and were soon engaged in sharp controversy with those who preferred the old ways. In the meantime Mr. Gladstone was again at work on the formidable task of preparing and carrying through the House of Commons a Home Rule Bill for Ireland, undeterred by the certain doom which awaited it at the hands of the House of Lords.

It was, for a man of eighty-five, an amazing performance to which even his most persistent opponents bore tribute. " I have known Mr. Gladstone for more than seventeen years," said Mr. Chamberlain in a speech at Birmingham shortly after Mr. Gladstone's retirement in 1894, " and never have I known his energy more remarkable, his resources more infinite, his eloquence more persuasive, or his skill in debate more admirable than during the last twelve months, and during the course of the discussions on the Home Rule Bill." Day after day and up to midnight and beyond the old Prime Minister was in his place in the House of Commons, drawing the fire and returning it, picking up every challenge, inexhaustible in persuasion and remonstrance, and no less in the parliamentary arts of turning corners and parrying thrusts. It was all useless. No argument about the strictly subordinate character of the proposed Irish Parliament prevailed against the view of its opponents that it meant separation and the disruption of the Empire. When the Bill reached the House of Lords it was rejected by a majority of 419 to 41 on its second reading

(September 8, 1893). Parliamentary Home Rule was thus buried for nearly twenty years.

Before the end of 1893 the Lords had attacked other Liberal legislation, laying heavy hands on the Parish Councils Bill, and so amending the Employers' Liability Bill that the Cabinet decided to abandon it. There was clearly little to be done by legislation which was liable to this handling in the second Chamber. Mr. Gladstone was for dissolving Parliament and making another appeal to the country, this time covering the whole issue of Lords and Commons. His colleagues thought otherwise, and saw advantage in pursuing Liberal ideas in the field of finance, at that time supposed to be out of reach of the House of Lords. But Mr. Gladstone's eyesight was failing, and he had little heart for other causes than that to which he had dedicated the last years of his life. In March, 1894, he found himself at variance with his colleagues about the Naval estimates which they thought necessary for the coming year. The stern economist in him rebelled against expenditure for more armaments in a world which he hoped would be at peace, and he insisted on resigning. He pleaded his eyesight as the cause, but there were other causes.

Queen Victoria parted from him without regret. She had never forgiven the defeat at his hands of her favourite Prime Minister, Lord Beaconsfield, and she considered the whole of his later career to have been mischievous and subversive. In the memorandum in which he has recorded his final audience with the Queen he describes the conversation as " neither here nor there." " There was not a syllable on the past, except a repetition, an emphatic repetition, of the thanks she had long ago amply rendered for what I had done, a service of no great merit, in the matter of the Duke of Coburg, and which I assured her would not now escape my notice if occasion should arise. There was the question of eyes and ears, of German versus English oculists, she believing in the German as decidedly superior. Some reference to my wife, with whom she had had an interview and ended it affectionately—and various nothings." She did not discuss public affairs with him or ask his advice about his successor. In this her parting with the most illustrious of her Prime Ministers after sixty years' service, Mr. Gladstone saw " a great sincerity."

Lord Rosebery, Prime Minister 1894–5

The Queen set speculation at rest about Mr. Gladstone's successor by sending for Lord Rosebery, then Foreign Secretary. It was within the discretion of the Cabinet to accept him or not, and by refusing to serve under him Ministers might have compelled a different choice. Sir William Harcourt, the Chancellor of the Exchequer, was greatly Lord Rosebery's senior, and he had all the advantages in what parliamentarians call "claims." But he had a quick temper, and though easily appeased himself when a storm had blown over, had inflicted wounds on a great many of his colleagues which they did not so easily forget. They asked themselves what, if he was so difficult as Chancellor of the Exchequer, would he be like as Prime Minister? The Queen's choice relieved them of the necessity of answering the question, and they accepted it without demur. But Harcourt, who was a formidable man in debate, had many warm supporters in the House of Commons and in the country, and these judged that a sound Radical and great House of Commons man had been passed over for a young peer who was supposed to be a Whig and a Jingo. Morley, who at the beginning had supported Rosebery, was dissatisfied with the distribution of places in the new Government, and became one of the Prime Minister's severest critics from that time onwards. This breach between the Prime Minister leading the party in the House of Lords and the Chancellor of the Exchequer leading it in the Commons led to perpetual friction in the Cabinet and division among the rank and file. A year of office on these conditions broke Lord Rosebery's nerve and reduced him to chronic sleeplessness. He said at the end that the position of a Prime Minister in the House of Lords was an impossible one unless he had a twin to lead in the House of Commons, and he vowed that he would never again be Prime Minister, or accept office in any Government except on his own terms.

Sir William Harcourt's Budget

The parliamentary honours of the last year of the Government fell nevertheless to Sir William Harcourt, whose Budget extending the old probate duties to all property, real and personal, passing at death, occupied the chief part of the session of 1895 and was the subject of heated controversy. The amounts levied, which rose to a maximum of 8 per cent. on the largest estates, may seem merciful by the standard set in later times, but the principle was new, and Conservatives professed to see in it the dismantling of ancient homes and the ruin of the countryside. It added to their exasperation that, according to the rule held inviolable until fifteen years later, this measure was beyond the reach of the House of Lords, which would have shown it scant mercy if it had had the chance. The Budget had its opponents even in the Liberal party, and the Prime Minister himself was supposed to have been only a reluctant convert, but Sir William had his way, and the taxes were carried substantially as he proposed. They had none of the immediate effects predicted of them; with wealth increasing, the rich men who were hardest hit easily absorbed them, and Conservative as well as Liberal Chancellors of the Exchequer came to regard them as an invaluable source of revenue. It was reserved for a future generation in stress of circumstances unimagined in 1894 to raise them to a level at which they had undoubtedly some of the results predicted by alarmists in that year.

The Government staggered on into the summer of 1895, adding to its other burdens a heroic attempt to pass a Welsh Disestablishment Bill with a majority which was seldom more than twenty, and which, with the slightest lack of vigilance, might be wiped out. Liberal members almost lived in the House of Commons and the session was long remembered as the most arduous in their experience. But the end was inevitable, and it came in a snap division on the vote for cordite in the Army estimates. The point at issue was trivial, but Ministers had reached the end of their tether and accepted the division with relief.

Liberal Achievements and Dissensions

When the Liberal Government was formed in 1892 very few had thought it possible that it could live for more than a year, and its survival for three years surpassed all expectations. Though its principal measures were doomed to failure, it played an important part in parliamentary history. It set a new example in administration, and some of its members, notably Asquith at the Home Office, and Acland at the Education Office, left a lasting mark on their departments. It gave the first serious impetus to social reform, and kindled new hopes in its younger supporters, who welcomed any departure from conventional party politics. It opened the battle with the House of Lords which was to come to its issue seventeen years later. In all these respects it blazed new trails, and made a definite breach between the new Liberalism and the Whig individualism of previous years.

Foreign affairs were by no means uneventful during the three years of this Government. There was perpetual friction with France, which pursued what was called at the time a " policy of pin-pricks " in Egypt, Siam, Madagascar, Morocco, and anywhere else in the world where the interests of the two countries were in contact. On the evening of July 30, 1893, a report reached London that a French naval squadron had peremptorily ordered the withdrawal of British gunboats in Siam, and for forty-eight hours it was in doubt whether this would not lead immediately to war. In the cool light of day the incident was explained as a misunderstanding, and was wound up by a suitable explanation ; but it caused great excitement while it lasted, and the German Emperor, who happened to be visiting Cowes, leapt to the idea of a great war in which France would be worsted and Great Britain compelled to join her fortunes to those of the Triple Alliance. This turned out to be only the dream—or nightmare—of a day.

These foreign affairs revealed a sharp line of cleavage in the Liberal party between Radical " little Englanders " who favoured a policy of non-intervention and disarmament, and " Liberal Imperialists " who wished their party to keep abreast of the movement towards expansion and self-assertion which was stirring all the nations in the last years of the century. Sir William Harcourt and Mr. Morley belonged to the former school, Lord Rosebery and the Under-Secretary for Foreign Affairs, Sir Edward Grey, to the latter. The " little Englanders " had looked on uneasily when Lord Rosebery used firm language to the French about the incident in Siam in 1893, and again in 1895 when the " Grey declaration " was formulated warning the French that their appearance in the Upper Nile would be regarded as an "unfriendly act" by the British Government. Though Harcourt and Morley were parties to these proceedings, they detected "jingoism" in the tone and manner of their colleagues, and a schism started between the two schools which lasted right up to the Great War, if indeed it ended then. It was the old contention between Palmerston and John Bright in a new form, and represented a real difference of temperament and outlook which was not easily composed between men of the same party. Lord Rosebery and Sir Edward Grey stood frankly for continuity of foreign policy through changes of Government; the "little Englanders" regarded the established policy, when the Liberals took office in 1892, as a legacy from the Tory jingoism of Lord Beaconsfield and greatly wished it to be changed.

These personal and political differences threw the Liberal party into confusion when the election came in August, 1895. Different leaders hoisted different standards, the Prime Minister appealing for a majority to deal with the House of Lords, while Morley put Home Rule first, and Harcourt, who lost his seat at Derby, devoted the chief part of his campaign to Local Option for public-house licences. In the result the Liberal party was heavily defeated, and the Unionists returned to power with a majority of 152.

The Liberal leaders continued to be distracted by their dissensions out of office as in it. In 1896 Mr. Gladstone came out of his retirement to advocate strong action against the Turks for the prevention of Armenian massacres, whereupon Lord Rosebery resigned his leadership on the gound that Mr. Gladstone had made his position impossible by advocating a policy which he thought too dangerous. Two years later Sir William Harcourt resigned his leadership on the ground that it had been made impossible by the action of Lord Rosebery and his friends. Sir Henry Campbell-Bannerman, who succeeded Harcourt, was a man of tough fibre and more equable temperament, but he too lived an uneasy life before his position was secure.

CHAPTER III

BY the middle of August, 1895, Lord Salisbury was again in office, and the Unionist party entered upon its longest continuous stretch of power. It was now the Conservative party with a difference, for the Liberal Unionists had decided to enter the Government, the Duke of Devonshire (as Lord Hartington had now become) being appointed Lord President of the Council, and Mr. Chamberlain Colonial Secretary. The main object of the Government in domestic politics was to resist Home Rule, and except for a serviceable extension of Employers' Liability and certain cautious changes in the Irish land laws, its legislation was unimportant. But its general tone and spirit were in harmony with the spirit of the times. Imperialism was the watchword of the hour, and in the popular mind the new Government stood not only for the integrity of the Empire threatened by Irish separatists, but for its expansion by a spirited colonial policy. Poets and literary men, Kipling, Henley and others, wrote of the glories of Empire, sang songs of the sword, and extolled the martial virtues; statesmen and politicians abounded in eloquent perorations on the same theme. A new Elizabethan era was said to be dawning. The fame of Cecil Rhodes was at its highest, and his great design of British dominion from the Cape to the Zambesi and an " all-red " British route from the Cape to Cairo was in high favour. To develop new markets for British traders threatened by competition in Europe, and with that object to carry the flag into all promising but unexploited regions was the declared policy of the new Colonial Secretary, Mr. Chamberlain, who seemed to have exactly the pushful and enterprising spirit that the times demanded.

Venezuela and the U.S.A.

Lord Salisbury had not been many months in office before he found himself involved in a sharp dispute with the United States on the question of the boundary between the State of Venezuela and British Guiana. It was in itself a trivial affair, concerning a few square miles of swamp and jungle, but President Cleveland saw in it a challenge to the American Monroe Doctrine, which since the beginning of the nineteenth century had been a diplomatic sign-post warning European Governments off intervention on the American Continent. In their dispute with Great Britain, the Venezuelans appealed to the Government of the United States, which warmly espoused their cause and announced through the President that it " would resist by every means in its power as a wilful aggression upon its rights and interests " the appropriation by Great Britain of any territory which " after investigation it had determined of right belonged to Venezuela." President Cleveland added that in saying this he " was fully alive to the responsibility incurred and to the consequences that may follow." (December, 1895.)

Lord Salisbury, who appears to have forgotten the Monroe Doctrine, was greatly astonished at this language, and for a short time there was ominous talk about the " consequences " indicated in this passage. Angry dispatches passed between the two Governments, and for some months it looked as if no solution could be found. But both the British and American publics were keenly alive to the absurdity and wickedness of starting a great war on a matter about which neither of them cared two straws, and after an interval in which it remained dormant, the question was settled amicably by arbitration (1899). The incident was, nevertheless, a sharp warning of possible causes of trouble with the United States to which, till then, scarcely a thought had been given. In 1903, when it was a question of collecting debts with the aid of gun-boats in the same Central American State, Germany drew down upon herself an even sharper warning, but on this occasion the British Government, which had learnt from experience, was careful not to offend American susceptibilities.

The Jameson Raid

Before the year 1895 was out, South Africa, on which the highest hopes were built, had involved the Government in serious trouble. The discovery of gold in the Transvaal had caused a bitter quarrel between Dutch and British in that State. President Kruger and his Dutch burghers, though very willing that the gold should be worked in so far as it enriched their country, were extremely unwilling to admit the gold-seekers on terms of equality with their own citizens. They saw themselves in danger of being swamped by a crowd of new-comers under British influence, and sought safety by imposing disabilities which the new-comers greatly resented. All through the years 1894–1895, the latter were laying their plans to throw off the Kruger yoke. There was to be a " bloodless revolution " in Johannesburg, the centre of the mining industry, and this was to be supported at the critical moment by an incursion of Chartered Company's troops, which the Colonial Office had somewhat incautiously per-mitted to be brought down from the north to a strip of territory on the Bechuanaland border of the Transvaal. Kruger, it was anticipated, would be helpless between the rising from within and the attack from without, and would accept the inevitable without serious resistance.

The sequel unfortunately was far otherwise. Dissensions broke out among the conspirators; some wanted the new regime to be under the British flag; others wished for a new independent republic; very few were willing to face a struggle in arms with President Kruger, who had learnt of their plans and was evidently preparing to meet them. In the middle of this confusion Dr. Jameson broke loose and made a dash for Johannesburg with his 500 troopers. (December 31, 1895.) It was a feather-brained enterprise, doomed to failure from the start, and he and his men were easily intercepted and captured by the Boers. A falsely dated letter, evidently prepared beforehand, suggesting that he had acted on an urgent call to rescue women and children in Johannesburg added to the mortification of the whole sorry business.

Results of the Raid

The effects were lamentable both in Africa and in Europe. Rhodes's life-long policy of working with the Dutch was destroyed at a stroke. All the Dutch throughout the sub-continent rallied to the Transvaal; the foundations were laid for an alliance between the Transvaal and the Orange Free State, which hitherto had been friendly to the British.

This was bad enough, but European complications followed. The German Emperor, who all through the previous year had been manifesting his sympathy with the Boers, now sent a telegram to President Kruger, expressing " sincere con-gratulations that, supported by your people, without appealing for the help of friendly Powers, you have succeeded by your own energetic action against armed bands which invaded your country as disturbers of the peace, and have thus been enabled to restore peace and safeguard the independence of the country against attacks from outside." (January 3, 1896.) At the same time he instructed the German Ambassador in London to inquire " at once in the proper official quarter whether the British Government approves of the crossing of the frontier of the Transvaal State by the Chartered Company's troops," and, if he gained the impression that it did, to ask for his passports. The Ambassador wisely kept this communication in his pocket, and having, as he records, " spoken no word to Lord Salisbury which could be construed as a threat," easily obtained the desired disclaimer and an assurance that the raiders would be faithfully dealt with when the facts had been ascertained. But the Emperor's telegram kindled wrath in Great Britain, and turned mortification at Jameson's fiasco into a new channel. President Kruger was now said to be displayed in his true colours—intriguing with the German Emperor and relying on his aid to defy the British power in South Africa. Self-respect was restored; the Government mobilized a flying squadron, and it was widely believed that the raid was a gallant, if misguided effort, to thwart a German conspiracy in South Africa.

The South African Committee

All this was highly unfavourable to the cool counsels and even-handed justice which the situation demanded. The

Boer Government acted wisely in releasing Dr. Jameson and his troopers and handing them over to the Imperial authorities for trial at home, but largely neutralized this act by proceeding rigorously against the Johannesburg conspirators, four of whom were actually sentenced to death, though the sentence was afterwards commuted to fines and terms of imprisonment. London retaliated by making a hero of Jameson, and he and his men were thought to have more than expiated their offence when they were tried and sentenced to short terms of imprisonment. The Government meanwhile had promised a strict inquiry into the whole affair, including the allegations of its own complicity, and a Select Committee of the House of Commons was appointed to pursue the investigation.

This committee sat during the first six months of 1897, and finally produced a Report which denounced Rhodes and gravely censured two colonial officials in South Africa, but returned a decisive negative to the question "whether the Colonial Office officials at home had received information that could be assumed to convey a warning of the impending incursion." The proceedings of this committee were far from satisfactory. Instead of taking the whole blame upon himself, Rhodes let it be known that his agents had been in constant communication with the Colonial Office before the raid, and that they had sent him a series of telegrams which he had used to "support his action." His representatives refused to produce the most important of these telegrams, and the committee took no steps to compel them to do so. It was Rhodes's case that Jameson had acted without his consent, and in so doing had "upset his apple-cart," but he seemed to suggest that the Colonial Secretary, Mr. Chamberlain, had an equal responsibility for the conspiracy, of which in the original plan, the raid was to have been the climax, and the fact that the Colonial Office had sanctioned the assembling of the troops on the Transvaal border, lent colour to the suspicion. It was in any case a fine line which divided the precautionary measure which the Colonial Office ought to have taken, if it had reason to expect trouble in the Transvaal, from the appearance of encouraging or fomenting trouble from which it ought rigidly to have held aloof; and suspicion was greatly aggravated when in the debate on the Report in the House of Commons (July 26, 1897), Mr. Chamberlain, apparently acting under extreme pressure, gave Rhodes a certificate that nothing " affecting his personal position as a man of honour " had been revealed in the inquiry. This was a shock to other members of the committee and especially to Sir William Harcourt, who held that it was by no means compatible with their report.

In the end, Rhodes saved his Privy Councillorship and the South African Company its charter, but the opportunity had been lost of doing what the Boers and the rest of the world would have regarded as courageous and even-handed justice. Rhodes largely redeemed his reputation by the skill and daring with which he ended the formidable Matabele rebellion of March, 1896, when he went alone and unarmed to the Matoppo Hills to palaver with the chiefs. But peace between British and Dutch had by this time become all but hopeless in South Africa; the trouble in the Transvaal was increasing and President Kruger had declined Mr. Chamberlain's invitation to come to London and negotiate amicably for a solution. In 1897 Sir Alfred Milner, who had won a distinguished reputation for himself, first as a journalist and afterwards as a civil servant and Chairman of the Board of Inland Revenue, was appointed Governor of the Cape, and it was generally believed that British policy was entering on a new course.

The Diamond Jubilee

In 1897 Queen Victoria celebrated her Diamond Jubilee. The Royal Family had suffered many losses and changes since the previous celebration. In 1892 the Prince of Wales's eldest son, Prince Albert Victor, Duke of Clarence, had died after a short illness ; and his brother, Prince George, Duke of York, was now in the direct line of succession to the throne. The following year (1894) Prince George married Princess May (daughter of the Duke and Duchess of Teck), who had formerly been affianced to his elder brother. A year later the Queen suffered a heavy loss in the death, from fever in the Ashanti Expedition, of her favourite son-in-law, Prince Henry of Battenberg, the husband of Princess Beatrice. The ten years had aged her, and in 1897 she was not equal to the ceremonial in Westminster Abbey which had been the climax of the previous Jubilee. But she drove through the streets, appearing as " the little old lady in black " in the heart of a great procession symbolic of her Empire; and stopped in front of St. Paul's Cathedral, where a brief service was held. Empire was the note of this celebration as of the last, and at the moment there seemed to be no shadow on the imperial scene. But the glittering display suggested some quieter reflections, and as the Captains and the Kings departed, Mr. Kipling wrote his famous " Recessional."

The Reconquest of the Sudan

Apart from South Africa, foreign policy in the years 1897 and 1898 was mainly concerned with the affairs of Egypt and the Far East. In Egypt it had long been recognized that the reconquest of the Sudan, which had been left severely alone after the death of General Gordon in 1885, would sooner or later become a necessity. That vast region and the head-waters of the river which is the life of Egypt was in the hands of fanatical tribes under a religious zealot who might at any moment take it into his head to invade Upper Egypt and raise the banner of the prophet among the fellahin. Lord Cromer and the British Administration in Egypt considered it their duty to relieve the country of this chronic danger, and to bring back under orderly government a great stretch of territory which had once been attached to Egypt. Mingling with these practical considerations the idea of avenging Gordon undoubtedly played some part in the British mind and with the British public.

The task was accomplished between 1896 and 1898 by the systematic construction of a railway and accompanying military expeditions to make good the ground as it advanced. Sir Herbert (afterwards Lord) Kitchener, who had been appointed Sirdar of the Egyptian army in 1892, was the presiding genius, and by the end of 1896 he had recovered the Province of Dongola and driven the Dervishes south. So far, he had carried his railway along the right bank of the Nile, but in 1897 he conceived the bold idea of running it straight across the Nubian desert from Wady Halfa, and so cutting off the great angle of the Nile between that place and Abu Hamed, which was within striking distance of Khartoum. At the beginning of 1898 the Mahdi, seeing himself threatened, began to send his forces north, and Kitchener engaged and defeated them on the Atbara on April 8. The way was now clear for the final advance to Khartoum, and at the battle of Omdurman on September 2, the Mahdi's army—40,000 strong under the Khalifa—was practically destroyed, losing 10,000 killed, as many wounded and 5000 prisoners. Two days later Kitchener crossed the river from Omdurman to Khartoum, where on Sunday, September 4, a service was held in memory of General Gordon, close to the spot where he had met his death in 1885. The Egyptian army played a gallant part in these operations, but in the last phases it had been largely reinforced by British troops, and the charge of the 21st Lancers at a critical moment in the battle of Omdurman is one of the immortal memories of that regiment. For sheer bravery the Dervishes could scarcely be surpassed. They came on, as was said at the time, in great white clouds, one following another without blenching, though each in turn was scattered and devastated by the British guns.

The Fashoda Crisis

Kitchener had scarcely time to look round before he learnt of the arrival of a French expedition at Fashoda on the White Nile, 600 miles to the south. Within a week he started up the river with five gun-boats and a small expedition, and four days later reached Fashoda, where he found Major Marchand with 120 Senegalese troops entrenched in a fort on which the French flag was flying. The Frenchman's position was critical, for he had been attacked by Dervishes three weeks earlier, and would probably have been attacked again and destroyed, but for the British victory at Omdurman and the arrival of Kitchener. But the French flag and the presence of Senegalese troops were serious facts in face of the warning of the British Government that the presence of a French expedition in the valley of the Nile would be regarded as "an unfriendly act."

Kitchener treated the immediate situation with tact and discretion, and contented himself with hoisting the British and Egyptian flags a little to the south of the French fort. But the incident reported home caused a serious diplomatic crisis, and for a few weeks there was great excitement both in London and Paris and even talk of war. But the French position was not a strong one, as Delcassé, the Foreign Secretary, recognized from the beginning. Before the Sudan was reconquered, it might have been argued that a mere British warning could not affect the right of France to possess herself, if she could, of desirable territory not in British or Egyptian hands. After the reconquest, the British-Egyptian title was legally beyond challenge, and an expedition which had started in ignorance of the facts might be withdrawn without the appearance of surrender. It required some courage for the French Minister to reach this conclusion in face of the public excitement, but Lord Salisbury made it as easy as possible, and the courtesy with which Marchand had been treated and the facilities given him to extricate himself and his expedition from a dangerous situation greatly contributed. The affair was skilfully handled on both sides and showed the old diplomacy at its best.

The Far East

In the Far East during this year the scramble of the European Powers for points of vantage in the China seas came to its climax. In the previous November the Germans had seized Kiao-Chow on the plea or pretext that the murder of two German missionaries required this satisfaction. In March, 1898, the Russians countered this by peremptorily demanding from China a lease of Port Arthur and the adjoining roadstead of Talien-Wan—much more important places than Kiao-Chow. Russia in Port Arthur at the southern end of Manchuria would have a commanding position in that province, and be under a strong incentive to extend her railway from the north to this warm-water port in the south. Simultaneously with their demand upon China the Russians requested the British Government to withdraw two British cruisers which were then anchored at Port Arthur, " in order to avoid friction in the Russian sphere of interest." It was disagreeable for British Ministers to comply with this request, and still more to accept the assumption that the whole of this important region should be written off as a " Russian sphere of interest." For several weeks the situation looked mortifying and dangerous, and British Ministers talked of resisting the pretensions of Russia " even at the cost of war." Finally, they decided to follow the general example, and obtained from China the lease of Wei-Hai-Wei on the opposite side to Port Arthur on the Gulf of Chih-li. The Chinese were helpless, but after Russia and Germany had planted themselves in important positions on their coast, they were not unwilling that Great Britain should come in to check the other two.

These events led to the great resurgence of national feeling in China which found vent in the Boxer Rebellion of 1900, when savage retaliations took place and China was for nearly six weeks cut off from communication with the outside world. For a time it was believed that the Pekin legations had been stormed and their inmates slaughtered, but though this proved to be untrue there was savagery enough to lead to further savagery when an international force appeared on the scene to restore order. The German contingent had been instructed by the Kaiser to " behave like Huns " and " show no mercy," and they reflected this instruction in their conduct. The Russians flung 5000 Chinese—men, women and children —into the Amur at Blagoveschensk and left them to perish. Order was for a time restored, but the Powers, which in a temporary panic had joined forces in these proceedings, were left glowering at each other from their respective stations, and meditating the new moves which in the next five years were to revolutionize the situation in the Far East.

The Death of Gladstone

For a multitude the sun was darkened by the death of Mr. Gladstone on May 19, 1898. Controversy was stilled, while thousands filed past his body, which lay in state in Westminster Hall before its burial in Westminster Abbey. Party leaders vied with one another in their tributes to his power and influence. Lord Salisbury spoke of him as " a great example of which history hardly furnished a parallel of a great Christian man." Mr. Balfour said he was the " greatest member of the greatest deliberative Assembly the world had ever seen." All agreed that he had " kept the soul alive in England."

Changes in the Newspaper Press

These years saw the beginning of the changes which were largely to transform the newspaper press. The new rotary printing presses had made it possible to print an immensely greater number of papers from the same office, and there was now waiting a great new public—the product of the Education Acts—which demanded lighter fare than was provided by the " heavy dailies " with their devotion to public affairs and long reports of Parliament and the speeches of public men. The pioneer of what was then called the " new journalism " was W. T. Stead, the brilliant editor of the *Pall Mall Gazette*, who startled and shocked the readers of that serious evening paper by introducing the " interview " and borrowing various other features from American journalism. But Stead was a serious political journalist, with a comparatively small circle of readers, and it was reserved to Alfred Harmsworth to make the first great experiment in popular journalism by producing the *Daily Mail* in 1896. That, at its then price of a halfpenny, was an immediate success, and provided a great circle of new readers with a light and variegated bill of fare covering all manner of subjects and interests which the older papers had thought beneath their notice.

The effect of this was felt over the whole field of journalism. Other papers of the same type came into existence, and many of the older journals were put to the choice of following the new fashion or going out of existence. " Amalgamations " followed, and public companies with vast capitals controlling groups of newspapers and themselves controlled by powerful " magnates " took the place of individual proprietors. The " newspaper magnate " has thus become a rival power to Ministers and politicians.

The general tendency in the subsequent years has been to substitute a few popular newspapers with immense circulations for a larger number with small circulations. Scarcely any new journal has been successfully established in the last forty years, and many of the journals of opinion which in former days influenced the public mind, though their circulations were small, have disappeared. There were at one time eight evening papers in London, whereas there are now only three, though the population has greatly increased.

Conditions were made more difficult for the serious newspapers by the course of party politics in the eighties and nineties. Mr. Gladstone's conversion to Home Rule transferred blocks of Liberal readers to Unionist newspapers and detached advertisers in the same proportion. Political writers who were unable to follow their party, either ceased writing on politics or lost their appointments. In 1892, when the *Pall Mall Gazette*, then edited by Mr. (afterwards Sir) E. T. Cook, was transferred from a Liberal to a Conservative proprietor, the whole political staff resigned, and a refuge was found for them later by the founding of the *Westminster Gazette*. The Boer War was to present special difficulties to Liberal journalists, and many of them resigned or lost their appointments in the capture of their newspapers by one section of the party or the other. Thus Mr. Cook, who was now editor of the *Daily News*, was compelled to resign from that position when the paper passed into the hands of the pro-Boers, and Mr. Massingham quitted the editorship of the *Daily Chronicle* when the contrary process delivered that paper into the hands of the Liberal Imperialists. In later years the *Standard* was supposed to have perished from a gallant adhesion to Free Trade, when its party was streaming after Tariff Reform. Individual journalists who wrote with conviction had great influence in these years, but their tenure was often very precarious, and they had no secure retreat or alternative platform if they resigned, or were ejected from their appointments.

CHAPTER IV

THE SOUTH AFRICAN WAR

THE South African question simmered during the year 1898, but the Boers were reported to be spending large sums of money on armaments, and the " Outlanders," *i.e.* the British and foreign residents in the Transvaal, were more than ever persistent about their grievances, and more and more looking to the British Government to assist them. The shooting of a British subject named Edgar by the Boer police brought agitation to a climax at the end of December, 1898, and a few weeks later a petition calling for British intervention received 20,000 signatures. The Government now decided to demand the franchise for the Outlanders, but when presented with this demand at a conference between him and the High Commissioner held at Bloemfontein on May 31, President Kruger flatly refused it. It was suggested afterwards that if they had met at some wayside inn and the old President had smoked his pipe and Sir Alfred Milner a cigar, the result might have been different. But both were men of stubborn disposition, and the ground taken left little room for manœuvres. The proposed franchise was valuable to the Outlanders only in so far as it would enable them to swamp the Dutch burghers, and for the same reason it was unacceptable to the Boers.

The Government now burnt their boats by publishing a dispatch from the High Commissioner in which the situation was described as intolerable, and the case for intervention said to be " overwhelming." " The spectacle of thousands of British subjects kept permanently in the condition of helots, constantly chafing under undoubted grievances and calling vainly to Her Majesty's Government for redress," said Sir Alfred Milner, " does steadily undermine the influence and reputation of Great Britain and the respect for British government within the Queen's Dominions." Various efforts were made at conciliation in the subsequent weeks, but without success. As the weeks passed the controversy grew shriller, and was extended from the franchise to a clash between the claim of the Transvaal to be a sovereign independent State and the claim of Great Britain to be the paramount power in South Africa. At the end of August Mr. Chamberlain in a public speech spoke of " the sands running down in the glass," and said that " the knot must be loosened or else we shall have to find other ways of untying it." There was a last stage in which preparations for war were obviously going on while the Governments exchanged uncivil dispatches, and then on October 9 President Kruger issued an ultimatum which left the British Government no option but to pick up what was now his challenge

British Reverses

There was a widespread opinion that the negotiations had been mishandled, and that so difficult a case as that of the rights of a new population which had gone to seek its fortunes in a country where an old population was already in possession needed much more careful and patient consideration than had been given to it. But the Kruger ultimatum was couched in language which no self-respecting Government could have accepted, and large numbers who had objected to Mr. Chamberlain's diplomacy agreed with Lord Rosebery when he appealed to the country to be " one people " in the coming war, and said that he " dated from the ultimatum as Moham- medans date from the Hegira."

Unfortunately, as now appeared, the ultimatum had taken the Government by surprise, for it had been led to believe that Mr. Kruger would give way, if he were addressed in sufficiently firm language, and had not at all foreseen that the Orange Free State would join forces, as it immediately did, with the Transvaal Boers in their declaration of war. Ministers were now faced with the united hostility of the Dutch States as well as a high probability of disaffection among the Dutch at the Cape, and they had only a comparatively small force on the spot. The Boers at that moment could place about 50,000 men in the field, the British had less than half that number available on the spot to meet them.

Seizing the offensive the Boers immediately invested

Mafeking and invaded Natal, driving all the advanced British posts in upon Ladysmith, which also they proceeded to invest. The story of the next five months was that of repeated failures or dearly bought successes which could not be followed up. The country was difficult and unfamiliar; the Boers, who were mounted on ponies, knew every inch of the ground, moved rapidly and practised tactics which took orthodox soldiers by surprise. British soldiers fought gallantly, but British generals were always being outwitted and out-manœuvred. Buller, who had been sent out from England to take command, failed to relieve Ladysmith, and horrified the Government by advising its surrender, but a further effort ended in the disastrous defeat of Spion Kop, where a British force became a concentrated target for the Boers and had to be withdrawn after heavy losses. (January 24, 1900.) When the New Year came it was doubtful whether the British public were angrier with the Boers for having defied the power of Great Britain, or with the Government which had landed itself and the country in such a position. But all forces were now being rallied, the Dominions offering assistance, and volunteers responding eagerly to the call for a special force to act with the regular army. Ministers rose to the occasion and deciding that a radical change was needed in the conduct of the war, appointed Lord Roberts as Com-mander-in-Chief, with Lord Kitchener as his Chief of Staff.

Lord Roberts's Campaign

The situation looked black when the new command arrived in Cape Town on January 10, 1900. Kimberley, as well as Ladysmith and Mafeking, was being besieged, and the Boers were threatening Cape Colony. It seemed at one moment as if the reconquest of South Africa would have to be under-taken systematically from Cape Town to the north. But the situation offered many openings to a skilful strategy. The Boer forces were dangerously scattered and any rapid move-ment which threatened their communications might compel them to relax their hold on the beleaguered places and to retreat for their own safety. This compulsion Roberts applied by concentrating his army on the Modder River and advancing on the Free State from the west. A Boer force, 4000 strong, found itself isolated at Paardeberg, and had to surrender; the Boer army in Natal withdrew to meet the new threat; Kimberley was relieved on February 15, Ladysmith on February 28, and Roberts entered Bloemfontein, the capital of the Free State, on March 13.

The march had been exhausting, and owing to the capture of transport, the troops had been reduced to half-rations during some part of it. A period of reaction followed during which the Boers had some minor successes, and again made an attempt to invade Cape Colony and were driven back. On May 1 Roberts continued his advance and invaded the Transvaal, meeting with comparatively little resistance. A flying column was thrown out for the relief of Mafeking, the stout resistance of which, under Colonel Baden-Powell, had won great applause; and this was accomplished on May 17. Roberts, meanwhile, had crossed the Sand River and entered Johannesburg on the 28th. On June 5 he marched into Pretoria, from which President Kruger had fled, taking with him the archives and an unknown quantity of "Boer gold." Various other operations were undertaken during the next few weeks to clear the Transvaal up to the Portuguese border, and by all the tests applied to ordinary warfare the Boers were decisively beaten.

A Guerrilla War

These successes had been rapid and spectacular, and when Lord Roberts returned to England in the autumn it was generally believed that the war was over. The two Boer Republics had been annexed, their Presidents were in flight, their capitals were in British hands; they had no War Office, Treasury, munition factories, or any other means of making organized war. But the Boers were no ordinary warriors, and they took advantage of the dispersal of their regular army and the removal with it of any focus for British attack, to start a harassing guerrilla war, which for nearly two years longer defeated all efforts to deal with it. Knowing the ground intimately, and being well supplied with ponies and rifles, the Boer commanders, Botha, De Wet, De la Rey, Smuts, performed miracles of rapid movement, sudden attack and as sudden retreat, inflicting many mortifying reverses upon British generals, who only very gradually learnt the means of dealing with this kind of warfare. In the very last weeks of the war De la Rey surprised and captured Lord Methuen and his column. The British people watched with many misgivings certain of the methods which were improvised, especially the farm-burning with its necessary consequence, the establishment of concentration camps for women and children rendered homeless by this expedient. Many of the camps were insanitary, epidemics broke out and the mortality was heavy. Gradually, by establishing blockhouses, using mobile columns and instituting systematic " sweeps " of separate areas, Lord Kitchener found a key to the problem, and on March 23,1902, Boer delegates came to Pretoria to negotiate peace.

The Negotiated Peace

In a remarkable speech at Chesterfield on December 16, 1901, Lord Rosebery had entered a strong plea for a negotiated peace in contradistinction to the unconditional surrender for which Sir Alfred, or as he now was, Lord Milner, was still supposed to stand. This speech made a strong appeal to the public, which in spite of its exasperation had been impressed by the gallant last stand of the Boers, and was more and more coming to the conclusion that they ought to be treated with all possible consideration. This also was the view of Lord Kitchener, who played an honourable and conciliatory part in the negotiations which followed. Technically the Boers had become rebels after the annexation of the Boer States, and a few stubborn counsellors desired advantage to be taken of this legal fact or fiction to deprive them of any general amnesty. Wiser counsels prevailed, and on declaring themselves subjects of King Edward the burghers of the former States were granted immunity from any proceedings for legitimate acts of war and from deprivations of their property or civil rights. They were also promised that the existing military administration should be superseded as quickly as possible by a civil administration which should lead up to self-government, and in the meantime, given a grant of £3,000,000 as compensation for the destruction of farms. At the same time a Commission was set up for the repatriation of the men in the field or in exile, and sundry concessions were made to their fears or susceptibilities. The Dutch language was to be allowed in the law-courts and taught in the public schools on the request of parents ; land was not to be taxed to pay for the war, and the enfranchisement of natives not to be considered until after the introduction of self-government. In these ways the door was kept open to the reconciliation of Dutch and British.

The war had cost Great Britain 7790 killed in action or died of wounds, 13,000 died of disease, and 22,800 wounded, and added £250,000,000 to the National Debt. By the standard of the times it was counted a great and costly war, and the cost was felt the more because there was little glory to be won and much odium to be incurred in the defeat of the two small rural communities by the whole weight of the British Empire. The outside world saw only the disparity of the forces and not the effort which was required to fight a prolonged campaign over a vast territory 6000 miles distant from Great Britain. The political results of the war were fortunately more important and enduring than a mere settlement of the quarrel between Dutch and British about the gold-fields with which it started. The inevitable British victory removed the chief obstacle to the unification of South Africa under one flag or Government, and prepared the way for the co-operation of British and Dutch over the whole area. That was still to be the work of many hands, but it may fairly be said that Lord Kitchener and General Botha laid the foundations at the Conference of Vereeniging.

The First Hague Conference

The times had scarcely been propitious for the Disarmament Conference to which the Tsar summoned the nations in 1898 and which took place at The Hague in the following summer. All the Governments, the British included, thought that the Tsar had fallen a victim to a sentimental craze, and some suspected a Russian trap. When the conference came, the experts vied with one another in proving disarmament to be totally impossible, but the Tsar's effort was not quite useless, for the conference agreed to the establishment of the first International Arbitral Court, on the understanding that recourse to it should be purely optional.

CHAPTER V

THE END OF A REIGN

THE South African War threw British politics into great confusion and, as will be seen presently, had serious consequences in foreign affairs. For the time being it added to the misfortunes of the Liberal party, which found itself divided into three sections on the dominant issue. At one end of the scale were the Liberal Imperialists who declared the war to be " inevitable and just " and gave a general support to the Government; and at the other end the pro-Boers, who openly and courageously proclaimed their belief that the Boers were rightly struggling to be free against financial and other conspirators seeking to possess their gold-fields. Between the two stood a centre party which, though thinking that the war might have been avoided by a wiser and more patient diplomacy, yet judged it to be inevitable after the Kruger ultimatum, and was willing to support the Government in its prosecution up to the point when a negotiated peace on reasonable terms was possible. The Liberal Imperialists included Rosebery, the ex-Prime Minister, Asquith, a future Prime Minister, and Haldane, the future Secretary for War; while another future Prime Minister, Lloyd George, won his parliamentary spurs and first became a figure in the country by his unflinching advocacy of the Boer cause. The titular leader of the party, Campbell-Bannerman, yet another future Prime Minister, led an uneasy life between these sections, and after a vain endeavour to keep them together leant more and more to the pro-Boers. While the Opposition was in this distracted condition the Government suddenly dissolved Parliament (September 18, 1900), pleading that the war was practically over with the capture of the Boer capitals, and that it was necessary to obtain the sanction of the country for whatever further measures might have to be taken against the enemy, and for the peace which was expected to follow.

The Khaki Election

There followed what was known at the time as " the Khaki election "—khaki being the new colour adopted for the uniform of the troops whose original scarlet had proved too easy a mark for the Boer rifles. It was, like the election which followed the Great War eighteen years later, a very excited and turbulent occasion, the slogan of the hour being " every vote for a Liberal is a vote for the Boers." Liberal Imperialists found themselves, equally with pro-Boers, the object of this attack, for it was said to be a paramount necessity that the Government should have not merely a normal but a striking and exceptional majority of whole-hearted supporters in order to convince the Boers of the uselessness of further resistance. This method of electioneering left a smouldering resentment which was to flare up in the subsequent years, and it did not, as was generally expected, wipe out the Opposition. The Government majority was actually 18 lower than at the previous General Election, and if the Government slogan meant anything, no fewer than 2,105,518 electors had " voted for the Boers " against 2,428,492 who had voted the other way.

The result, nevertheless, was a heavy blow to the Liberal party. Before the war, the tide of opinion, as measured in by-elections, had been running strongly in their favour, and if there had been no war, it is highly probable that they would have returned to power in or about the year 1900. Now they were in the wilderness again for another long period with the pro-Boer stigma added to the unpopularity of their Irish policy. The prospect did not sweeten tempers or make for unity. Grave dissensions broke out between the different sections of the party, and Campbell-Bannerman's now un-concealed sympathies with the Boers all but produced a complete rupture between him and the Imperialist group.

The trouble came to a climax when in a public speech at the Holborn Restaurant, he denounced farm-burning and the concentration of women and children in refugee camps as " methods of barbarism." A wave of indignation swept over the country; he was said to have insulted the British army, defamed the British people, and rendered himself for ever impossible as leader of one of the great British parties, let alone as a future Prime Minister. More important for his personal position, he was gravely rebuked by Asquith and other of his Liberal Imperialist colleagues, and though he rallied his friends and challenged his opponents at a party meeting which gave him a unanimous vote of confidence, the schism continued till the end of the war, and at one moment all but led to the disruption of the Liberal party. In the course of these events Lord Rosebery announced his " definite separation " from the party, and Asquith, Grey and Haldane followed him in founding the " Liberal League " which looked like a direct challenge to the official leader. The quarrel went to dangerous lengths and, if pursued, it might have had momentous consequences in the future history of the country, but as the war drew to its close, the sections became reconciled, largely through Asquith's mediation. By this time both he and Rosebery had become advocates of a generous negotiated peace.

The Rise of Campbell-Bannerman

Contrary to expectation at the time, the stubbornness with which Campbell-Bannerman held his ground, and his refusal to withdraw or explain away what he had spoken, served him well in the long-run. All that he could be induced to say under pressure about his notorious phrase " methods of barbarism " was that he blamed the system and the Government which sanctioned it, and not the soldiers who acted under instructions, but he insisted to the end that the system was barbarous, and his insistence undoubtedly led to the reform of the abuses which had grown up in the hastily improvised camps and had led to a lamentable amount of suffering and mortality in some of them. But whether he was right or wrong, the public judged in the end that he was an honest and courageous man, who had refused to bow to the storm on a question on which he felt deeply ; and General Botha in after years testified that his action, so far from encouraging the Boers to a hopeless resistance, had touched their hearts and led them to think seriously of reconciliation. The future, they said, could not be quite hopeless, if the leader of one of the great English parties had had the courage to say this thing and to brave the obloquy that it brought upon him. When the war ended the storm subsided, and there was no longer any question of Campbell-Bannerman's fitness to lead the Liberal party or to be Prime Minister, if the opportunity offered. He was from this time specially qualified to play the part in the reconciliation between British and Dutch which was to be one of his chief titles to fame.

The War and Foreign Affairs

The effects of the South African War on Great Britain's relations to her neighbours in Europe proved in the long run to be among the most serious and lasting of its results. In the months following the Jameson Raid, Germany had toyed with the idea of a combination of European Powers to make trouble for Great Britain, and Baron Holstein, the famous Under-Secretary for Foreign Affairs, had actually made a list of objects which each of them might gain at her expense, if they acted together. But when it was broached to the French and Italians neither would have anything to do with this plan, the French because the " lost provinces " still counted for more than anything that Germany could offer them, the Italians because they judged that they could gain nothing which could compensate them for the hostility of Great Britain. The Kaiser was, thereupon, left with the dangerous reflection that Germany would be helpless against the British unless and until she possessed a fleet which they would fear and respect. The young Tirpitz, passionate advocate of sea-power, seized the occasion to point the moral and was vehement and eloquent in expounding it.

In 1899 when the war broke out, the Kaiser seemed to be in a more friendly mood. In the famous *Daily Telegraph* interview nine years later he even claimed to have stood between Great Britain and a hostile combination against her, and it is true that he rejected a suggestion of joint intervention which came to him from Russia, and promptly informed the British Ambassador and his royal relatives in London that he had done so. But the war was nevertheless fatal to the closer relations with Germany which the British Government at this time desired. The Kaiser visited the Queen at Windsor, accompanied by Count Bülow, the German Foreign Secretary, shortly after it began, and Mr. Chamberlain, who was among the Queen's guests, a few days later made a speech at Leicester in which he launched the idea of a British-German alliance. He had supposed himself to have had sufficient encouragement from Count Bülow to warrant him in doing this, and he had looked for a favourable reply. Instead a storm broke out in Germany at the very suggestion of a partnership with the "bloodhound of the Transvaal," and when Bülow spoke in the Reichstag on his return to Germany, he poured cold water on the project, and spoke flatteringly of France and Russia. The German Navy League now turned the anti-British feeling to account for the new Navy Bill of the year 1900, which was regarded in Great Britain as a definite challenge to British sea-power. From now onwards to the outbreak of the Great War the naval question was to prove the great obstacle to good relations between Britain and Germany.

The Kaiser came again to England in the following year when Queen Victoria was on her death-bed, and remained for her funeral. In the emotions of these days the word alliance was again spoken and the Foreign Office went so far as to draft a treaty. But recriminations about the Boer War were at a high pitch between the British and German peoples, and Lord Salisbury, who had always been lukewarm to projects of alliance, saw little advantage in this one. Once more, as on the occasion of Bismarck's last overture in 1890, the project "lay on the table," and at the end of the year disappeared in a heated debate between Mr. Chamberlain and Count Bülow about the behaviour of British and German soldiers in their respective wars. Now and for the next three years Great Britain seemed to be without a friend in the world. Denunciation of her conduct in South Africa came equally from both the European camps, and the smaller nations who had generally been her friends were warm in sympathy with the little Dutch Republic about to be extinguished by the Great Empire. France at this time was being shaken by the Dreyfus affair, and British comments on her military justice added to the resentment which had been kindled by the Fashoda crisis. Nothing in these years stood between Britain and a hostile European combination but the British fleet and the unappeasable feud between France and Germany. Angry as Frenchmen might be with England, nothing would induce them to join Germany in any adventure.

The Death of Queen Victoria

Queen Victoria died in January, 1901, after reigning more than sixty-three years. At the end of her life she had become an institution as well as a Queen, and in her character she reflected both the virtues and the limitations of the well-to-do English. By her integrity, simplicity and devotion to duty she inspired a respect which was a high service to the monarchy, but she lived into an age which was moving rapidly from the ideas that she cherished, and in the last years of her life she watched with growing concern the development of tendencies that she deplored—the spread of democracy, the demand of Ireland for Home Rule, the emancipation of women, the clash between Lords and Commons, the departure from old solemnities and conventions. Twenty years earlier she had favoured all spirited policies in foreign or imperial affairs and had vented her displeasure on Ministers whom she thought backward or indifferent to the prestige and interests of the country, but she had wished for peace in her last years, and was greatly saddened by the war in South Africa. The grief at her death was genuine and widespread throughout the Empire and even the least sensitive seemed to be aware that a period had ended.

If there was any period in the world's history in which life was easy for rich and moderately well-to-do people, it was the sixty-three years of Queen Victoria's reign. To their eyes British institutions and the framework of British society seemed secure beyond challenge. Freedom broadened down from precedent to precedent; moderation was the watchword of both the great parties; the occasional ebullitions of the poor were easily dealt with, and never looked dangerous as in the less favoured continental countries; a wise Parliament made timely concessions and all went on as before. Such wars as there were, were conducted by professional soldiers in remote parts of Europe or the world, and left the general current of life undisturbed. Great literary figures and scientific leaders commanded a respect and obtained a hearing seldom vouchsafed to their kind in other ages. Trade advanced by leaps and bounds, British ships covered the seas, the Empire expanded, and solved its problems by the magic of self-government. If there were occasional sets-back, the general assurance of progress was never shaken. Science went hand in hand with industry and helped it with new inventions, health improved, the death-rate declined, education spread to the masses, falling prices made low wages tolerable, and, so far as Government was concerned, it was generally believed that no one had any excuse for not being happy. Well-to-do men and women living in the Victorian age had a vision of a permanent, orderly and progressive state of society seldom vouchsafed to human beings in other centuries.

The New Voices

But the period was running out some years before Queen Victoria died. The Victorians, it was being discovered, had purchased their comfort by passing on many of their problems to their successors. Arnold Toynbee and Barnett of Whitechapel had already in the 'eighties raised powerful voices against the growing gulf between rich and poor typified in the contrast between West and East London, and a few years later Charles Booth's monumental survey of London revealed that an inordinate number were living " on the poverty line," that is, had no more than the bare necessaries of existence, and that the conditions in which they were housed made a decent life all but impossible. The industrialists of a previous generation had immensely extended their factories and given employment to a constantly increasing number of wage-earners in the great towns, but neither they nor the local authorities in these towns had thought it part of their duties to provide in an orderly way for the housing of the workers. From the year 1885 onwards there was a gradual awakening to the urgency of the social problem, the slum problem and the poverty problem, and the debates about these were to play a large part in the warfare of parties, and in the struggles between Lords and Commons during the subsequent years. When the Victorians extended the franchise, they said that " we must educate our masters," but they had perhaps failed to realize that universal education would awaken in the newly educated a lively sense of their own abilities and disabilities, and bring on the scene a new class of workman-politician who would upset the established order by a growing demand that the inequalities between rich and poor should be redressed.

King Edward comes and Lord Salisbury goes

For several years yet this movement was to work below the surface, and in the meantime King Edward came to the throne and the Government occupied itself in ending the South African War. The King's coronation fixed for June 26, 1902, had to be postponed to August 9, in consequence of his sudden and serious illness which necessitated an immediate operation. Between the two dates another reign was ended by the resignation of Lord Salisbury, who slipped from the scene almost unnoticed on July 11, when all thoughts were centred on the King's illness. Lord Salisbury, too, like Queen Victoria, had become an institution, having been Prime Minister for thirteen years out of the previous sixteen, and, for the greater part of the time, Foreign Secretary as well. He was immensely respected, he had a longer experience than any other eminent man in the world, his presence at the head of affairs inspired confidence. What part, if any, he played in domestic politics was always difficult to discover. He had long been removed from the House of Commons where his brilliant nephew, Mr. Arthur Balfour, led the Unionist party to its complete satisfaction, and kept it true to the few and simple purposes that its followers expected of it in these years.

Lord Salisbury, meanwhile, concentrated upon foreign affairs, which he pursued with a cautious sobriety on the general line of working with Germany and Triple Alliance whenever possible. It seemed as if, having had his one adventure in a spirited foreign policy under Lord Beaconsfield in the days of " peace with honour " he was resolved for the rest of his life to have no other. Bismarck in 1887 succeeded in drawing him temporarily out of his reserve and induced him to sign the Mediterranean Agreement, which for a time made Britain a naval partner of the Triple Alliance, but after that he withdrew quickly into his shell and returned evasive answers to all invitations from Germany to advance further into her camp.

He had a habit of thinking aloud in public which was often disconcerting to his admirers, as when he said that "village circuses would be better than Parish Councils," or when he told the House of Lords in 1897 that in backing the Turks, according to the policy which was traditional in his party, Great Britain "had put her money on the wrong horse." He advised imperialists and strategists to "consult large maps," and observed that much of the territory in Asia and Africa which they were so anxious to annex was "very light soil." He had spoken firmly to the French when Marchand appeared at Fashoda in 1898, but he was only with great reluctance drawn into the competition for points of vantage in the Far East, and he was generally supposed to have felt considerable sympathy with the Boers under the hard driving of his pushful Colonial Secretary, Mr. Chamberlain.

Most important of all, Lord Salisbury was among the last firm believers in the policy of splendid isolation. In 1899 Mr. Chamberlain told the German Ambassador that a majority of the Cabinet was in favour of a German and a minority of a French Alliance. Lord Salisbury was of neither school. In one of the last memoranda that he wrote on foreign affairs (May 29, 1901) he put his opinion on record that it would not be wise to "incur novel and most onerous obligations in order to guard against a danger in whose existence we have no historical reason for believing." The British Government, he said, "cannot undertake to declare war, for any purpose, unless it is a purpose of which the electors of this country would approve. If the Government promised to declare for an object which did not commend itself to public opinion, the promise would be repudiated and the Government would be turned out. I do not see how, in common honesty, we could invite other nations to rely on our aid in a struggle which must be formidable and probably supreme, when we have no means whatever of knowing what may be the humour of our people in circumstances which cannot be foreseen." Here in what was almost his last word Lord Salisbury raised the vital questions to which his successors were to give the answers in the next thirteen years, and, it may be said not untruly that, when he laid down the reins, the last of the great exponents of splendid isolation had passed from the scene. He died in 1903.

Lord Salisbury was succeeded as Prime Minister by his nephew, Mr. Arthur Balfour, who had long led the House of Commons with the entire approval of the Unionist party. There were no changes of importance in the Government and outwardly everything went on as before. But great changes were pending which in the next four years were profoundly to affect both the domestic politics and the foreign relations of Great Britain.

THE END OF BRITISH ISOLATION

FROM the beginning of the twentieth century onwards British Ministers were more and more beginning to doubt if Lord Salisbury's preference for the policy of isolation could be maintained or whether it could properly be described as "splendid." In all European countries public opinion was raging against Great Britain for her supposed oppression of the Boers, and it was only a question whether feeling was stronger in Berlin, Paris or St. Petersburg. But furiously as the other nations might rage, she could still up to this point rely for her safety on the supreme fleet which rendered them impotent for action. From 1900 onwards, however, two new facts called for serious consideration. First, the Germans were evidently preparing to challenge British sea-power; second, a situation was developing in the Far East which, unless very carefully handled, might leave Great Britain at the mercy of a hostile combination. The first was to develop over a period of years; the second was urgent and immediate.

During the year 1898 Japan had watched uneasily while Russia occupied Manchuria which she had marked down for herself, and for the next few years she wavered between the two alternatives of making her peace with Russia while installing herself in Corea, and of forming an alliance with a European Power which would strengthen her hands against Russia. To Lord Lansdowne, who had succeeded Lord Salisbury as Foreign Secretary in the year 1900, the former alternative seemed full of menace for British interests. Britain could not single-handed undertake the task of bolstering up China against foreign aggression, and, strong as her fleet might be, it could not in these distant waters be equal to a combination of Russia and Japan with an unfriendly Germany awaiting her opportunity. Lord Lansdowne concluded that the only way out of this situation was to make common cause with Japan.

The Japanese Alliance and its Consequences

Japan by this time was feeling her way simultaneously with both Russia and Great Britain. During the year 1901 she made overtures for a British Alliance through the Japanese Ambassador, Baron Hayashi, in London, and sent the Marquis Ito to explore the possibilities with the Russian Minister, Count Lamsdorf in St. Petersburg. Lord Lansdowne and Baron Hayashi were quicker on the ground than Count Lamsdorf and the Marquis Ito; and the party in Tokio which objected to the Russian occupation of Manchuria proved stronger than the party which was willing to make terms with it. In the end Lord Lansdowne won the race and the Marquis Ito received instructions to leave St. Petersburg and repair to London, where an Anglo-Japanese Treaty was signed on January 30, 1902. It covered British interests in China, and Japanese interests both in China and in Corea, but only in the event of either Power being attacked by more than one Power did it engage the other to come to its assistance. In all other events the observance of a strict neutrality and " efforts to prevent other Powers from joining in hostilities against its ally " was the limit of what was pledged, though the two Powers undertook to " communicate with one another fully and frankly " when the interests of either were in jeopardy and " not to make arrangements with other Powers to the prejudice of their agreement without consulting one another."

Lord Salisbury was still Prime Minister, though not Foreign Secretary, when this Treaty was concluded, and he must therefore be presumed, in this special case, to have waived his objections to engaging the British people to go to war in circumstances which could not be foreseen. Great Britain was now the senior member of a powerful partnership in the Far East and she was pledged to make war in circumstances which were by no means remote. It is probable that British Ministers considered their engagement to Japan as an exception for exceptional circumstances in a distant part of the world to their established policy for Europe, but if so, they reckoned without Japan, which was now free to pursue a policy which was to have momentous consequences in Europe as well as in the Far East. Being secured by the Anglo-Japanese Treaty against intervention by any third Power she was from this time onward more than ever determined not to submit to the permanent occupation of Manchuria by Russia, and began to prepare in earnest for the struggle to evict her. Manchuria might or might not be desirable colonizing ground for the Japanese people, but the Power which possessed it controlled the ways in and the ways out of the Sea of Japan, and she had persuaded herself that to prevent Russia or any European Power from being in a position to exercise this control was vital to her existence.

It appears not to have dawned upon the Russians that a mere yellow race could have the audacity to challenge them, or that, if it did, its fate could be in doubt. They now pushed forward their scheme for exploiting Manchuria and, ignoring their definite promise to evacuate the country, were evidently preparing to make their occupation permanent. Japan expostulated and negotiated; Russia procrastinated and dispatched a big fleet and large army to the Far East; Japan broke off negotiations and declared war (February 8, 1904). There followed, instead of the easy and expected triumph for the European Power, the long series of reverses and disasters which were to put an end to Russia's adventure in the Far East.

The Dogger Bank Incident

The Russo-Japanese War was brought home to the British people by the Dogger Bank incident of October 21, 1904, when the Russian Baltic fleet on its way to the Far East fired on the Hull fishing fleet, sinking one trawler, killing two men and wounding six, and injuring other boats. This was thought at the time to be a deliberate outrage, and an indignant public demanded immediate redress. The Government at one moment came near to giving orders to the British fleet to challenge and intercept the Russian fleet on its way to the East, but cooler counsels prevailed, and on the 28th the Prime Minister was able to announce that the Tsar had expressed his regret and that an international Commission would investigate the circumstances with a view to the punishment of any responsible parties. The Commission, composed of British, Russian, French and American Admirals (with an

Austrian Chairman), met in Paris early in 1905, and while absolving the Russian Admiral and his officers from any discredit attaching either to their " military qualities " or their "humanity," reported that the fear of hostile torpedo boats which had caused them to fire was not justified. Upon this the Russian Government paid compensation and the affair was wound up.

The British-French Entente

This was but a passing incident, but the adversities of Russia had lasting results upon policy in Europe, and may even be said to have prepared the way for the British-French Entente which was the most important event in the British history of these years. The French had looked on with alarm while their ally staked his fortunes on this remote adventure, and were in two minds as to whether his defeat or a success which permanently diverted a large part of his strength and resources from Europe to the Far East would be the greater evil for them. Either event disastrously lowered the value of their alliance for European purposes. For precisely the same reasons the Germans had for years past encouraged the Russians to pursue their Far-Eastern adventure, and the Kaiser had used high-flown language about the sacred mission of the Tsar to uphold the Cross against the yellow races. As the Russo-Japanese rivalry developed the Germans saw in it a unique opportunity of squaring accounts with France, and the French became aware that they were once more being thrown back into the dangerous isolation from which they supposed themselves to have escaped through their alliance with Russia. It thus became a matter of high importance to them to find another friend in Europe ; and stifling their grievances about Fashoda and the Dreyfus affair they began to look to Great Britain. She had made a breach in her isolation policy in favour of Japan ; why not another in favour of France ?

Lord Lansdowne and British Ministers looked at it from a purely British point of view. They had for years past been harassed and irritated by the policy of pin-pricks, as it was then called, which had embittered British-French relations all over the world. In Egypt, Morocco, Siam, Sokoto, Madagascar, the New Hebrides—wherever the two countries came into contact—the friction had been vexatious and incessant. Thus, when after the peace in South Africa the atmosphere began to change and the war of words in the Foreign Offices and the newspapers suddenly died down, they were more than ready to reciprocate. To be on bad terms with both the European groups was uncomfortable, if not dangerous ; to make friends with one, when opportunity offered, seemed wise and right.

Early in 1903 Chambers of Commerce were passing resolutions in favour of an Arbitration Treaty between Britain and France ; a group was formed in the French Chamber to advance that project, and 200 deputies gave it their support. The idea was broached that King Edward should visit Paris and this was received with warm approval by French newspapers. The way being thus prepared, the King arrived in Paris on May 1, and had an enthusiastic reception. By making himself popular in Paris and overcoming the hostility of the French people he did a work which was beyond the power of any Minister.

At the beginning of July the French President, accompanied by the Foreign Secretary, M. Delcassé, came to London and had a similar reception. During this visit Lord Lansdowne had serious conversations with M. Delcassé, and before he left regular negotiations for an Agreement were on foot. These lasted for the next nine months, and at some points presented serious difficulties. The French needed substantial compensation for waiving their traditional objection to the British occupation of Egypt; the British Dominions were not pleased at the concessions which had to be made in the New Hebrides and other regions where their interests were affected. There was a critical moment in March, 1904, when the negotiations seemed on the point of breaking down, but in the next fortnight all obstacles were smoothed away, and the British-French Convention was signed on April 7, 1904. It settled the more distant colonial questions by mutual concessions and wound up the long-standing quarrel about Egypt by giving France what was practically a free hand in Morocco.

Europe and the Entente

British Ministers felt that they had done a good day's work. They had removed long-standing and possibly dangerous causes of quarrel, put the peace on a firm footing with their nearest neighbour, paved the way for friendly co-operation instead of mutual obstruction wherever the two Powers came into contact. The public warmly approved, Conservatives seeing in the Entente a great achievement for a Unionist Government, Liberals welcoming it as a substantial step towards a Liberal and conciliatory foreign policy. In Europe the interpretation was far different. To the Continental observer it seemed that British Ministers, whether knowingly or unknowingly, had plunged into the heart of the European quarrel and given their casting vote—the one remaining prize for both the alliances—to the Dual as against the Triple Alliance.

For European purposes the importance of the Convention lay in its last article in which the British and French Governments " agreed to afford one another their diplomatic support to obtain the execution of the clause of the present Declaration regarding Egypt and Morocco." Lord Lansdowne and British Ministers actually relied on these words to prove that they had not pledged military support or compromised the right of the British Parliament to keep the decision of peace and war in its own hands. But to the diplomatists of Europe the line which divided diplomatic from military support seemed a very thin one, and they judged that diplomatic support would only be effective if there was a strong presumption that in case of necessity it would be backed by military. This from the beginning was in the minds of European statesmen in both camps, and they could with difficulty be brought to believe that it was not in the minds of British statesmen. In England Lord Rosebery alone issued a warning note. All others, when the question came to be debated in the British Parliament, welcomed the Agreement as a wise and pacific step in British policy.

The Germans were greatly disturbed. It had been one of their most cherished beliefs that the possibility of an understanding between Great Britain and France was too remote to need serious consideration. Baron Holstein, the famous Permanent Secretary of the German Foreign Office, had for years been saying that Germany had only to bide her time to purchase British friendship on her own terms, and in the meantime not to seem eager, but even to step back when Great

Britain advanced, was the way to strike a good bargain and to win the respect of the nation of shopkeepers. It now seemed that by acting on these principles Germany had missed her market and left the door open to an Anglo-French *rapprochement*.

German Reprisals

But it was the practice of diplomatists, when taken by surprise, to pretend that nothing had happened, and this for a time was the attitude of the German Government. The agreement, they said, was a purely local and colonial event which not only caused them no displeasure but even gave them a certain satisfaction. In May, 1904, Count Bülow told the Reichstag that Germany could take no objection to British policy and need feel no uneasiness about her interests in Morocco. During the next few months the German Government busied itself itself in obtaining the same commercial privileges for itself as France had obtained in Egypt, and there was no difficulty about that. But during these same months alarming events were taking place in the Far East. Russia met with disaster on disaster; her army was driven back, her fleet destroyed, and revolution threatened to break out in St. Petersburg and Moscow. Before the year 1905 was far advanced, it was evident that she was out of action for any European purpose, and the Germans concluded that they were now in a position to take a high line with France without running the risk which had hitherto deterred them of the " war on two fronts " with Russia and France in alliance.

In encouraging the Tsar in his Far-Eastern adventure the Kaiser, as the " Willy-Nicky " correspondence shows, had given him an assurance that he would " guard his rear in Europe," and this might have been supposed to exclude the possibility of making trouble for the Tsar's Ally, while he was occupied elsewhere. But this was too high a doctrine for Bülow and Holstein who argued that Germany would be failing in her duty to herself and her Ministers be justly branded with neglect and incompetence, if they failed to take advantage of circumstances so providential and so favourable to German interests as now offered. In a book called *Germany's Road to Ruin*, Herr Nowak, who is supposed to record the views of the ex-Kaiser, has recorded (English translation, p. 312) that at this juncture Count Schlieffen, the German Chief of Staff and author of the plan for the invasion of France through Belgium, adopted in the Great War, "was in favour of the earliest possible thorough clearing up with France at arms. No waiting ten or twenty years for a world war, but so thorough a settlement that thereafter there should be no fear of a world war. France should be provoked until she had no course left but to take up arms." Whether Bülow and Holstein were prepared to go that length may be doubted, but they decided on a policy which the authority above quoted describes as a "deep and deliberate provocation to France." To make its meaning clear, the ground chosen was Morocco, on which the British had pledged their diplomatic support to France, and which was bound to afford a test of the meaning and value of the British-French agreement. It now appeared that the Germans had only been waiting a favourable moment for their return blow to this act of policy.

Provocation and Intrigue

The German plan revealed in the year 1905 had two phases. It was first an attempt to intimidate the French by challenging their policy in Morocco and next an attempt to wean the Tsar from the Franco-Russian Alliance, and induce him to make a treaty with Germany to which France too, under pressure, would be compelled to adhere. The first part was inaugurated on March 31 by the Kaiser's landing at Tangier, where he ostentatiously offered his patronage and protection to the Sultan, then in a state of friction with the French, who desired to "reform" his administration in ways that he disliked.

From this beginning the Germans went on to demand that the whole question of Morocco should be submitted to a European conference and were so threatening that the French Government became alarmed and sacrificed their Foreign Minister, Delcassé, who had resisted this pressure to the point at which Bülow, the German Foreign Minister, had declined to have further dealings with him. (June 6, 1905.) Instead of being appeased by this sacrifice the Germans renewed their pressure, and on the threat of "standing behind the Sultan with all their forces" compelled the French to accept the conference (September 28), and even then continued to use language

E

which led the French to fear that, when it came, they would make impossible demands which would break it up and precipitate war.

In the meantime the Kaiser had taken up the second part of the German plan, and on July 24, six weeks after the fall of Delcassé, he visited the Tsar on board his yacht off the Island of Bjorkoe in Finnish waters, taking in his pocket the draft of a treaty which had been prepared by Bülow and Holstein. There followed, according to the Kaiser's account, a highly emotional interview, in which the two Emperors fell into each other's arms and the Tsar signed the treaty on the spot. It contained three clauses: (1) in case either Germany or Russia was attacked by a European Power, its Ally was to " come to its aid in Europe with all its forces on land or sea "; (2) neither was to make a separate peace with a common enemy; (3) the Tsar was " after this Treaty comes into force " to take the necessary steps to inform France, and to associate her with it as an Ally. France, therefore, was to know nothing about it until it came into force—the date fixed for that being the conclusion of peace between Russia and Japan—and then was to be faced with the fact that her Ally, Russia, had behind her back entered into an alliance with her opponent, Germany. The Tsar appears to have forgotten that his Government and the French had pledged themselves to " take counsel together upon every question of a nature to jeopardize the general peace," for he could scarcely have supposed that a secret treaty between Russia and Germany lay outside this stipulation.

The Kaiser specially prided himself on the last clause of this treaty. It ruled France out of all previous consultation and ensured that she should be faced with the accomplished fact of a Russo-German Alliance. She would then have had to take her choice between submission and complete isolation. In the condition in which she was after the fall of Delcassé, the Kaiser confidently assumed that she would submit.

The Bjorkoe Treaty and its Miscarriage

The plan, nevertheless, misscarried, for though the Kaiser obtained the Tsar's signature, there were others who had to be reckoned with. On returning to Berlin, the Kaiser found to his dismay and surprise that his Chancellor, Prince Bülow, took strong exception to a change that he (the Kaiser) had made on his own responsibility in the treaty as originally drafted. He had added the words " in Europe " to the clause defining the action which Russia was to take in support of Germany, if she were attacked by another Power. This, Prince Bülow objected, took all the sting out of the treaty, for what he specially had in mind when he drafted the treaty was Russian action against Great Britain in India. This would have been a " strong bullet " which would have stopped Great Britain, but with Russian action confined to Europe, the treaty was a weak one which would provoke without intimidating, Great Britain. There followed a crisis in which the Chancellor held stubbornly to his point, and the Kaiser threatened to abdicate, and even, according to Bülow's account, to commit suicide, if he did not have his way. " The morning after the receipt of your resignation would fail to find the Kaiser alive. Think of my poor wife and children." Such, if we are to believe Bülow, was the appeal which the distracted Emperor made to his Chancellor.

The Tsar too had trouble when he got back to St. Petersburg. His Foreign Minister, Lamsdorf, pointed out that the treaty was in direct conflict with not only the spirit but any honourable interpretation of the letter of the Franco-Russian Treaty of Alliance. It was, therefore, a flagrant breach of faith, the probable consequence of which would be that France would decline to submit and Germany, being guaranteed against Russian opposition, would crush her and become unchallenged mistress of Europe, including Russia. The Tsar, who was a man of weak and vacillating character, was easily persuaded that he had made a mistake, and the crisis in Berlin was averted by his repentance. Thus between the German Chancellor and the Russian Foreign Secretary, the second part of the German scheme broke down, and the Franco-Russian Alliance remained intact for what it was worth.

Thanks to President Roosevelt, who played a useful and important part in negotiating the peace between Russia and Japan, the former was spared the mortification of yielding Russian territory or paying an indemnity, as the Japanese desired, but her power of intervening in Europe was shattered for the time being. France, therefore, seemed more than ever isolated and the Germans continued their pressure with the now undisguised intention of driving a wedge between her and Great Britain. By the autumn of 1905 it had become clear that Mr. Balfour and Lord Lansdowne would hand on a very dangerous legacy to their successors, whoever these might be.

The Shrinkage of the World

The process which was binding the whole world in a chain of cause and effect, obliterating distance and requiring statesmen everywhere to keep their eyes on the ends of the earth, had made rapid progress since the beginning of the century. The South African War had roused the Germans to a sense of their impotence in the absence of sea-power and started them on building the great fleet which was to be the chief cause of contention between them and Great Britain in the coming years. The British-Japanese Alliance had afforded Japan the opportunity of challenging Russia in the Far East; the defeat of Russia had deprived France of her principal support in Europe and led her to look for help from Great Britain; Anglo-French friendship had incensed Germany and led to reprisals against France. Finally, the return of Russia to Europe and the substitution of the Near East for the Far East as the goal of her ambitions, was to be the occasion of the clash between the European Alliances in the Great War.

But the consequences of their action were mostly hidden from statesmen at the time. Lord Salisbury and Lord Lansdowne did not foresee that their alliance with Japan would pave the way to a war between Russia and Japan; the Russians were so confident of their ability to defeat Japan that they were not deterred by an agreement which only came into operation if a third Power intervened. Still less did British statesmen foresee that in ending a series of vexatious quarrels with France and paying what seemed the modest price of " diplomatic support " on strictly defined ground, they would be supposed to have committed themselves to taking sides in the rivalry of the European groups. Nor, finally, did the Germans foresee that in resenting the Anglo-French Convention and threatening France on ground on which Great Britain had promised this " diplomatic support," they were taking the one step which was calculated to draw France and Britain closer together and to convert their Entente into a fighting alliance.

A Memorable Date

On December 17, 1903, at Dayton, Ohio, the brothers Wilbur and Orville Wright made a flight of 260 yards in a heavier than air machine fitted with a petrol motor, and two years later at the same place flew thirty-six miles. They received little encouragement at the time from their own countrymen, and transferred their activities to France, where the principal developments in aviation took place during the next few years. In 1910 the French airman, Bleriot, flew over the English Channel, thus making an historic breach in the insularity of the British Isles.

CHAPTER VII

MEASURED by its consequences in after years the British-French Entente was by far the most important act of Mr. Balfour's Administration, but in home affairs also this Administration started policies and raised controversies which were to occupy politicians for a generation to come.

It was the view of the Liberal party that having appealed to the electors to suspend party politics in the national interest at the election of 1900, the Government were bound to refrain from legislation of a partisan character, and they were loud in protest, when in 1902 Mr. Balfour introduced an Education Bill abolishing School Boards and setting up Education Committees of County and Borough Councils to take over their work and to " control all secular education " in voluntary schools. There was much to be said for unifying education and giving the new authorities wide powers over all schools, secondary as well as elementary, but Liberals and Nonconformists took strong exception to the terms made with voluntary schools and especially to the provision that these schools should be wholly maintained out of the rates, while the public authority appointed only a third of their managers, and, in respect to the appointments of teachers, was given only a veto which was not to be exercised " except on educational grounds." The Government replied that the denominations—mainly Church of England and Roman Catholic—provided the buildings and kept them in repair; the Opposition retorted that this was but a trifling contribution compared with the complete maintenance out of public funds which was now proposed.

Nonconformists challenged the whole scheme as a new State-endowment of religion, and strongly objected to paying rates for the support of schools teaching religious doctrines of which they disapproved. The Bill was hotly contested through all its stages in the House of Commons, and gave rise to a vehement agitation in the country which by no means ceased when it passed. For several years to come, Nonconformist " conscientious objectors " submitted to having their goods seized rather than contribute through the rates to the support of voluntary schools, and the measure undoubtedly helped to swell the reaction which by this time was rapidly rising against the Government in the country. A later generation which has lost interest in denominational controversies may look back on this agitation with surprise, but at the time it seemed to raise tremendous issues of conscience and principle.

The Licensing Bill

Two years later (1904) the Government's Licensing Bill caused a similar agitation and brought all schools of Temperance reformers into the field against them. A judgment of the House of Lords in the case of Sharpe v. Wakefield had laid down, that in law a public-house licence was for one year and one year only, and could be revoked by the justices at their discretion without evidence of misconduct on the part of the licensee. This upset the commonly accepted assumption that a licence was automatically renewable except in evidence of misconduct, and brought consternation to " the trade " and to the great brewing companies which had invested immense sums in " tied houses," and saw their property becoming extremely precarious, if they had no more than a yearly tenure at the discretion of the magistrates.

It was generally admitted that some change in the law was necessary, and the Government now proposed that except for misconduct or because the premises were unsuitable, the licence should never be refused unless the " persons interested " were compensated. At the same time a compensation fund was provided by a tax on existing licences and a special payment on the issue of new licences. The Government argued that this would set magistrates free to extinguish redundant licences, whereas even if they had the power to revoke the yearly licence, they would hesitate to exercise it, if by so doing they inflicted hardships on the licensee. This was far from pacifying opponents of the measure, who held it to be quite unnecessary to convert the licence into the legal property of the licensee, and by so doing to disarm Parliament in any future efforts in Temperance reform.   Instead they proposed a time-limit of fourteen years during which compensation should be paid on a descending scale, and at the end of which, magistrates should have unhampered discretion to treat the licence as a yearly and no more than a yearly permit to sell liquor.

The Government had their way and carried their Bill by guillotine closure, but by this time they had challenged the two most militant sections of the Liberal party, the Non-conformists and the Temperance advocates, and in the meantime another controversy was growing up which not only united the Liberal party but divided their own party.

The Challenge to Free Trade

The beginning of this was the proposal by Sir Michael Hicks Beach, then Chancellor of the Exchequer, of a shilling duty on corn.   He called it a "registration duty," expressly disclaimed any Protectionist intention and said it was so small that it could not raise the price of bread.   This, however, was not the view of the bakers, who at once added a halfpenny to the price of the loaf.   More embarrassing still, Sir Wilfred Laurier, the Canadian Prime Minister, made a speech in the Canadian Dominion Parliament in which he stated:

> He was going to England to discuss commercial relations on the invitation of the Imperial Government, and he could not conceive that Mr. Chamberlain would invite the Colonial representatives to discuss that subject unless the British Government had something to propose.   There was now a duty on wheat and flour which placed Canada in a position to make offers which she could not make in 1897.   A step had been taken which would make it possible to obtain preference for Canadian goods. (May 12, 1902.)

Here was the germ of a controversy which was to occupy the country for the next thirty years.   The entire policy by which, at the end of that period, Great Britain was to impose duties on foreign imports and remit them or part of them for the benefit of the Dominions was foreshadowed in this speech.

Thus in six weeks the bakers had stamped the shilling tax as Protectionist and Sir Wilfred had hailed it as the foundation of Colonial Preference. The two things together plunged Mr. Balfour's Government into a controversy which was to be its ruin, and rallied Free Traders to the support of the Liberal party which instantly took up the challenge. Three days after Sir Wilfred Laurier had spoken, Mr. Chamberlain, the Colonial Secretary, told his constituents that he too favoured the policy of Preference and was ready for a wide departure from the " old shibboleths " and " antiquated methods " of the Free Trade system. This brought confusion to the Cabinet, which contained a powerful group of convinced Free Traders ; and Sir Michael Hicks Beach, the author of the corn tax, now declared it to be " the most perfect delusion that can be conceived " that the Government would " encourage trade with our Colonies by initiating a tariff war with all those foreign countries who are our largest and greatest customers."

For the next few months the controversy simmered. Sir Michael Hicks Beach stood firm against the remission of the tax in favour of the colonies, but in the autumn resigned from the Government and was succeeded as Chancellor of the Exchequer by Mr. Ritchie, who was, if anything, an even stauncher Free Trader. In the Budget of 1903 the corn tax was withdrawn, and the Free Traders had won the first round, thanks to the efforts of their friends in the Cabinet.

Mr. Chamberlain's Manifesto

Mr. Chamberlain, meanwhile, had paid a visit to South Africa and on his return acquiesced for the moment in the remission of the corn tax as being from his point of view slightly better than its retention and the refusal of Colonial Preference. But he had no idea of accepting defeat at the hands of Mr. Ritchie, and shortly after the introduction of the Budget he made a speech at Birmingham (May 15, 1903) in which he enlarged his demands and declared a policy of Protection, including food-taxes and preference, to be imperative for the Empire and announced his intention of making it the issue at the next election. A few hours before this speech was delivered Mr. Balfour, the Prime Minister, had defended the repeal of the corn tax to a Unionist deputation on the ground that it could not be a permanent part of our fiscal system and had described it as " a tax which revived old controversies, which was attached to no new policy believed in by the people at large, and which, being thus the battledore and shuttlecock of the two contending parties, was singularly ill-fitted to be of that permanent armoury which every Chancellor of the Exchequer needed to have at his command."

The Prime Minister and Colonial Secretary thus made speeches on the same day in which the former seemed to be in full retreat from the policy which the latter declared to be imperative. Hot debates followed in Parliament, and it soon became evident that a schism had been created in the Unionist party which threatened the existence of the Government. Sir Michael Hicks Beach said bluntly that Mr. Chamberlain's proposals had divided, and, if persisted in, would destroy the Unionist party. Mr. Ritchie, the new Chancellor of the Exchequer, declared himself a convinced Free Trader and threatened resignation if the Government committed itself to Protection.

Mr. Balfour's " Unsettled Opinions "

In this emergency Mr. Balfour, the Prime Minister, found safety by announcing that his own opinions were unsettled and promising an inquiry. This kept both parties at bay for the next few months, and in the meantime the Board of Trade set to work to collect all available facts and figures bearing on the fiscal question, and early in September produced an elaborate blue book covering the whole subject but expressing no opinion. About the same time Mr. Balfour issued a pamphlet entitled " Insular Free Trade " in which he announced his conversion to the use of tariffs for retaliation, but reserved his opinion about all other aspects of the question. On September 18, Mr. Chamberlain, Mr. Ritchie and Lord George Hamilton, the First Lord of the Admiralty, resigned from the Government, and three days later Lord Balfour of Burleigh, the Secretary for Scotland, and Mr. Arthur Eliot, the Secretary for the Treasury, followed their example. The public were greatly mystified by these resignations. Why, they asked, if Mr. Chamberlain had resigned, should the other Ministers, who were well known as Free Traders, have thought it necessary to quit the Government? Why, above all, did the Duke of Devonshire, who was known to be one of the staunchest of

Free Traders, remain, if his Free Trade colleagues thought it necessary to go?

The answer was that the fact of Mr. Chamberlain's resignation had been disclosed by the Prime Minister to the duke, but withheld from his other colleagues. The duke therefore had stayed in the Cabinet with the knowledge that Mr. Chamberlain was leaving it, and they had resigned in the belief that Mr. Chamberlain was remaining. A fortnight later, when these circumstances had been brought to the duke's knowledge, he too insisted on resigning. In the meantime, Mr. Ritchie's place as Chancellor of the Exchequer had been filled by the appointment of Mr. Chamberlain's son, Mr. Austen Chamberlain, an appointment which gave great satisfaction to the Protectionists and was taken to mean that there was no serious difference between Mr. Balfour and Mr. Joseph Chamberlain.

Mr. Chamberlain's Agitation

Mr. Chamberlain, it turned out, had resigned in order to set himself free to start an independent Protectionist campaign in the country and he was quickly on the war-path. He now went far beyond Imperial Preference, and arraigned the entire Free Trade system. Protection, he now said, was as necessary for British trade as Preference for the British Empire. The great home industries were being battered to death by the assaults of foreign competitors who paid nothing for the privilege of entering our markets. Cotton was going, wool was going, iron and steel were threatened, and it was imperative to arrest the process of decay. With great courage he faced the fact that it would be necessary to tax food in order to give Preferences of any value to the Dominions and endeavoured to beat down the strong instinct or prejudice which put a multitude on the defensive against any measure which would increase the cost of living. This proved the principal stumbling-block to the large number of Unionists who were willing to advocate tariffs on foreign manufactured goods, but unwilling to brave the storm aroused by the proposal to tax food. But nothing daunted Mr. Chamberlain, who brought immense energy and supreme organizing skill to what his opponents called his " raging and tearing propaganda."

For the next two and a half years, the country rang with the controversy. Wherever Mr. Chamberlain went the Free Traders followed, challenging his theory, arraigning his figures, upholding the hitherto accepted views that trade was exchange, that imports could not be excluded without exports being correspondingly reduced, that the consumer would pay and in far greater measure than the Exchequer would profit. Mr. Asquith, the future Liberal Prime Minister, was specially hot on this scent, and greatly increased his reputation by the formidable speeches he made in answer to Mr. Chamberlain. Lord Rosebery, whose imperialism was beyond suspicion, said he did not envy the man who staked the unity of the Empire on taxing the food of the British people, and declared his conviction that the controversies which would arise over the proposed preferences were much more likely to divide than to cement the Empire.

Mr. Balfour at Bay

Seeing his party threatened with a disastrous schism, Mr. Balfour sought to gain time. His position seemed all but desperate. There were enough Free Traders in the House of Commons to make the defeat of the Government highly probable, if he went all lengths with Mr. Chamberlain, and enough whole-hearted supporters of Mr. Chamberlain's policy —" whole-hoggers " as they were called at the time—to make it quite certain, if he rejected that policy. For more than two years he managed to keep a precarious balance between these alternatives, and showed extraordinary skill and wariness in avoiding the traps which were laid for him by his opponents. When hard pressed early in 1905 he evaded his pursuers by " walking out " with all his supporters and leaving a hostile Free-Trade resolution to be carried by 254 to 2; and on three other occasions in the same month similar resolutions were carried *nemine contradicente* in the absence of the Government and its supporters. It was by common consent a most remarkable feat in parliamentary strategy, but it mystified the public, which had no eye for the subtle gradations of colour perceived by the Prime Minister between the black and white of Protection and Free Trade and expected the Government either to resign or to stand up to the challenge of its opponents. Wherever opinion was tested at by-elections it was clear that the tide was running strongly against the Ministry. In the spring, 1905, the great Tory stronghold of Brighton returned a Free Trader by a majority of 800.

It was a maxim of those days that ailing Governments never recover, but unexpected troubles now came to aggravate Mr. Balfour's difficulties. The sudden resignation of Mr. Wyndham, who had angered Irish Unionists by appearing to sanction a cautious move in " devolution," revealed serious differences on Irish policy among Ministers. A Redistribution Bill, in which it was intended to cut down the Irish representation in the House of Commons and proportionately increase the representation of England, foundered on a point of order to the great disappointment of Ministerialists. Worse than all was the question of Chinese labour in South Africa, which from 1904 onwards became a subject of agitated controversy both in that country and in Great Britain.

Chinese Labour

Many reasons combined to give prominence to this question. The South African War had been followed by the usual reaction, and this had been aggravated by the report of the War Commission which revealed grave defects in the military system, and by the failure of the Government to recover any part of its cost from the mine-owners of the Rand. The final touch of disillusion seemed to have been given when these mine-owners procured an ordinance from the Government which enabled them to import Chinese labour under conditions which, when scrutinized by critical eyes, seemed little distinguishable from slavery. The war, as the Government claimed, had been fought to prevent the retrograde Boer civilization from being imposed on South Africa, and to open a new and promising field to British emigration. It was now to be followed by an influx of Chinese. There was something ironical in this result which, apart from all else, must have evoked strong protest.

A violent agitation followed. The Liberal leaders laid hold of the ordinances and denounced as slavery the provisions which segregated the Chinese in compounds; forbade them to hold fixed property or mineral rights, or to engage in any business but unskilled labour; denied them access to the

Courts and required those who imported them to re-export them when their contract expired. The Government replied that similar provisions were to be found in other ordinances sanctioned by other Governments, Liberal as well as Conservative, and that in any case the Chinaman, if he entered into such a contract, would do so voluntarily, knowing the conditions. Lawyers exercised their ingenuity in finding distinctions between the proposed ordinances and previous ordinances, and Asquith was strong on the point that, whereas the previous ordinances confined themselves to securing the execution of the contract between labourer and employer, this one " sought deliberately to prevent the labourer from getting into free contact or communication with the community and to keep him in a situation which no Government had ever ventured, or ever would venture, to keep any subject of the King, however humble he might be or from whatever quarter of the Empire he might come." The great majority cared for none of these distinctions. They said if the previous ordinances contained similar provisions so much the worse for them ; it was time all such ordinances were ended and it was outrageous that the British effort in South Africa should end in a large importation of " Chinese slaves " into the Transvaal.

A Heated Campaign

Tempers rose to a high pitch on both sides, and Mr. Lyttelton, the Colonial Secretary, one of the gentlest of men, was dressed up in a pigtail and presented on posters as a Chinese slave-driver, with a procession of manacled coolies behind him. The Government protested that it was the victim of a malicious propaganda and it had good ground for complaining of the excesses committed in the course of this campaign. But it had challenged something vital in the public consciousness, and mingled with the party spirit which grasps at electioneering good things, there was a very genuine feeling that it had lost touch with the fundamental regard for liberty expected from British statesmen. The Unionist regime seemed suddenly to have come to its climax on Chinese labour. In their Education Bill, their Licensing Bill, their attack on Free Trade, and now finally in this Chinese ordinance, Ministers in the space of three years seemed to have challenged every

Liberal principle in turn, and large numbers of electors who had voted for them at the Khaki Election of 1900, in the belief that they could rally to the common cause without prejudice to their own ideas in domestic politics, were now preparing to have their revenge.

When Parliament rose at the beginning of August it was with the expectation that it would meet again in the following year for another session in which the Redistribution Bill and other legislation which the Government had promised would be proceeded with. But the Unionist dissensions continued all through the autumn, and invaded the Cabinet. Ministers made speeches in public which were evidently aimed at one another; Unionist Associations rejected Mr. Balfour's compromise and adopted the " whole-hog " policy of Protection and Preference; Mr. Chamberlain himself protested vehemently against further concessions to Unionist Free Traders, and compared the Unionist party to an army which was being led into battle on the principle that the lamest man should govern its march. By the end of November Mr. Balfour had come to the conclusion that his position was impossible, and on December 4 he handed his resignation to the King.

Liberal Difficulties

He was possibly influenced in the choice of this moment by the fact that the Liberal party also had relapsed into one of its periodic dissensions. For in a speech at Bodmin on November 25 Lord Rosebery had challenged the Irish policy announced two days earlier by Sir Henry Campbell-Bannerman —the policy of proceeding step by step instead of at one stride into Home Rule—and announced emphatically and explicitly and once for all "that he could not serve under that banner." This speech made a sensation which for the moment threw the Unionist quarrel into the background, and seemed to threaten a revival on the eve of the election of the schism between the Liberal Imperialists and other Liberals which had all but wrecked the party during the South African War. But it turned out that the other Liberal Imperialists, Mr. Asquith, Sir Edward Grey and Mr. Haldane, approved, and had been parties to, Campbell-Bannerman's declaration of Irish policy, and that Lord Rosebery was almost alone in his protest. The Bodmin speech proved in the end to be mainly important in that it ruled Lord Rosebery out of any Liberal Government that might be formed, and ended for Ministerial purposes a career on which the highest hopes had been built. This was widely regretted, but the Irish question played so small a part in the composite volume of opinion which was bringing the Liberal party back to power, that the defection of one man, however eminent, on one issue could have little effect on the course of events. The Bodmin speech gave Mr. Balfour his cue for a heroic effort to divert attention from the fiscal question and Chinese labour, and to bring the battle back to the Irish question, on which he believed the Unionist party to be on favourable ground, but the electors at this moment insisted on thinking of other things, and the cry of the Union in danger fell mostly on deaf ears.

Not a few Liberals were of opinion, that in resigning before the election, Mr. Balfour had laid a trap for his opponents and strongly urged Campbell-Bannerman to follow the example of Disraeli in like circumstances, and to decline to form a Government until after the election. He, however, took the simple view that to refuse the opportunity when it offered would be shirking the task which he had again and again declared himself ready to undertake, and proceeded at once to form a Government.

Even then, he was not free from difficulties. Two very important members of the party, Sir Edward Grey and Mr. Haldane, at first made it a condition of joining the Government that the Prime Minister should go to the House of Lords and leave the leadership in the House of Commons to Mr. Asquith. Campbell-Bannerman who, as recorded in his biography, was largely influenced by his wife, declined this proposal and for two days there was deadlock. But Asquith himself was unwilling to take any position which appeared to reflect on his Chief, and Grey and Haldane were not prepared to press their demand to the point of making serious trouble for their party at this critical moment. In the sequel the inclusion of these two men, Grey as Secretary for Foreign Affairs, and Haldane as Secretary for War, had momentous consequences, and the curious may speculate on the possible differences to the history of the country and

even of the world if they had persisted in holding aloof. All
else went smoothly and the new Government was complete
by December 10.

The Great Liberal Victory

Thus, after ten years in the wilderness of Opposition, the
Liberal party came back to power and succeeded in forming
a Ministry which was acknowledged to be one of all the
talents. Within the Cabinet were Asquith, Grey, Lloyd
George, Haldane—names to be famous in the coming years—
and with them were distinguished men of letters, Morley,
Bryce, Augustine Birrell, a son of Mr. Gladstone, Lord Ripon,
who had sat in Cabinet with Lord Palmerston, Lord Crewe,
who had been Mr. Gladstone's Irish Viceroy in the days of
the First Home Rule Bill, Sydney Buxton, who was to be
High Commissioner for South Africa during the Great War,
John Burns, the first workman to obtain Cabinet rank. Mr.
Balfour called them the " apostles of imperial disintegration "
and appealed to the country to turn them out a month after
he had put them in. It had apparently been the calculation
of some Unionists that the mere appearance of these dangerous
men would cause a revulsion of feeling among the electors
and lead them to seek safety by recalling the Unionist party
to power. But the volume of opinion calling for new men
and new methods was by this time irresistible, and when the
election of January, 1906, was over, the new Ministry found
itself installed in power by an enormous and all but unprecedented majority. In the new House of Commons the
Liberals alone were 377 strong apart from their Irish and
Labour allies (83 and 53 respectively), whereas the Unionists
were reduced to 157, of whom 109 were pledged to Mr.
Chamberlain's and 33 to Mr. Balfour's fiscal policy, and
11 held Free Trade or " Free food " opinions. The Liberal
tide had swept over the whole country and submerged the
Unionist strongholds in London and the Home Counties no
less than the north. Several Unionist Ministers shared the
fate of their supporters, and the late Prime Minister, Mr.
Balfour, was defeated in East Manchester. This was the first
of the great sweeps which were to be characteristic of politics
in later years.

GREAT BRITAIN, FRANCE AND RUSSIA

THE outgoing Ministers apparently had not taken their successors into their confidence about the foreign affairs described in a previous chapter, for, if they had, Sir Henry Campbell-Bannerman could scarcely have said, as he did in his first speech as Prime Minister (Albert Hall, December 21), that the " outlook abroad was most pleasing." By the beginning of January the new Foreign Secretary, Sir Edward Grey, had discovered that it was most unpleasing. The French Government, which was in the middle of its Morocco crisis with Germany, and, in spite of the sacrifice of its Foreign Minister, was still subject to German threats, inquired rather anxiously whether the new British Government would give the same support that had been promised by their predecessors. Since the Prime Minister had pledged himself in his Albert Hall speech to maintain the Entente with France, the answer to that extent was easy. Sir Edward Grey " promised diplomatic support in accordance with Article IX of the British-French Convention," and for the moment no more was said.

On January 9 the French Ambassador came to the Foreign Office and put the question more explicitly. He said that his Government feared an attack by Germany, and that the best guarantee against that possibility would be the certain knowledge that Great Britain would stand behind France. Sir Edward replied that, though he personally was of opinion in the event of an attack on France by Germany arising out of the Anglo-French Moroccan Agreement, public feeling in England would be so strong that no British Government could remain neutral, he had no authority to give any pledge which would transform the Entente into a military alliance, and such a step could not be taken without the assent of Parliament.

M. Cambon replied that war might arise so suddenly that the need for action would be a question not of days but of minutes, and that, if it was necessary for the British Government to consult and to wait for the manifestations of British opinion, it might be too late to be of use. He therefore urged that, if even the possibility of war had to be contemplated, the British and French naval and military authorities should consult together and concert a plan for joint action, as in fact they had already begun to do under the previous Government. To this Sir Edward Grey agreed and obtained the consent of the Prime Minister.

Thus began the " military conversations " of which so much was to be heard in future years. There was no denying the force of the French argument. If it was conceded on the British side that the diplomatic support promised in the British-French Convention might lead on to military intervention, it was from the French point of view folly for the two Governments to be without a concerted plan of action. Far remoter contingencies were habitually provided for by the War Offices of Europe, and to provide for them was part of the A B C of the military business. That was true, and in the circumstances as they now were between France, Germany and Great Britain, no British Government could have refused to take this precaution, unless it had intended to repudiate the Entente with France. This was certainly not the intention of the new Government.

But however logical and necessary the institution of "military conversations" might be in the circumstances, it undoubtedly gave a new emphasis to the British-French Convention. In French eyes the value of " diplomatic support," promised in that Convention, lay in the probability that it would be followed in case of necessity by military support; and the fact that British and French soldiers were engaged in concerting plans together rendered it so much the more probable that this would be its result. The French, moreover, were at no pains to conceal from Germany and the other nations that this step had been taken, and rumours were soon in circulation which greatly exaggerated the extent of the British commitment.

In after years it became a subject of complaint that the Cabinet had not been consulted before so important a step was taken, and though it is extremely improbable that the

Cabinet could or would have come to a different conclusion, the omission afforded a legitimate grievance to certain Ministers who, like Lord Salisbury, in earlier days, feared and mistrusted all entanglements in European politics. All parties afterwards acknowledged that the Cabinet should have been consulted, but the subject had been sprung upon the Prime Minister and Sir Edward Grey without notice at a moment when Ministers were scattered over the country in the election campaign, and the crisis had passed before they returned to London.[1]

The Algeciras Conference

The belief that Great Britain stood behind France undoubtedly helped to moderate German policy, and the Morocco Conference which assembled at Algeciras—under the shadow of the Rock of Gibraltar—on January 17, 1906, passed off in relative peace. The main French demand, that of the right to organize an international police in co-operation with Spain, received the support not only of Great Britain but of Russia and Italy, and President Roosevelt used his influence behind the scenes to induce the Kaiser to consent to it. Germany, finding no support except from Austria, her "brilliant second" as the Kaiser called her, gave way; and the main point having thus been gained, British influence was used to moderate other French demands, and France conceded the equal rights for foreigners and the establishment of the new State Bank financed in equal parts by all the Powers which Germany desired.

This served to turn the corner, but the whole transaction had definitely clouded the relations of Britain and Germany, and the Kaiser and Admiral Tirpitz once more drew their favourite moral that Germany was exposed to mortifications at the hand of Great Britain by her lack of sea-power. A new naval agitation was now on foot in Germany, and preparations were being laid for the next great enlargement of the German fleet. In the meantime efforts were being made on the British side to heal the quarrel. A party of German burgomasters visited England in May and were everywhere warmly welcomed and entertained. King Edward visited the

[1] Sir Edward Grey was prevented from returning by a fatal accident to his wife a few days after the elections were over.

Kaiser at Cronberg in August and listened patiently while the latter explained that his visit to Tangier had been an innocent excursion warmly welcomed by British and Spanish residents. Mr. Haldane, the Secretary for War, went to Berlin, where he was warmly welcomed by the Kaiser and permitted to study the great German military machine. Theologians, men of science, journalists and authors paid visits and return visits and exchanged compliments. All endeavoured to believe that the British-German estrangement was a passing quarrel due to misunderstandings which had only to be discussed in an amicable spirit to be cleared up. But behind it all was the permanent fact of the great schism between the two European Alliances, and the belief in Germany that the casting vote of Great Britain had been given to the anti-German group.

Great Britain and Russia

If ever a Government was determined to keep the peace and to abate the competition in armaments which was more and more becoming a burden and a danger to all the nations, it was the Government of Sir Henry Campbell-Bannerman. But events seemed to conspire to thwart its good intentions. No sooner was the Algeciras Conference over than a crisis arose with the Sultan of Turkey, who, by hoisting the Turkish flag to the west of the Gulf of Akabah in what was supposed to be Egyptian territory, was plainly threatening to jump the Sinai Peninsula and bring the Turkish frontier up to the Suez Canal. In the end he gave way but not until he was faced with an ultimatum threatening forcible measures.

There followed a period of perplexity and difficulty in our relations with Russia. Just as in after days Conservatives objected to all dealings with a Communist Russian Government, so in these days Radicals and Labour men regarded the Tsardom as a detestable tyranny which a British Government, and above all a British Liberal Government, should keep at arm's length. But Russia was the friend of France which greatly desired us to be friends with her friend, and it was much to be desired that we should make an end of the incessant trouble and friction in Central Asia and on the Indian frontier which had followed from our strained relations with her in recent years. A British-Russian agreement, therefore, seemed the natural counterpart of our agreement with France; and Russia having expressed her willingness, the Government set to work to prepare the ground for it in the usual way, by arranging for a visit of the British fleet to Cronstadt in July of this year (1906).

But the announcement of this brought angry remonstrances from Radicals, who thought it intolerable that British sailors should fraternize with "Tsarist assassins," and seeing the storm that threatened, the Russian Government intimated that it would prefer the visit postponed. When July came, there was further embarrassment. The Government had relied on the establishment of the Russian Parliament or Duma as proof of a change of heart in the Russian tyrant, but on July 22 this newly created assembly was abruptly suspended by imperial ukase after an existence of only six weeks. On the following day it fell to the Prime Minister to address the Inter-Parliamentary Union, a body comprising representatives of all the European Parliaments (and on this occasion including a special representation from the Russian Duma) which was to hold its opening Conference in the Royal Gallery of the Palace of Westminster. There could hardly have been a more testing occasion. It was impossible to rebuke a friendly Government in public before such an audience, but even more impossible to pass over in silence the one subject which was in the minds of all present. The Prime Minister met the occasion in a speech which was long remembered as a triumph of fine feeling and skilful expression:

I cannot refrain from saying for myself, and I am sure for everyone in this great and historic assembly, how glad we are to welcome among us to-day the representatives of the youngest of Parliaments—the Russian Duma. We deeply regret the circumstances of their appearance in our midst. It is, I venture to think, of good augury for your movement and for the future of Europe that the first official act of the Russian Parliament in regard to affairs outside the Russian Empire has been to authorize its delegates to come here to Westminster and to join hands with us in the assertion of those great principles of peace and goodwill which were so incalculably advanced by the head of the Russian State, the author and convener of the Hague Conference. I make no comment on the news which has reached us this morning; this is neither the place nor the moment for that. We have not a sufficient acquaintance with the facts to be in a position to justify or criticize. But this at least we can say, we who base our hopes on the parliamentary system—new negotiations have often a disturbed, if not a stormy, youth. The Duma will revive in one form or another. We can say with all sincerity: " La Duma est morte, vive la Duma." (July 23, 1906.)

It was not foreseen in those days that the proletarian masters of Russia would have even less use for Dumas than the Tsar, and the speech was received with immense enthusiasm by the parliamentary audience. The next day, when the Russian Ambassador expressed his fear that it might be misunderstood by his Imperial master, Campbell-Bannerman reassured him by pointing out that he had said no more than the Tsar himself had said, for he too had expressed the hope that the Duma might reassemble at some more convenient season. He had, nevertheless, between the lines of his speech contrived to say a good deal that that potentate certainly would not have said.

The British-Russian Convention

The Radical objectors were reassured, and being convinced that dislike of the constitution of a foreign country should not be a bar to political relations which were desirable on their merits, the Government proceeded with negotiations for an Anglo-Russian Convention on approximately the same lines as the Anglo-French Entente. This was concluded in August of the following year after a prolonged exchange of views in which Mr. John Morley, as Secretary for India, played an important part. In the main it delimited the Russian and British spheres of interest in Persia and Central Asia, giving the north to Russia and the south to Great Britain. Some critics objected that since the north was by far the richer territory, Russia had got the best of the bargain ; but in the view of the Government this was more than outweighed by the strategic and military importance of the free hand secured to them in the south. This finally extinguished the fear of a Russian invasion of India, which for fifty years and more had weighed on the British people, and relieved the Government of India of the necessity of keeping watch against Russian intriguers in Afghanistan and elsewhere on the Indian frontier. It had been a point much debated whether Russia would actually have ventured the daring and difficult risk of invading India across the great natural barrier of mountains which protects her on the north, but the threat of such an invasion had been kept alive by the Russian military party and used with considerable effect as a diplomatic weapon; and to be rid of it was at least a great practical convenience.

It cannot be said that the Persian part of the Anglo-Russian Convention worked smoothly. The officers and officials of the Tsarist regime were with difficulty persuaded to moderate their traditional anti-British instincts or to respect Persian interests and feelings in the way that we thought right and reasonable. There were many difficult moments in the subsequent years, in which the British Government had to weigh the great political interest of friendship with Russia against the necessity of consenting to and condoning Russian proceedings in North Persia to which they took strong objection.

The agreement was judged in England mainly on the broad ground that it ended the Anglo-Russian quarrel; and though it was coldly received by Radical objectors to the Russian tyranny, it was generally approved by the public which saw in it only, as they had seen in the Anglo-French Entente, a step towards peace by the removal of differences between the two friendly Powers. European observers judged it somewhat differently, and saw Great Britain taking a further step into the camp of the Dual Alliance. The Germans especially detected in it the hand of King Edward whom they believed to be engaged in a conspiracy to encircle Germany, being inspired thereto by dislike and envy of his nephew, the Kaiser. This suspicion was groundless, for though the King had undoubtedly been very outspoken about the behaviour of his nephew in the Morocco crisis, and had gone out of his way to show his sympathy with French Ministers, he had kept strictly within his constitutional limits, and was in no sense the author of either the French or the Russian agreements. The responsibility for both, nominal and actual, rested with his Ministers, who in each case were thinking only of composing their differences with France and Russia, and had no hostile intention against any other Power. To Sir Edward Grey and Sir Henry Campbell-Bannerman as to Lord Lansdowne and Mr. Balfour it seemed impossible that Great Britain should be prevented from making friends with France and Russia because Germany or the Triple Alliance thought it more convenient that they should be estranged, and all said with perfect sincerity that they had no desire for anything but peace and friendly relations with Germany.

Campbell-Bannerman and Disarmament

If there was one thing on which Campbell-Bannerman had set his heart when he became Prime Minister, it was to procure some abatement in the competition in armaments which was rising steadily in these years. The Second Hague Conference was due to take place in 1907, and it seemed to him that his Government ought to be early in the field giving a lead in this direction. It therefore announced its intention to cut down battleship construction by 25 per cent., destroyer construction by 60 per cent., and submarine construction by 33 per cent. (July, 1906.) In March of the following year, to make his intention clear, the Prime Minister wrote an article which was published in the weekly paper then called *The Nation*, in which he offered to reduce armaments still further, if other Governments would do the same, and urged strongly that the subject should not be excluded, as the German and certain other Governments were supposed to desire, from the Hague Conference.

To Campbell-Bannerman's surprise, this article, entirely pacific in intention, was regarded by the Germans as a menacing communication. Great Britain, they said, was calling on her neighbours to stop at the moment most convenient to herself, the moment when she was at the top of her own naval power, and when she had just launched a new type of battleship, the far-famed Dreadnought, which she asserted to be vastly superior to any possessed by her rivals. She was claiming an unchallengeable superiority for all time, and probably preparing to enforce this claim by arms, if it were not conceded. Nothing could have been farther from Campbell-Bannerman's thoughts, and he was unfeignedly astonished that any human being could have put such an interpretation on his language. It nevertheless required much patient explanation and tactful diplomacy to convince the Germans and certain other European Governments that Great Britain did not intend, when she launched her Dreadnought, to make a peremptory demand on other nations to cease their competition with her.

The Germans were now more than ever determined to keep the subject of disarmament out of the Hague Conference. The Kaiser said that the mere proposal to discuss it was an invasion of his sovereign right to build what fleet and raise what army he chose and that he might as well abdicate as entertain it. What, he asked, would be said if France proposed that the German army should be reduced? What answer but the drawn sword would a patriotic German give to such a suggestion? The circumstances were, indeed, somewhat untoward. While the Prime Minister was in-geminating peace, Sir John Fisher, the energetic First Sea-Lord of the British Admiralty, could not refrain from singing the praises of the Dreadnought, his own special invention, and just as in the previous year Count Schlieffen had declared the moment to be uniquely favourable for Germany to try conclusions with France, so he was supposed to have said that Great Britain would never again have such an opportunity as the present for disposing of the menace of the German fleet. It was also known to the Germans that Great Britain was drawing nearer to Russia, and they saw the hostile combination against them in Europe correspondingly strengthened.

The project of a mutual reduction of armaments thus fell still-born from the beginning. The Kaiser was adamant that the German delegates should not debate it at the Hague Conference, and though the subject remained on the agenda, it was relegated to a pious resolution declaring it to be " highly desirable " which was carried at the fag-end of the proceedings in the absence of the German delegates. These delegates, in the meantime, had contrived very adroitly to turn the tables on Great Britain. By supporting an American resolution in favour of the immunity of private property at sea, which the British Admiralty stoutly resisted, they made her appear as holding out almost single-handed for the largest belligerent rights for the greatest fleet against the humane opinion of the rest of the world. When the Great War came all the Allies, including the United States, combined in the exercise of these rights for the discomfiture of Germany, but at the moment all Europe scoffed and said that British hypocrisy had once more been exposed.

The Great Competition

The way was now open to the great competition in Dreadnoughts which was to continue up to the Great War. In April, 1906, a new German Naval Law had been introduced, which provided for the widening of the Kiel Canal, and a considerable increase in the previous ship-building programme. At the end of the year Great Britain created a Home Fleet to be concentrated in the North Sea, and in the following year the British Secretary for War, Mr. Haldane, introduced his military scheme which provided an Expeditionary Force of 120,000 men to operate, in case of need, on the continent of Europe. In less than two years the Liberal British Government had discovered that it was living in a fighting world in which it dared not go unprepared. Men might agree in the abstract that the competition in armaments was collectively folly, but each nation judged that armaments were imperative for itself.

 CHAPTER IX

THE GREAT LIBERAL PARLIAMENT

WHEN the new Parliament assembled for business on February 19, 1906, the Liberal party had been out of power for nearly eleven years, and being now in an immense majority, it looked confidently to the Government to make up for lost time. To the Government this majority was embarrassingly large. So many ardent spirits panting to be at work on plans and programmes which they thought to be of supreme importance; so many independent minds claiming liberty to criticize and amend, had never in living memory been ranged behind any Government. They overflowed the Government benches and thronged the side galleries and even invaded the Opposition side of the House. Many were entering Parliament for the first time, and came with the ardour of new men determined to attend every sitting and to seize every opportunity of taking part in debate. How to satisfy them, how to avoid the schisms and discontents to which great majorities, and especially great Liberal and Radical majorities, were liable, were from the beginning anxious questions for the new Ministers.

These Ministers were aware, as many of their supporters were not, that a shadow lay over the scene from the beginning. Whatever the country might have said at the election, the House of Lords remained unchanged—an overwhelmingly Conservative body with the last word in legislation. A Unionist leader said, soon after the election, that whether in power or in Opposition the Unionist party would still control the destinies of the country, and at that moment many thousands of his party reckoned on the House of Lords to save them from the Radical measures which otherwise threatened them. Whether or how far that House should exercise this control was for the next five years to be the dominant issue in domestic politics, but though they expected the peers to assert their power, if, or when the Liberal tide ebbed, Ministers did not look for any serious challenge from that quarter immediately after their great triumph at the polls. Thinking this danger to lie rather in the future than in the present, they decided to push forward as quickly as possible with Bills on which their supporters had most set their hearts, and the King's speech for the first session promised an Education Bill, a Trades Disputes Bill, an Agricultural Holdings Bill, a Bill for the abolition of Plural Voting, an Irish Government Bill and numerous other minor measures.

The Education Bill

While taking objection to nearly all these Bills the Unionist party concentrated its attack on the Education Bill. That was to a large extent a repeal of Mr. Balfour's Act of 1902, since it proposed to obliterate the distinction between voluntary or " non-provided " schools and publicly provided schools, and to bring all alike under the local authority. In all schools, public or voluntary, undenominational teaching, as defined in the " Cowper-Temple clause " of the original Education Act, was to be given by the ordinary teachers, unless they pleaded conscientious objection; and in the former voluntary schools, now to be transferred to the local authority, facilities were to be given for special denominational teaching on two days in the week. But this special teaching was not to be given by the regular teachers, the ground alleged for this being that an option to give it would be tantamount to compulsion, since in most cases the teachers would be unable to decline without disqualifying themselves for the appointment. Finally, to meet the case of Roman Catholics and Anglo-Catholics, it was provided in Clause IV that a school might remain denominational, though maintained out of public funds, if four-fifths of the parents desired it.

The Bill, which was introduced by Mr. Birrell, the Minister of Education, on April 9, 1906, raised a storm of protest. The bishops in a meeting at Lambeth denounced it as " confiscation " and " tyranny " and declared uncompromising opposition on behalf of the Church of England. The Roman Catholics refused the concession offered for their schools and made common cause with the Anglicans. Joined in opposition were a certain number of Radicals who objected to any religious teaching under State auspices and stood out for "complete secularization," and a few High Churchmen who objected so strongly to "Cowper-Temple" teaching that they were willing to accept secularization in preference to it. All through the summer the battle raged in the House of Commons on these rather confused lines, and the Bill was smothered with amendments which were only disposed of by a drastic use of the guillotine closure. The Irish were hostile, but Liberals and Nonconformists stood solidly behind the Bill, thinking it a reasonable solution that the denominations should concentrate on a certain number of purely denominational schools, and leave the rest to the local authorities on the conditions for religious teaching laid down in the Bill.

The First Struggle with the Lords

The Bill passed its third reading by a majority of 192 in the Commons at the end of July, when the Lords gave it a second reading but postponed the Committee stage till November. Then they took it clause by clause and turned it inside out. As reconstructed by the peers, the Bill practically restored the Act of 1902 and, as the Government contended, even gave the denominations further privileges, since the area of the Clause IV schools had been extended from town to country, and the "right of entry" was claimed for denominational teachers into the public schools. The Lords were of course aware that the Government could not accept the "changeling" thus offered them for their own child, and Ministers retorted by moving the Commons to reject the Lords' amendments *en bloc*. A period of negotiation followed, and at one moment compromise seemed possible, but in the end all efforts broke down on the stubborn question whether the regular teachers should be granted the option of giving denominational teaching, and when the Lords persisted on this point, the Government abandoned their Bill.

The greater part of the work of the first session was thus destroyed in spite of the great triumph at the beginning of the year. It may be added that another effort was made to settle the question in 1908 when Mr. Asquith's Government offered the "right of entry" for denominational teaching into *all* schools on two days in the week, provided that all came under public control, and was willing to permit assistant, though not head-teachers, to volunteer for this teaching.[1] But though Archbishop Davidson appears to have favoured this settlement, the other bishops required many more concessions, and this last effort too was abandoned.

The Lords, meanwhile, had rejected the Plural Voting Bill and drastically amended other Liberal Bills such as the Irish Town Tenants Bill and the Agricultural Holdings Bill. The only important measure which they left intact was the Trades Disputes Bill, which restored the right of peaceful picketing and the immunity of Trade Union funds from civil proceedings and saved strikes from being treated as offences under the laws of conspiracy. In effect the law was brought back to the position in which all parties had assumed it to be until certain recent judgments in the law-courts, but there was much controversy among lawyers as to the proper way of reaching this conclusion; and though the Lords accepted the Government Bill, they did so frankly on the tactical ground that it was not expedient at the moment to challenge organized labour on this issue.

With this exception, the peers made it clear that they were not to be deterred by the largest Liberal majority from dealing as they thought fit with Liberal legislation, and in the following session they made short work of the Government's land legislation for Scotland, and so amended an Irish " Evicted Tenants " Bill that Irish members declared it to be quite valueless. Liberals were now saying loudly that, if this went on, appeals to the country would be quite useless, when they resulted in a Liberal majority. The measures they had proposed were entirely in line with the programme they had put before the country; they had received an enormous majority for that programme and yet they had been prevented from fulfilling their promises and carrying out their programme, by a second Chamber which had accepted without demur or any serious amendment, the whole of the legislation presented to them by Unionist Governments in the previous ten years. Whatever second Chamber might be desirable, said the Prime Minister, it ought not to be one which was

---

[1] An exception was made for existing head-teachers in voluntary schools which would have been transferred to the local authorities.

completely at the disposal of one party and uniformly hostile to the other.

Unionists retorted that if Liberals were aggrieved they could dissolve Parliament and appeal again to the country, to which Liberals replied that the power of forcing dissolutions was precisely what they were not prepared to concede to a second Chamber which, as they had good reason to believe, would use it against a Liberal party but never against a Conservative party. The Government considered seriously whether they should dissolve after the destruction of their Education Bill, but decided that to appeal to the country on an issue which did not greatly stir the mass of the public and thus end a Parliament on which such high hopes had been built within twelve months of its assembling was not practical politics. But the two Houses were now committed to the conflict which, as Mr. Gladstone had predicted twelve years previously, would " go on to its issue."

Finding a Way

At the end of 1906 Campbell-Bannerman had been able to do no more than promise his angry supporters to " find a way " to make the popular will prevail, but on June 24 of the year following (1907) he produced the scheme of the " suspensory veto," *i.e.* permitting the House of Lords to hold up legislation for two sessions but no longer, which had in the meantime been evolved by the Cabinet, largely on his own initiative, and which, with slight modifications, was from henceforth to be the policy of the Liberal party. This, embodied in a resolution which was intended to lay the foundation for legislation in the following year, was carried by 432 to 147, but not until after a stormy debate in which Mr. Balfour charged the Government with seeking to pick a gratuitous quarrel with the House of Lords, and certain Radical and Labour representatives demanded the total abolition of that assembly. There were many gems of speech in the three days over which the debate extended. Mr. Lloyd George said that the House of Lords had been called the watch-dog of the Constitution, but was in reality " Mr. Balfour's poodle "; Mr. Winston Churchill called it " a one-sided, hereditary, unprized, unrepresentative, irresponsible absentee."

The Unionist party took the passing of this resolution with composure. Liberals might fulminate but the House of Lords remained a solid fact, and if legislation threatening its powers were attempted, it would know what to do. The Prime Minister, they said, had been obliged to do something to appease his supporters and the resolution was a convenient way of doing that, and at the same time, putting an awkward question on the shelf. In the meantime there were signs that the Liberal tide was ebbing from the high-water mark of 1906, and Unionists believed that as it ran out, the Government would be more and more discredited by the failure of its legislation and its manifest inability to return the blows inflicted on it by the House of Lords. Liberals talked of " filling up the cup " of the House of Lords until its iniquities ran over in public wrath; their opponents retorted that they were " ploughing the sands," and that the public showed no sign of being displeased at their discomfiture. Threatened institutions live long, and it was confidently predicted that the House of Lords would survive this as it had all other assaults.

An Irish Failure

The Government, meanwhile, had suffered a serious blow in the failure of the " step by step " policy for Ireland—the policy of proceeding to Home Rule by instalments which it had put before the country at the General Election. At the beginning of May, Mr. Birrell, who was now Chief Secretary for Ireland, introduced a Bill setting up a Central Irish Representative Council, composed of 82 elected and 24 nominated members, to which should be transferred a large part of the control over Irish Departments then exercised by Dublin Castle. Mr. Redmond, the Irish leader, gave it a cautious welcome and led the House of Commons to suppose that it would probably be accepted by Irish Nationalists as a step in advance. This was no doubt his honest belief, but the Bill was nevertheless rejected unanimously by the Irish Nationalist Convention which assembled in Dublin in Whitsun week. The Convention, influenced largely by the clergy and the new Sinn Fein movement, declared itself unalterably opposed to the acceptance of anything less than full Parliamentary Home Rule. It was clearly useless to proceed with a measure intended to conciliate Ireland in the teeth of Irish opposition, but Ministers were much blamed by their supporters for having failed to discover the state of Irish feeling before exposing themselves to this rebuff.

This occasion must be noted as one of the landmarks in the development of the Irish question. In a letter to the Prime Minister, Mr. Birrell pointed to the combination of the clergy and the new independent National movement which called itself "Sinn Fein" (Stand by Ourselves) as equally threatening to the Government and to the Irish Parliamentary party. The Irish parliamentary leaders, he said, were now in a position in which the slighest appearance of yielding an iota of the full Irish demand would be instantly fatal to them. The entire parliamentary party would be " kicked out " if the suspicion gained ground that they were conniving at the weakening of British Liberals on Home Rule. It had not till then been in the minds of either of the British parties that the delay in the settlement of the Irish question and the suspicion that the British advocates of Home Rule were weakening in the cause would lead to an extreme movement which would await its opportunity for a more drastic settlement. But the more ardent Nationalists were now beginning to point out that twenty-one years had elapsed since Mr. Gladstone introduced his first Home Rule Bill, and that so far from progress having been made towards Parliamentary Home Rule, the British Liberal party had gone to the recent election unpledged to anything but a step in advance. Many voices were already enlarging on this theme in the year 1907.

CHAPTER X

In the eyes of the historian of the British Empire the grant of self-government to the conquered Boer States will probably rank as the most important and, in its consequences, the most durable of the events of the year 1906 and 1907. This was the decisive step which rendered possible the Union of South Africa under the British flag two years later.

The name of Sir Henry Campbell-Bannerman will always be associated with this great act of policy. He had accepted the annexation of the two Boer States as an inevitable result of the war, but he was for that reason the more determined that annexation should carry with it at the earliest possible moment the free institutions which were the pride of the British Commonwealth of Nations. When he became Prime Minister, he found in existence the scheme of a constitution for the Transvaal promulgated in March, 1905, which proposed to set up a Legislative Assembly composed partly of elective and partly of nominated members, but reserved all executive functions and the control of finance to the Lieutenant-Governor, who was also to have the right of reserving legislation for the veto of the crown. This in the opinion of the then Colonial Secretary, Mr. Lyttelton, was as much as " prudent and sensible men " whether at home or in South Africa could be expected to approve, or as any Government would be wise in conceding within three years of the war. The Treaty of Vereeniging had promised " representative institutions leading up to self-government " and the limited constitution now proposed was a strict fulfilment of this promise.

Campbell-Bannerman was for sweeping it all away and proceeding at once to Responsible Government on the Dominion model. Such audacity took away the breath of some even of his own Liberal colleagues, and there were serious arguments before the Cabinet consented to cancel

99

the Lyttelton Constitution.   Among the obstacles was the opposition of the High Commissioner, Lord Selborne, an able and sincere man, who did not easily adjust himself to the new circumstances.   The principle having been decided, the next step was to send out a committee to the Transvaal, under the chairmanship of Sir Joseph West-Ridgeway, to report on the proper method of representation on the basis of manhood suffrage.   The committee set out on April 7, 1906, and came back on July 14, with a complete scheme arranged between British and Boers.   Inquiry had elicited the fact that the British in the Transvaal were no more enamoured than the Boers of the " Downing Street Government," which they detected in the Lyttelton scheme, and were ready for an amicable settlement which would enable Responsible Government to be set up without delay.   On this basis the Government proceeded to frame a complete self-governing constitution for both the Transvaal and the Orange River Colony, and it was presented to the House of Commons on July 30, 1906, by Mr. Winston Churchill, then Under-Secretary for the Colonies.

Seldom can a Goverment have acted with more expedition in a matter of high importance.   But the opponents of the scheme were correspondingly incensed, and long and heated debates followed in both Houses of Parliament.   To the great majority of Unionists, and indeed to almost all outside observers in the world, it seemed something like madness to give the Boers the opportunity, as the current phrase ran, of " winning back by the ballot-box what they had lost in the war." Was it for this that we had sacrificed 30,000 lives and spent 250 millions of money?   Wrath was poured out on the Government for what Mr. Balfour described as " a dangerous, audacious and reckless experiment," and in the debate in the House of Commons its opponents spoke at such length that the Prime Minister was left no time to defend his own measure. Lord Lansdowne and Lord Milner, the former High Commissioner, were equally vehement in their denunciations when the House of Lords debated the scheme.   But these were only temporary and expiring protests.   When the finished work was presented to both Houses of Parliament on December 17 the necessary resolutions were agreed to without a division, with general public approval.   There was an instinctive feeling that the Government had placed itself in line with the greatest and wisest of British traditions.

But the credit was not alone due to the British. There were among the Boers generous and high-minded men, especially General Botha and General Smuts, who could not have accepted anything less than the equality of status enjoyed by British citizens in all the Dominions, but who were ready to work for peace and conciliation on that basis. To General Botha especially, belongs the credit of having persuaded the old Dutch burghers to consent to what for many of them was a difficult act of submission.

Chinese Labour

Another burning South African question, that of Chinese labour, found its solution through the grant of self-government to the Transvaal. This, as often happens with electioneering topics, had proved a much more difficult subject for a Government to handle than for Opposition speakers to exploit on the platform. While the election of 1906 was in progress, the Law-officers and lawyers in the Government had warned the Prime Minister that a literal fulfilment of his promise to " stop forthwith the recruitment and embarkation of Chinese coolies " would involve the Government in large claims for compensation for the breach of contracts already entered into. The Prime Minister thereupon explained that the word " forthwith " must be construed as applying to " further embarkations when those already authorized were exhausted." Eventually the Government decided that, while further recruitment and the embarkation consequent upon it should be stopped, the question of dealing with the 47,000 coolies already in the country should be left to the Transvaal Government now about to be set up. This encountered some opposition from Radicals who denounced it as compromising with an evil thing, but it was in line with the new self-governing principle, and it led in practice to the speediest elimination that could have been expected of the coolie labour. After a short trial the Transvaalers, both British and Boer, decided that the drawbacks and dangers of keeping 50,000 Chinese in compounds on the Rand far outweighed the advantages of a cheap labour supply, and in June, 1907, General Botha, who was now Prime Minister, announced that the Chinese would be sent home immediately on the expiry of their contracts.

The Death of Campbell-Bannerman

When Campbell-Bannerman became Prime Minister in December 1905, he was warned by his doctors that, if he added the leadership of the House of Commons to the other duties of his office, he would certainly shorten his life, and by the winter of 1907 he was an exhausted and dying man. The death of his wife, to whom he was entirely devoted, had greatly shaken him in the previous year, but he had rallied from that blow and in the subsequent fifteen months applied all his energy to public affairs. His short period as Prime Minister is his chief title to fame. For though the fibre of his character had been tested in the South African War, and he had won great respect by the tenacity with which he held to his then unpopular opinions he had not, up to that point, shown any high capacity as a leader or debater in Parliament, and the doubt whether he would be equal to the task of leading the House of Commons when he became Prime Minister was by no means ill-founded. But accession to that high office seemed to make him a new man, and in the two years that followed he obtained a mastery over the House of Commons and developed a skill and resourcefulness in debate of which his best friends had scarcely thought him capable. The great throng of Liberal, Labour and Irish were divided on many things, but they were at one in the affection for " C.B.," and in their readiness to submit to his control. He was by no means without astuteness, but he gained much in their eyes from the contrast between his simple and direct methods and the subtle dialectics and skilful casuistry which Mr. Balfour displayed in the leadership of the Unionist party. Politics in these years presented themselves to a vast number as a duel between Balfour and "C.B.," recalling to an older generation the longer and more famous duel between Disraeli and Gladstone. The famous occasion on which he answered an elaborate and skilful but highly dialectical speech of Mr. Balfour's on Free Trade with " enough of this foolery " (March 13, 1906) threw suddenly into a high light the contrast between the two men.

The Succession of Asquith

Campbell-Bannerman resigned on April 2 and died three weeks later (April 22). There was no doubt as to his successor. As far back as 1898, when Sir William Harcourt resigned the leadership of the Liberal party, Asquith had been regarded as one of the only two possible successors, and in April, 1908, he was without rival or competitor. King Edward happened to be at Biarritz, and by a daring departure from convention which caused much criticism at the time he " sent for " the new Prime Minister to " kiss hands " at that French watering-place. Asquith went on April 5, and two days later returned to London with the list of his Ministers. In that the most important change from the previous Administration was the appointment of Mr. Lloyd George, previously President of the Board of Trade, to be Chancellor of the Exchequer.

If Asquith's promotion was a foregone conclusion, some members of his party were by no means sure of its results. In many ways he belonged to the old school of statesmen, being a son of Oxford and Balliol, a man of high academic distinction and wide culture. No one questioned his supremacy in debate or his immense capacity for handling all sorts of subjects, but there was a certain aloofness in his character which was in strong contrast with the homespun familiarity of his predecessor, and the question was asked rather anxiously whether he would keep touch with and control the great democratic party of all sorts and conditions which he was now appointed to lead. The question was to be answered in ways undreamt of at the time, but in April 1908 there were not many who predicted a long tenure of office for the new Prime Minister.

The circumstances, indeed, were far from encouraging. Some reaction from the great Liberal triumph of January, 1906, was to be expected, and in the past few months the by-elections had shown a decided turn in the tide. But the Government had suffered blow upon blow from the House of Lords, and if the constituencies showed no sign of resenting its action, that Assembly would almost certainly be encouraged to do its worst. The Government and the Liberal party were thus faced with a crucial dilemma. They had exhausted practically all that they could do with the consent of the House of Lords, and had now to choose between abandoning the chief part of their programme and going on to a conflict which would compel them to dissolve Parliament in the near future. Liberals, who saw an enormous majority panting to do its work, shrank from either conclusion. To govern on the sufferance of their opponents and proceed only with such measures as they would agree to was, they said, intolerable; but it was scarcely less intolerable to be compelled by these opponents to break off their work and end the Parliament half-way through its normal term of existence. The Unionist party might as well be in power continuously as compel the Liberal party to submit to these conditions.

From the beginning Asquith warned his followers of the difficulties ahead. " There is," he told them, " a lot of country still to traverse, steep hills to climb, stiff fences to take, deep and even turbulent streams to cross before we come to the end of our journey, but we know where we are going and we shall not lose our way." He spoke even better than he knew, for at that moment no one foresaw or could foresee the course of events which was to prolong the stubborn conflict of wills up to the Great War and make Asquith the protagonist in the greatest constitutional struggle of modern times. His decision for the moment was to proceed with Liberal legislation in the House of Commons and leave the House of Lords to do what they would, in trust that the country would eventually decide to arm the House of Commons with the new powers proposed in the previous session. At this moment it seemed quite probable that the country would take the Unionist view and condemn Liberal persistence in proposing measures which were doomed to destruction in the House of Lords as futile and unpractical.

The Licensing Bill

Certainly it was doubtful whether the first measure which Asquith's Government produced in the session of 1908 would evoke any popular enthusiasm. This was a Licensing Bill, the object of which was to re-establish the theory upset by the Act of 1904 that the licence was an annual permit to sell drink which could be revoked without compensation by the authority which gave it, and on that basis to pave the way

for a drastic reduction in the number of public-hc
was to be a period of delay during which all part.
have notice of the new conditions and compensatio.
licences extinguished. Asquith pleaded for it as a n.
and reasonable remedy for admitted evils, but 1.
immediately denounced by his opponents as " spoliat. ᴗ ´
and " blackmail," and in spite of offers to prolong the period
of delay and increase the amount of compensation, it was
summarily rejected on its second reading by the House of
Lords. King Edward had watched with much misgiving the
rising conflict between the two Houses of Parliament, and did
his utmost to persuade the peers to take a more conciliatory
view of these proposals, but he argued in vain. The peers
and the Unionist leaders were convinced that in this matter
they had popular feeling behind them, and that the Government
would not venture to appeal to the country on the issue of more
or less beer; and the Government, it must be said, was by no
means sure of what would happen, if they did make such an
appeal.

Old-Age Pensions

But there was one subject, finance, which was still supposed
to be beyond reach of the House of Lords, and in the Budget
which he had prepared as Chancellor of the Exchequer in
the previous months, and which he now introduced as Prime
Minister, Asquith found the opportunity to introduce old-age
pensions. In the previous years he had made the distinction
between earned and unearned incomes for the purposes of
income-tax, and by careful economy brought the revenue
to a point at which the pensions could be financed without increasing taxation. He now proposed to give pensions of five
shillings a week to persons of the age of seventy who had not
more than £21 a year and smaller sums on a descending scale
to those who had not more than £31, 10s. a year. It was, as
he described it, a " modest and tentative " measure, but
Conservative opinion at the time deemed it a dangerous and
costly experiment. When the Budget reached the House,
of Lords, Lord Lansdowne said he thought the arguments
against it to be conclusive, but that he feared the misrepresenta-
tion which would follow if the peers gave effect to that view.

He therefore contented himself with certain amendments including one which would have limited the duration of the measure to seven years, but these the Speaker ruled out of order as breaches of the Commons' privileges in dealing with the conditions under which public money should be spent and the original proposal was passed intact.

This "modest and tentative" measure, an Eight Hours Bill for miners, which the Lords let pass under protest, and a Scottish Education Bill were all that survived at the end of Asquith's first session. The Lords had rejected the Licensing Bill, which was the chief part of the work of the Commons, rejected the Scottish Landholders Bill, and so amended the Scottish Land Values Bill that the Government thought better to drop it. There was by now practically nothing left in the Liberal programme which had any chance of escaping destruction at the hands of the peers, and on all the major issues which interested Liberals—Education, Temperance reform, Land reform, Welsh Disestablishment, Irish Home Rule—the way seemed hopelessly blocked. The Government had only carried its old-age pension scheme by asserting the privileges of the Commons in finance, and on this ground they still thought themselves secure. But with this exception there seemed at the end of the year 1908 to be no legislation open to the Liberal party, unless it consented to act within the limits laid down by the Conservative party acting through the House of Lords.

Asquith put the case to his supporters in a speech at the National Liberal Club on December 11. "To put the thing plainly," he said, "the present system enables the leader of the party which has been defeated and repudiated by the electors at the polls to determine through the House of Lords what shall and what shall not be the legislation of the country. The question I want to put to you and to my fellow Liberals outside is this: 'Is this state of things to continue?' We say that it must be brought to an end, and I invite the Liberal party to treat the veto of the House of Lords as the dominating issue in politics—the dominating issue, because in the long-run it overshadows and absorbs every other."

These were resounding words, but Mr. Gladstone in 1894 and Lord Rosebery in 1895 had used almost exactly the same language and nothing had happened except that the Liberal party had lost the subsequent elections and been continuously out of power for more than ten years. Was there any reason why anything different should happen now? Lord Lansdowne and Mr. Balfour said confidently not, and were able to point to by-elections as proof that opinion was turning against the Government. The Liberal measures to which a few zealous persons attached such immense importance created no enthusiasm in the country, which was glad to see them rejected or amended by the House of Lords. What purpose, they asked, could a second Chamber fulfil if it was not to be a Conservative bulwark against dangerous, pernicious and unconstitutional innovations? The House of Lords had a duty as well as the House of Commons to stand by its convictions, and it would be an act of cowardice for it to surrender because the Liberals had a large temporary majority in the House of Commons. It was precisely on such an occasion that it needed to stand firm.

Thus on one side and on the other parties braced themselves for the coming struggle.

THE TROUBLES OF EUROPE

WE must now take up the story of affairs in Europe from the end of the Hague Conference in 1907—the point at which it was left in a previous chapter. It has been necessary for the moment to describe the course of British affairs as if these alone filled the thoughts of the British people and their rulers. The reality was far otherwise. All through these years incessant and dangerous crises in Europe ran simultaneously with the conflict in home affairs, increasing the strain upon Ministers and adding to the unrest and anxiety in the public mind.

Read by itself as a chapter in British history, the year 1908 may be reckoned a comparatively quiet one, but it was marked in Europe by the Revolution of the " Young Turks " who deposed the blood-stained Sultan, Abdul Hamid, and announced their intention of introducing parliamentary government and making radical reforms in Turkish administration ; by the sudden proclamation of Bulgarian independence (October 5) and the equally sudden annexation on the following day (October 6) of the nominally Turkish provinces of Bosnia-Herzegovina by Austria-Hungary—events which were to have far-reaching consequences in the next few years. In the last week of October, Asquith, the Prime Minister, told Balfour, the leader of the Opposition, in confidence, that he had never known Europe nearer to war than at that moment.

In spite of their rebuff at the Hague Conference, and in spite of the large increase in the German navy provided in the new law of April, 1908, British Ministers persisted in their efforts to come to terms with the Germans about the naval competition. When King Edward visited the Kaiser at his castle at Cronberg in August of that year, Sir Charles Hardinge, the permanent Under-Secretary for Foreign Affairs, who accompanied him, broached the question to the Kaiser with very discouraging results. The Kaiser, according to his own account, "looked Sir Charles in the eye till he blushed scarlet," and told him that Germany would fight rather than yield to British remonstrances at the increase of her fleet. Sir Charles's version of this conversation is pitched in a lower key, but he was left in no doubt that the door had been banged, barred and bolted against any possible accommodation at this time. The mere raising of the question was in the Kaiser's eyes an offence to his imperial dignity and a challenge to his sovereign rights.

The Kaiser was at no pains to conceal his part in this business, and a few days later the story of the Cronberg interview reached Vienna, where it had immediate consequences which he had by no means foreseen. At that moment Aehrenthal, the Austrian Foreign Secretary, was seeking the consent of his Hungarian colleagues to the annexation of Bosnia-Herzegovina, and they naturally asked him first of all what would be the attitude of their German ally. To this he replied (August 19) that they could be absolutely sure of the support of Germany, since after her rejection of King Edward's overture, she was now dependent on Austria alone. So sure, in fact, did Aehrenthal feel on this point that when he launched his project on October 6 he had not even taken the precaution of telling his German ally. He was nevertheless right in his calculation, for though the Kaiser was greatly incensed and at first inclined to demand that the annexation should be revoked, his Chancellor, Bülow, pointed out that in the circumstances in which she now was Germany could not afford to quarrel with Austria, and with whatever reluctance he yielded and promised his support. In this way the German quarrel with Great Britain had the unexpected and undesigned results of throwing Germany into the arms of Austria.

The Bosnia-Herzegovina Crisis

The annexation of Bosnia-Herzegovina raised a storm in Europe. It was not so much the thing in itself as the way in which it was done that caused the trouble. Austria was already in occupation of the two provinces, and the change from occupation to annexation made little practical difference. But the Powers still attached great importance to the shadowy suzerainty of the Sultan and the theory which it symbolized of the "integrity" of the Ottoman Empire; and they felt instinctively that if the suzerainty could be abolished and the theory upset by one Power acting alone, there would be no end to the mischief, as indeed the event proved. Russia had a special grievance. There had long been an understanding between her and Austria that if either changed the *status quo* in the Balkans the other should obtain "compensation"; and in the previous summer Isvolsky, the Russian Foreign Minister, had met Aehrenthal, the Austrian, at the villa of their friend, Berchtold, at Buchlau in Moravia, and supposed it to have been arranged between them that they should simultaneously obtain the consent of the Powers to the annexation of Bosnia-Herzegovina by Austria and the opening of the Straits, *i.e.* the Bosphorus and the Dardanelles, to Russian war-ships. After the Buchlau conversations Isvolsky started on a tour round Europe in order to obtain the consent of the Powers to the Russian part of the programme, but when he reached Paris at the very beginning of this mission, he received a telegram from Aehrenthal saying briefly that he had been compelled to push forward the annexation of the two provinces, and before Isvolsky had time to answer the annexation was announced.

Aehrenthal's excuse was that Prince Ferdinand of Bulgaria had forced his hands by announcing the independence of that country, and proclaiming himself sovereign on the previous day (October 5). There is little doubt that this move had been arranged between Aehrenthal and the Bulgarian prince in order to provide the former with the pretext that he wanted. In any case the result was that Austria and Bulgaria between them had shattered the Treaty of Berlin without asking the leave of the other Powers, and that Russia had been cheated of the compensation for which she had stipulated as the price of her consent. Isvolsky was now in a deplorable position. It was quite probable that if Austria and Russia had approached the other Powers simultaneously, with a joint proposal for the annexation of Bosnia-Herzegovina and the opening of the Straits, these Powers would have consented with whatever reluctance. But there was little prospect that Russia alone would persuade Britain, France and Italy to reverse their traditional policy of keeping the Straits closed to Russian war-ships after Austria had annexed the two provinces without asking their leave.

British Action

So when Isvolsky came on from Paris to London he had but a chilly reception. In regard to the Straits he was asked a simple question—whether in return for Russian war-ships being permitted to go through the Bosphorus and Dardanelles into the Mediterranean, Russia would permit the war-ships of other Powers to go through them from the Mediterranean into the Black Sea. Since this was by no means what Russia wanted, he evaded the question and left London without having advanced his original idea. The circumstances, indeed, were very unfavourable to the Russian demand. The "Young Turks" had just carried through their revolution in Constantinople, making an end, as the world hoped, to the blood-stained tyranny of Abdul Hamid, and high hopes were built on their capacity to reform the Ottoman Empire. Apart from all other considerations, it seemed to Sir Edward Grey and the British Government a most untimely moment to inflict on them, in addition to the loss of Bosnia-Herzegovina, the mortification of being compelled to open the Straits to Russian war-ships.

Grey and other British Ministers took a serious view of the whole situation. They thought that, if one Power acting alone were permitted to tear up the Treaty of Berlin without even going through the form of consulting the other Powers, a most dangerous precedent would have been set to which no limit could be assigned. They therefore proposed a European Conference to consider the whole situation in the Balkans, and at least to "regularize," if it could not change, what Austria had done. This proposal found few sympathizers in Europe. Russia cared little about "regularizing" the Austrian annexation, if she could not obtain the opening of the Straits. Austria opposed the conference as a reflection on her conduct, and Germany, though using polite language about Sir Edward Grey's proposal, was bound to support Austria. France wished only to avoid a crisis, and though British opposition to the opening of the Straits accorded with her own traditional policy, was ready to concede anything which would avoid trouble, with or without a conference. Serbia, meanwhile, the most spirited and inflammable of the Balkan States, who saw in the annexation of the two provinces the irretrievable ruin of her ambition to absorb the Slavs of the Ottoman Empire, was demonstrating wildly and demanding compensation; and Russia was supporting Serbia. After a few weeks the British Government found itself the sole supporter of the conference, and in the meantime the question had resolved itself into a dangerous duel between Austria and Russia, who stood glaring at each other across their frontiers, with armies half mobilized and making noisy preparations for war.

For some weeks longer the British Government held its ground, so far as the conference was concerned, while endeavouring to moderate these passions and to abate the Serbian demands. But the practical statesmen of Europe failed to understand " the British passion for abstract justice," as some of them termed it; Austrians and Italians confided to each other that they found it " totally unintelligible," and even the French were mystified and troubled. The British, it was said, could not be as simple as they seemed, and in some quarters the absurd theory was thrown out that British Ministers were engaged in the " encircling policy " of King Edward, and endeavouring to force a war in which they would look on cheerfully while the other Powers exhausted themselves. Nothing could have been farther from the truth, as the records of these years show, but Europe in these months was in a state of nerves and suspicion in which almost anything was believed.

Russia's Submission

For many weeks war seemed inevitable, then Austria made her peace with Turkey on the basis of a money compensation, and Russia suddenly collapsed, withdrawing all her demands and giving an undertaking not to support Serbia (March 22, 1909). Europe was utterly mystified at the time, but it appeared afterwards that Germany had presented what was tantamount to an ultimatum in St. Petersburg intimating that she would give Austria *carte blanche* to do what she chose with German support against Serbia and Russia, and demanding an answer

" yes or no " on the spot. Being by no means ready for another war within so short a time of his disasters in the Far East, the Tsar yielded, as his opponents had confidently reckoned he would do, and the crisis was over.

But only temporarily over. " It was with surprise and indeed with bewildered consternation," wrote Sir Arthur Nicolson, the British Ambassador in St. Petersburg, " that the public learnt that the Russian Government, who were supposed to have under their special care the interests of the smaller Balkan States, and whose influence in the Balkan Peninsula has been endangered, had consented suddenly to abandon the position which they had hitherto assumed, and to sanction the act which Austria-Hungary had executed some months ago. It was considered not only in the Press but in all classes of society that Russia had suffered a deep humiliation and had renounced the traditional part which she had hitherto played in South-East Europe, and in the prosecution of which she had made so great sacrifices in the past." These feelings were intensified when in the following year the German Kaiser visited Vienna and claimed in a public speech to have stood behind his ally, Austria, " in shining armour," while Russia suffered this humiliation. One thing was clear from this time forward : the Tsar was very unlikely to submit again to a similar threat, for, if he did, he would risk losing all authority among his own people, if he did not actually lose his throne.

The DAILY TELEGRAPH Interview

The Bosnia-Herzegovina affair was by no means the only trouble in the year 1908. Right in the middle of the annexation crisis came the publication in the Daily Telegraph (October 29, 1908) of the famous interview in which the Kaiser protested his regard for Great Britain and his grief at the lack of reciprocity which his many efforts to be of service to her had encountered. He said he took as a " personal insult " the distortions and misrepresentations of his repeated offers of friendship to England by a considerable section of the English Press, and added that his own position in seeking British friendship was the more difficult because only a minority of his countrymen —though it was true an influential minority—shared his feelings. He further claimed credit for having refused the request of

France and Russia to join them in saving the Boer Republics and " humiliating England to the dust," and for having with one of his officers worked out a plan of campaign for England in the darkest days of the South African War which " as a matter of curious coincidence " was on much the same lines as that subsequently adopted by Lord Roberts and by him successfully carried out. Finally he protested that Germany was not building her fleet against England, but to be ready for eventualities in the Far East—presumably for action against Britain's ally, Japan.

It was, no doubt, well intentioned, but so much that was calculated to give offence both in England and Germany could scarcely have been packed into the same space by a deliberate mischief-maker. The English by this time were accustomed to the Kaiser's ebullitions and soon forgot all about it, but the Germans were extremely angry both at the picture of them which the Kaiser had presented to the English and at his implied claim to have helped in the conquering of the Boers with whom they greatly sympathized. A crisis followed in Berlin in which, if we may believe Bülow, who was then Chancellor, the Kaiser came near abdicating, and was for a time reduced to great prostration. Bülow, who tells the story in his Memoirs, would have it believed that he acted with great generosity and sacrificed himself to save the Kaiser. It can only be said that his own conduct in having let pass through his hands without comment or even inspection a manuscript which was specially sent to him for revision needs more explanation than he has given it. In the end the Kaiser had to submit to a mortifying debate in the Reichstag and a defence by the Chancellor which was equally wounding to his pride. The affair led to an estrangement between him and Bülow which ended a year later in the latter's downfall and the appointment as Chancellor of von Bethmann Hollweg, a well-meaning man whose misfortune it was to be unfamiliar with Foreign affairs. This also had momentous consequences for Germany and Europe.

The Kaiser crisis in Berlin was followed by a short but acute crisis between French and Germans over an affair of police in the Moroccan port of Casablanca, which showed that the Moroccan quarrel between the two countries was suspended rather than composed. For a week or more Berlin used high language to Paris and the danger of a Franco-German war on ground on which British diplomatic support was pledged to France was by no means remote. But the Austrians at that moment were deeply concerned to prevent their own enterprise in the Balkans from being overlaid by any other dispute, and the Emperor Franz Josef, whom the German Kaiser happened to be visiting at this time, intervened with a strong plea for peace which proved successful.

The Naval Competition

The agitations on the matter of Bosnia-Herzegovnia were mostly behind the scenes, and the British people knew little about them at the time, but for those who did know they afforded a very uneasy background to the heated debates on the Naval Estimates, with the accompanying angry comparisons between British and German strength, which took place in the House of Commons in the spring of 1909. It was impossible to justify to a House predominantly Radical and pacifist the large increase in the Naval Estimates which the Government were now proposing without strict proof of its necessity. But this proof could only take the form of a comparison of British and German strengths and the treatment of Germany as at least a potential enemy. Since the corresponding argument was going forward in Germany with Britain playing the part of potential enemy, a growth of bitterness and suspicion between the two peoples inevitably followed and increased the danger that they would one day be actual enemies.

Metternich, the German Ambassador in London, endeavoured courageously to explain to his superiors in Berlin that the British Empire depended for its existence and the British people for their security against starvation upon the possession of a supreme fleet, and that any appearance of challenge to this was bound to raise suspicions and emotions exceeding all ordinary fears of military preparations. A beaten army might be replaced and the struggle renewed, but war-ships could not be improvised to replace a conquered fleet. There could, therefore, he warned his Government, be no hope of permanent good relations between Britain and Germany if the latter decided to continue building battle-ships which the British would inevitably regard as a menace to their security. This argument, combined with the debates in the House of Commons, seems to have caused uneasiness in Germany, for Metternich was summoned to Berlin to attend a Council of Ministers in which on June 3, 1909, he engaged in a grim argument with Tirpitz, the Minister of Marine who, with the Kaiser, was chiefly responsible for German naval policy. Metternich appears to have made some impression on the German Chancellor, Bülow, and even on General von Moltke, the Chief of the General Staff, but Tirpitz was obdurate in his view that British hostility was due not to the German fleet but to trade jealousy, and that Britain would become civil and friendly just in proportion as she was inspired with respect for the growing naval power of Germany. With the exception of Tirpitz, all who attended this conference appear to have agreed with Bülow that " the one black cloud at present was that which brooded over the North Sea," and that " this was heavy with thunder." The question thus came back to Tirpitz and the dialogue which followed is recorded in the German Documents :

> Admiral von Tirpitz: " In my opinion the danger zone in our relations with England will be passed in from five to six years, say in 1915, after the widening of the Kiel Canal and the completion of the fortifications of Heligoland. Even in two years the danger will be considerably less."
> The Chancellor (Prince Bülow): " That is all very fine, but the question is still : How are we to get over the dangers of that period ? "

Tirpitz's answer is not recorded.

The argument at this conference made a sufficient impression on the Kaiser to induce him to withdraw his unconditional negative on discussions of the naval question and to permit soundings to be made in London for a possible agreement. These were welcomed by British Ministers, and negotiations continued for some months in 1910. But it now appeared that in return for a cessation of ship-building on their part, the Germans required a " political equivalent " which seemed to be nothing less than the entry of Great Britain into a combination with Germany, and the sacrifice of her ententes with France and Russia. Whenever the naval question came up in the subsequent years, this demand reappeared in different guises and proved fatal to all attempts at accommodation. Greatly as they desired to end the naval competition and establish better relations with Germany, British Ministers were not prepared to sacrifice their friendships and go back upon their word to other Powers.

CHAPTER XII

THE PEERS AND THE BUDGET

I<small>F</small> the peers had remained within their own ground, as it was then supposed to be, and confined themselves to dealing with ordinary Bills sent up to them from the House of Commons, it is probable that they would have prolonged their struggle with the House of Commons for many years. But in the year 1909 they stepped out of their ground and invaded the sphere of finance which for 250 years had been supposed by all parties to be the preserve of the House of Commons, " the Gentlemen of the House of Commons " to whom alone the portions of the King's Speech relating to supply were addressed. In so doing they rallied a great body of opinion to the Government, and prepared the way for the disaster which befell them in the Parliament Act of 1911.

Two causes combined to make finance an acute issue in the year 1909. First, the German Navy Bill of 1908 with its undisguised challenge to British sea-power required a large expenditure on the navy; next, the plans which the Government were now preparing for sickness and unemployment insurance and other social reforms involved another considerable increase of expenditure. A sharp struggle took place in the Cabinet, and afterwards in the House of Commons, as to the number of new battle-ships which would be necessary to meet the German effort. The Admiralty said six, Radicals and pacifists said four would be enough, and finally after angry debates, in which tempers were greatly inflamed against Germany, and outside agitation had become violent, it was decided to build eight. But Liberals and Radicals were determined that if money was found for building battle-ships it should be found also for social reform, and it fell to Mr. Lloyd George, the new Chancellor of the Exchequer, to provide for both in his Budget of 1909.

Mr. Lloyd George's Budget

Judged by later standards of expenditure, the Budget of 1909 may well seem a mole-hill and scarcely one of the largest size. Mr. Lloyd George's task was only to raise fourteen millions in extra taxation, a sum which one of his successors in later years sacrificed with a light heart to reduce the taxation on beer. He proposed to raise income-tax on a graduated scale from 9d. to 1s. 2d. in the pound, to lay a super-tax beginning at £3000 on incomes which exceeded £5000; and to raise death duties to a maximum of 10 per cent. on estates of £200,000 and over. These proposals were hotly resented by the well-to-do, but the crowning controversy was over the land taxes which took a fifth of the "unearned increment," when land was sold or passed at death, and set up machinery for valuation for this purpose; and levied an annual duty of ½d. in the pound on "undeveloped land," i.e. land which had a site value but was not being used for building and was probably being held up until its value ripened. There was finally a 10 per cent. "reversion duty" on any benefit accruing to a lessor on the termination of a lease, and sundry new taxes on spirits, tobacco, motors and petrol.

Rejection by the Lords

The storm which raged round these proposals shook the country from end to end. In the House of Commons the Unionist opposition fought the Finance Bill line by line and prolonged the proceedings until November 4, when it was carried by a majority of 379 to 149. In the meantime a fierce battle was being fought in the towns and villages between rival organizations—Budget League and anti-Budget League—specially improvised for the occasion; and Mr. Lloyd George, the Chancellor of the Exchequer, went from platform to platform delighting Radicals, incensing Tories, shocking Whigs, and drawing rebukes from King Edward by the strong language in which he denounced his opponents and railed at the "dukes" and the "idle rich" who were resisting his taxes. At first it was not thought possible that the House of Lords would go to the length of rejecting a Budget. Much as he disliked Mr. Lloyd George's rhetoric, King Edward himself did his utmost to dissuade the Unionist leaders from this extreme course; and many of the elder statesmen of the Unionist party viewed the course of events which was driving them in this direction with grave misgiving. But when November came tempers were greatly inflamed, and both Mr. Balfour and Lord Lansdowne were of opinion that no compromise was possible. By this time the Tariff Reform group of the Conservative party had come to the conclusion that if it were let pass, the Budget would for many years to come be fatal to their alternative policy of raising revenue by taxing imports. In the end Tariff Reform zeal, combined with the strong objection of landowners and Conservatives to the land taxes and the valuation accompanying them, decided the issue; and on November 30 the peers, following Lord Milner's advice to act boldly and " damn the consequences," rejected the Budget by a majority of 350 to 75.

The Appeal to the Country

It was plain to all parties that if the House of Lords could do this and obtain public sanction for it, it would from henceforth have the whip-hand of the House of Commons, since it would be able at any time to bring a Government to a standstill and force a dissolution by holding up its provision for taxation and expenditure. Asquith immediately took up the challenge, and proposed and carried through the House of Commons the following resolution :

> That the action of the House of Lords in refusing to pass into law the financial provision made by this House for the service of the year is a breach of the Constitution and a usurpation of the rights of the Commons.

This was carried by 349 to 134 on December 2, and Parliament was dissolved the next day, the first day of the general election being fixed for January 14.

From the first Asquith made it clear that much more was at stake in the battle which was now pending than the passing of the Budget. " I tell you quite plainly and I tell my countrymen," he said in a speech at the Albert Hall a week after the dissolution, " that neither I nor any other Liberal Minister supported by a majority in the House of Commons is going to submit again to the rebuffs and the humiliations of the last four years. We shall not assume office and we shall not hold office until we can secure the safeguards which experience shows us to be necessary to the legislative utility and the honour of the party of progress. . . . We are not proposing the abolition of the House of Lords or setting up a single Chamber, but we do ask, and we are going to ask the electors to say that the House of Lords shall be confined to the proper objects of a second Chamber. The absolute veto which it proposes must go."

The Difficulties of the Government

It was easy to say but not quite so easy to do. The election which followed gave the Government a majority of 124, a large reduction of the unprecedented majority of 1906, but still in ordinary circumstances a handsome and even a generous majority. The circumstances of the 1909 Budget, however, were not ordinary. The Irish (82 in number) had taken great exception to certain parts of the Budget, especially the new taxes on spirits, and had abstained or voted against these taxes in the previous Parliament. No harm would be done if they abstained in the new Parliament, but if they voted against the Budget the Government would be defeated, the Budget rejected, and the peers justified. There followed a stubborn duel between Asquith and Redmond, the leader of the Irish party. As a condition of the Irish withdrawing their opposition to the Budget, Redmond desired a pledge from the Government that it would proceed immediately with a Bill dealing with the veto of the House of Lords and pass it within a year, and this Asquith declined to give. The Budget, he said, must be decided on its own merits, and if the Irish thought necessary to vote against it, they must do so and take the consequences.

For several weeks the Budget was held up, and the fate of the Government was in doubt. But English Radicals also were strongly of opinion that a House of Lords policy should at least be produced before the Budget was again submitted to the peers, and in the first fortnight of April the Government passed three resolutions through the House of Commons defining this policy, and procured a first reading for the Parliament Bill which was to give them legislative force.

This satisfied the Irish, and on April 20 the Budget was re-introduced and passed through both Houses, the Lords accepting it without a division. (April 28.)

The Parliament Bill and the resolutions on which it was founded restored the presumption that finance was beyond the competence of the House of Lords, and propounded the policy of the " suspensory veto " which since the year 1907 had been the solution of the second Chamber question accepted by the Liberal party. A Bill was to become law without the consent of the House of Lords if passed by the House of Commons in three successive sessions, whether in the same Parliament or in successive Parliaments, provided that at least two years had elapsed between the time of its first introduction into the House of Commons and its passing in that House for the last time. A Bill was to be treated as rejected by the House of Lords if not passed either without amendment or with such amendments only as might be agreed upon by both Houses. It was further provided that the duration of Parliament should be limited to five years.

There had been long discussions in the Liberal Cabinet as to whether or not this measure should be accompanied by an effort to reform the House of Lords, but the differences on that subject were acute and Ministers decided that, if they attempted both tasks at once they would probably fail in both. They did, however, qualify this decision by adding a preamble to the Parliament Bill, which still stands as a notification that they intended it to be only one part of the dual problem of " veto and reform " :

> Whereas it is intended to substitute for the House of Lords as it at present exists a second Chamber constituted on a popular instead of a hereditary basis, but such a substitution cannot immediately be brought into operation : And whereas provision will require hereafter to be made by Parliament in a measure affecting such substitution for limiting and defining the powers of the new second Chamber, but it is expedient to make such provision as in this Act appears for restricting the existing powers of the House of Lords.

That remains on the statute book as the expression of an intention which still awaits fulfilment. In the conflict which was now coming the Government limited themselves to two objects : (1) the restoration of the control of finance by the

House of Commons, and (2) the limitation of the Lords' veto to a period of two years.

A Political Deadlock

The transactions of the first months of 1910 and the delays and hesitations accompanying them had not improved the credit of the Government, and though the Lords had submitted to the popular verdict on the Budget it was clear to Ministers that a long and difficult struggle lay ahead of them. Politics were now at deadlock. Liberals were unanimous that it was impossible to go on as if nothing had happened, leaving the peers free to reject another Budget, and in the meantime to veto all legislation to which the Liberal party attached importance. At the same time it was quite certain that the House of Lords would not of its own free-will accept a Bill which greatly curtailed its privileges, and it could by no means be taken for granted that the King would consent to the creation of peers—by which alone their opposition could be overcome—on the strength of the Budget election of the previous January. He had in fact warned Asquith that he would require a second election directed to that issue alone before he would take this extreme course for the passing of the Parliament Bill. This in itself doomed the new Parliament to a very brief existence—a fact which most of its members had not realized and did not at all relish.

The position of the Unionist party was even more difficult. In advising the peers to reject the Budget, the Unionist leaders had played for the highest stakes and lost. Presumably their expectation had been that the Goverment would either be defeated at the subsequent election or so weakened that it would be unable to take any effective action. They had failed in that and left their opponents in a position in which they were bound to pursue the attack on the House of Lords, or abandon all policies to which that House took exception. Before the rejection of the Budget there had been many signs that the Liberal tide was running out; after it there was every probability that Liberals and Radicals would rally to the issue which the peers themselves had provided, and keep their majority at full strength. It was now generally acknowledged that the rejection of the Budget could only have been justified by success, and that its failure had placed the House of Lords and the Unionist cause in a position of great danger.

The Union of South Africa

The story of the great Budget controversy has been carried consecutively to this point, but we must go back a little to glance at the one measure which gave universal satisfaction in the troubled year of 1909. This was the Act establishing the Union of South Africa and giving statutory effect to a scheme which had been elaborated at a convention in that country and accepted by the Parliament of each of the four Provinces. This set up a Senate and a House of Assembly for the Union as a whole, and Provincial Councils, to which powers were delegated, for the four Provinces, the Cape, the Transvaal, the Orange Free State and Natal. The Bill was passed first in the Lords and then, on August 19, in the Commons, where the sole point of controversy was the "colour bar," *i.e.* the exclusion of natives from the new Constitution. Asquith said frankly that he greatly regretted this, but was not prepared to jeopardize the whole scheme and plunge into a controversy with white South Africa in order to maintain his objection. An amendment extending the franchise to natives was accordingly rejected, and the scheme accepted as it stood without a division. Generous tributes came from Conservatives who had played prominent parts in the struggle with the Boers and four years previously had strongly objected to the grant of self-government to the Transvaal and Orange Free State. Mr. Balfour described the measure as "the most wonderful issue out of all those divisions, battles and outbreaks, the devastation and horrors of war, the difficulties of peace." "I do not believe," he said, "the world shows anything like it in its whole history." It may be added here that General Botha, who became first Prime Minister of the Union, was four years later fighting for the British Empire, and took into his own hands the task of dealing with the brief Dutch rebellion under Beyers and De Wet which followed his decision to take part in the war.

CHAPTER XIII

THE PEERS AND THE PARLIAMENT ACT

WHILE party leaders were contemplating the unpleasing situation described in the previous chapter, the scene was suddenly changed by the death of King Edward, which took place after a short illness on May 6. The King had reigned only nine years, but he had won a unique place for himself by his genial character, and by the tact, good sense and strict impartiality between parties with which he had steered a difficult course. He had an uncommon flair for what the British people liked and expected in their sovereign, and had impressed them with a sense of character and personality which they greatly valued. He was thought to be a wise counsellor, and he sustained the dignity of his position without pomposity or self-assertion. His known approval of the Entente with France, and the friction between him and his nephew, the Kaiser, led the Germans to believe that he was deliberately aiming at the "encirclement" of their country, but British policy in these years was the policy of British Governments, and though he approved and helped, he kept strictly within his boundaries as a constitutional sovereign. The expectation of Europe that his death would lead to a change of British policy was, therefore, not fulfilled, but in Great Britain it created a sense of loss and bereavement which men of all parties felt instinctively should be reflected in the conduct of affairs.

The Constitutional Conference

This was the view of the Prime Minister, and immediately after the King's funeral he approached Mr. Balfour, the leader of the Unionist party, and proposed a conference between party-leaders on the subjects in dispute between them. Mr. Balfour agreed, and the conference started work on June 17. The Government was represented by the Prime Minister, Mr. Lloyd George, Lord Crewe and Mr. Birrell; and the

Unionist party by Mr. Balfour, Lord Lansdowne, Mr. Austen Chamberlain and Lord Cawdor. The subjects discussed were the relations of the two Houses in regard to finance; the provision of some machinery to deal with persistent disagreements between them whether by limitation of veto, joint sitting, referendum or otherwise; and the possibility of so changing the numbers or composition of the "Second House" as "to ensure that it would act and be regarded as acting fairly between the great parties in the State."

The conference met twelve times at longer or shorter intervals, but finally on November 10 Asquith was obliged to report that it had failed. There was some approach to agreement on the subject of finance, the Unionist leaders offering to surrender the right of the House of Lords to reject money Bills, provided the House of Commons consented to limit the scope of measures regarded as financial; but on all else the differences proved irreconcilable. There was a great variety of opinion on the composition and personnel of the "Second House," and the Unionist leaders demanded a referendum for certain important questions which they called "constitutional," but which Liberals thought should be treated as ordinary legislation and dealt with in the ordinary way.

What in fact the conference had been attempting was—as Asquith's biographers have put it—nothing less than to convert the immemorial unwritten into a written constitution with an explicit legal distinction between organic changes and ordinary legislation. Such a task would have been immensely difficult if undertaken by impartial men in a calm atmosphere, and it was beyond the power of political leaders who were deeply committed to promote or resist certain measures actually or soon to be before Parliament. On all these, and especially on such questions as Home Rule for Ireland and Welsh Disestablishment, the Liberal leaders greatly desired to remove obstructions and the Unionist leaders to block the way. To find a constitution to fit these circumstances was as difficult as insuring a house when it is on fire.

There was much talk behind the scenes in these months of a coalition between parties, and Mr. Lloyd George and Mr. Balfour explored the possibilities of a method which both were to favour in subsequent years. This too came to nothing. It meant at the time that the two parties should bargain with each other about the causes and principles which they had hitherto declared to be vital, that the Liberals, for example, should consent to Imperial preference and compulsory military service, and the Unionist to Home Rule and the limitation of the veto of the House of Lords. It was felt, when these proposals were seriously approached, that even if the leaders of parties were willing to bargain with each other on this ground—and the great majority were not—the effect on the public would be to destroy all confidence in the sincerity of politics. It was still in these days an accepted maxim that " England hates coalitions," and the traditional objection was not to be removed except under a compulsion which for the time being extinguished other politics.

The Approach to the Crown

When the conference failed, Asquith decided at once on another appeal to the country. It was certain that without it the Parliament Bill would be rejected by the House of Lords and he felt that the new king could not reasonably be asked to exercise his prerogative for the creation of peers to overcome their resistance, on the strength of the Budget election, which had taken place before he ascended the throne. But equally it was impossible for the Prime Minister to undertake a fresh appeal to the country within less than a year of the previous appeal, unless he had reasonable assurance that the result would be decisive, *i.e.* that in the event of a sufficient majority being obtained for the Government's policy, the King would use his prerogative if the peers prolonged their resistance. Asquith had been warned that King Edward would require a second election before using his prerogative to deal with the question of the House of Lords, and he now thought it necessary to ascertain whether, if such an election was held and gave a result favourable to the Government, King George would act as presumably his father would have acted. He therefore went to Buckingham Palace, accompanied by Lord Crewe, on the afternoon of November 16, and put the question to the King.

The situation was a painful and difficult one for both King

and Prime Minister. The King, new to the throne, was asked to take a decision which was likely to involve him in serious trouble with one of the great parties in the State, and the party which was most fervent in its professions of attachment to the throne. The Prime Minister was compelled to put the question, or resign and put upon the King the onus of finding a new Minister who would have been obliged at once to appeal to the country and to hold an election in which it would have been impossible to keep the action of the King out of public controversy. The King undoubtedly would have been within his rights in refusing to answer Asquith's question, but he could only have done so at the cost of adding a controversy about the Crown to the controversy about the House of Lords, and bringing the monarchy into question at an election which, according to all the signs, was likely to be unfavourable to the Unionist party.

In reporting the result of his interview to the House of Commons in the following year, Asquith said :

> His Majesty, after careful consideration of all the circumstances past and present, and after discussing the matter in all its bearings with myself and with my noble friend and colleague, Lord Crewe, felt that he had no alternative but to assent to the advice of the Cabinet.

It was suggested in the subsequent months that Asquith, as one of his opponents said, had " played the bully in the royal closet " and taken advantage of the youth and inexperience of the King to force his hand, but it is now generally agreed that the King's action was constitutionally correct and proper. In the circumstances he " had no alternative but to assent to the advice of the Cabinet," and the Cabinet had no alternative but to offer that advice. The warfare of parties had brought both to that position, and the King did no more than promise to give effect to the decision of the people, provided that decision was unambiguously expressed on an issue clearly explained to them. In order to place that beyond doubt the King insisted that the Parliament Bill, which had been read a first time in the House of Commons, should be submitted to the House of Lords also before the election, and to that Asquith agreed. Lords, Commons and public were thus apprised in detail of the proposals which were now submitted to the country. It was agreed between the King and the Cabinet that their understanding should be kept secret, and at the time it was the hope and expectation of both King and Prime Minister that the Unionist party would save the necessity of revealing it by accepting the Parliament Bill under protest if the verdict of the country were decisively in its favour.

The Second Election

The election took place in December and gave the Government a majority of 126—a figure which could not be impeached as less than the "sufficient majority" for which the King had stipulated. No question was asked, and no word said about the King's action during the election; it was taken for granted that if the Government took the extreme course of holding a second general election within one year, the result would this time be decisive. The argument was sustained on the high level of constitutional law and practice, of which the Prime Minister was an unrivalled exponent, and it was assumed by the electors that it would settle the issue between the two Houses. But this was not the view of the fighting spirits of the Unionist party. They were unaware of the understanding between the Cabinet and the King; there were many possible slips between cup and lip, and, above all, the controversy had aroused passions which were beyond argument or a cool calculation of consequences. Threatened with such a blow to their power and prestige, many peers and a large number of their friends in the Unionist party were of opinion that it was their positive duty to resist to the last, and only to yield, if yielding were necessary, to a declared threat to create peers, or even to an actual creation of peers. The lists were thus set for a continuance of the controversy to the end in the new Parliament.

The Parliament Bill in Parliament

The Parliament Bill, depriving the House of Lords of power over "Money Bills" and limiting its veto to two years, was introduced into the new House of Commons on February 22, 1911, and carried through all its stages by the second week in May. In the meantime the House of Lords occupied itself with the question of its own reform, a measure for that purpose having been introduced by Lord Lansdowne as an alternative to the Government policy of curtailing the power of the existing House. Lord Lansdowne proposed that a new second Chamber should be set up composed of 350 members, of whom 100 were to be peers elected by a specially qualified panel of their own order, 120 elected by members of the House of Commons, 100 nominated by the Crown in proportion to the strength of parties in the House of Commons, and the remaining 30 to consist of judicial dignitaries and spiritual Lords. In the event of differences between the two Houses, there were to be conferences, joint sittings, and in the last resort referendum. These proposals were received by the House of Lords, as Lord Lansdowne's biographer says, " in a dignified, if frigid silence," and it was by no means certain that, if they could have voted by ballot a majority of the peers would not have preferred the Government scheme, which limited their power, to Lord Lansdowne's, which deprived the great majority of them of any power at all as hereditary legislators. In the previous year when Lord Rosebery had introduced resolutions on similar lines, the veteran Lord Halsbury had advised his brother peers to " take their stand on their hereditary rights and stoutly resist any tampering with it," and at the end of the debate on Lord Lansdowne's proposals it remained very much in doubt whether the hereditary peerage would have abandoned the legislative part of these rights even at the bidding of the Unionist party.

The question was not put, for Lord Morley,[1] speaking on behalf of the Government, said bluntly, that though the Lansdowne scheme might be " a possible supplement or complement to the Parliament Bill, it could not be a substitute for or an alternative to it." Since the peers were in no mind to add the whips of their friends to the scorpions of their opponents, this sealed the fate of Lord Lansdowne's proposals, and no more was heard of them after the preliminary debate. The way was now clear for the Parliament Bill which came up

---

[1] In November 1910 Mr. John Morley had resigned the Secretaryship of State for India and been created a peer, under the title of Viscount Morley of Blackburn, and appointed Lord President of the Council. He was leading the peers on this occasion during the temporary absence of the Marquess of Crewe, the official leader.

from the House of Commons on May 23, and was given a second reading with warnings of " grave amendments " in the Committee stage.

There was an interval for the Coronation of the new king which postponed the Committee stage until June 28. Then the struggle began in earnest, and by the end of the next week the Lords had amended the Government Bill out of existence. A referendum was substituted for the suspensory veto for all measures of Home Rule, whether for Ireland, Scotland, Wales or England, and for all other measures which a joint committee might decide to be " of great gravity." The same joint committee was to be substituted for the Speaker as the authority to define " Money Bills," in order, as Lord Lansdowne said, " to prevent the House of Lords from being deprived of rights in the region of finance which they conceived to be theirs." With these changes nothing remained of the Government policy but the restoration, qualified by new safeguards, of the control of finance by the Commons, which until 1909 had been taken for granted.

The Threatened Creation of Peers

Up to this point the secrecy of the understanding between the King and the Cabinet had served the purpose of keeping the King out of public controversy. The election had come and gone without the mention of his name by any responsible man on either side. But secrecy had its drawbacks, as was now to be seen. Asquith had miscalculated in supposing that if he obtained a decisive majority, the peers would accept the inevitable after a show of resistance. It now appeared that they had every intention of resisting and meant to press to the utmost the drastic amendments which Lord Lansdowne had proposed or sanctioned when the Bill first reached them. Had he been aware of the understanding between the King and the Government, Lord Lansdowne would probably have committed himself less deeply, and he found himself in a position of great difficulty when the facts were communicated to him at the end of the Committee stage (July 18). To pull back was for the moment far more difficult than to press forward, and there was now on his flank a formidable and organized movement led by Lord Halsbury and sponsored by other important men who, as in 1909, were in favour of going all lengths at whatever cost.

There followed a sharp struggle in the Unionist party between the " Die-hards," as the Halsbury party were called, and the moderates, now led by Lord Lansdowne ; the former declaring that the threat to create peers was a bluff which could safely be called, the latter seeing the worst disaster of all in the " swamping creation " which now threatened. The issue was in doubt up to the last moment, for of the 600 peers some 400 had not been in the habit of attending the House; and whether these " backwoodsmen," as they were called, would follow Lord Lansdowne or Lord Halsbury, and whether they could even be reached in the short time now available, was uncertain. It now became impossible to keep the King's name out of the controversy, for Lord Lansdowne was in a position in which he could only withdraw under this visible pressure, and he accordingly communicated the facts to a meeting of Unionist peers which took place at his house on July 21.

The Last Phase

The Bill with the peers' amendments had in the meantime (July 20) received a third reading in the House of Lords, and four days later it returned to the Commons in an atmosphere of heat and confusion, little conducive to wise and sober counsels. When the Prime Minister rose to explain the intentions of the Government his voice was drowned in shouts from the opposite benches and he was obliged to resume his seat, leaving his speech to be reported in the next day's papers. The Unionists now moved votes of censure in both Houses declaring the advice given by Ministers to the King, " whereby they obtained from His Majesty a pledge that a sufficient number of peers would be created to pass the Parliament Bill in the shape in which it left the Commons," to be " a gross violation of constitutional liberty " ; and heated debates followed leading in each House to the foregone conclusion. On August 8 the Commons dealt with the Lords' amendments, accepted one, excluding from the operation of the Bill any measure extending the duration of Parliament beyond five years, made a small concession on another by providing that the Speaker should consult the Chairman of Ways and

Means and the Chairman of Committee on Public Accounts when called upon to decide what were " Money Bills," and rejected the rest. The decks were thus cleared for the final action which followed the next day (August 9), when the Bill was presented again in its original shape by the House of Commons to the House of Lords.

No one on that day knew what the result would be. Lord Lansdowne had a list of 320 Unionist peers who were prepared to abstain from voting, and Lord Morley a list of 80 Liberal peers who were pledged to vote for the Bill. The number of " Die-hards " who were determined to vote against the Bill at all costs was unknown, but they were supposed to be sufficient to defeat the eighty, if no more could be induced to vote for the Bill. There remained an unknown quantity of " backwoodsmen," who either had not been reached or who refused to disclose their intentions, and there were also the " spiritual peers " who kept their own counsel.

The debate was worthy of a great occasion. Anger and tumult had accompanied the final stages in the House of Commons, but the peers faced their enemy with dignity and composure, and kept a passionate argument on a high level of restrained eloquence. It became evident after the first day that a large number were still incredulous about the threat to create peers. Lord Morley, therefore, obtained authority from the King to make a still more explicit statement, and on the afternoon of the last day he read twice over the warning words which he had been authorized to use : " If the Bill should be defeated to-night His Majesty will assent to the creation of peers sufficient in number to guard against any possible combination of the different parties in opposition by which the Parliament Bill might be exposed a second time to defeat." This intimation had a profound effect on the waverers, which was presently enhanced by a speech from the Archbishop of Canterbury (Dr. Davidson), who said he had been moved from his resolve to abstain by " the callousness—I had almost said levity—with which some noble lords seem to contemplate the creation of some five hundred new peers, a course of action which would make this House, and indeed our country, the laughing-stock of the British Dominions beyond the seas, and of those foreign countries whose constitutional life and progress have been largely modelled on our own." Nevertheless the "Die-hards" remained true to their name, and when the division was called, the result, as Lord Morley has recorded, " was still profoundly dark, and dark it remained in the dead silence only broken by the counting of the tellers, down to the very moment of fate." The Bill was passed by a majority of 131 to 114, the great majority of the peers abstaining. (August 11, 1911.) That it was only passed by the votes of the bishops was a subject of angry comment in the following days.

The conflict between the Liberal and the Conservative forces which had continued without pause from 1906 onwards ended thus in the assertion of the democratic over the hereditary principle. But those who imagined that the House of Lords had been disposed of were destined to have a rude awakening. It was to be discovered in the next three years that the power which still remained to it of holding up legislation might play a vital part in the political life of the country.

In November 1911 Mr. Balfour resigned the leadership of the Unionist party, and was succeeded by Mr. Bonar Law, an ardent Tariff Reformer and unyielding opponent of Home Rule. Mr. Joseph Chamberlain had been incapacitated by a stroke of paralysis in July 1906, and was unable to take any further part in public affairs from then until his death in July 1914.

The South Pole

On December 14, 1911, a Norwegian expedition under Captain Roald Amundsen succeeded in reaching the South Pole, thereby forestalling a British expedition under Captain Robert Scott which came there a month later (January 18, 1912). The whole of Captain Scott's party perished on their return journey, and it was not till another winter that their bodies were found, together with the diaries which told the story of their last days. It was a tragic and heroic story of mutual support and endurance reaching its climax in the self-sacrifice of that " very gallant gentleman," Captain Oates, who, rather than be a burden to his comrades, walked out into the blizzard and was not seen again. The story survives all the clamour of these times.

CHAPTER XIV

HOME RULE AND ULSTER

IF Asquith and his colleagues looked for peace and quiet after the House of Lords question was disposed of, they were doomed to disappointment. The dangerous Agadir crisis, which will be described in another chapter, was at its acutest phase, and scrutiny of the measures to be taken in the event of war led to a sharp difference of opinion between the War Office and the Admiralty, leading to the reshuffling of the Cabinet whereby Mr. Winston Churchill became First Lord of the Admiralty and Mr. McKenna Home Secretary. The definite adoption of the plan by which the Expeditionary Force was transported to France immediately after the outbreak of the Great War dates from these days. But that was not the only trouble. While the foreign situation was still a gravely anxious one the Government was faced with a sudden and unexpected railway strike which threatened to paralyse the entire trade of the country, and to cut off the food-supplies of the towns. Asquith intervened at once with a warning that the Government would use all means to keep the railways open, with a hint of the gravity of the national situation in foreign affairs, and a promise to submit the questions in dispute immediately to a Royal Commission. This sufficed and the strike was called off after two days, but not before both Government and public had learnt something of the meaning of a railway strike, and the problems which would await them, if another took place and lasted for more than two days.

Industrial Trouble

The following year (1912) witnessed the first strike of coal-miners which extended to the whole country. This was called on February 29 by the Miners' Federation, an organization embracing all the district unions, after a ballot of its members, and evidently threatened the most serious consequences if it was prolonged. For a fortnight the Government laboured in vain to bring the parties to terms and both miners and mine-owners rejected its proposal that wages should be fixed for the various districts by conferences with independent chairmen. The miners wished minimum wages to be laid down by Act of Parliament; the mine-owners objected to any interference between them and their employees. The Government thereupon embodied its proposal in a Bill and passed it through both Houses of Parliament in a week. On this the Miners' Federation took a fresh ballot of their members, and though there was still a majority for holding out, they decided that it was too small to justify them in continuing the strike, and the men were back at work by the middle of April.

These two strikes and the procedure attending them may be said to have established a new precedent in labour disputes affecting great industries. Hitherto it had been the practice of Governments to remain impartial spectators of all industrial struggles, and employers had strongly resisted any appearance of Government interference in their dealings with their workmen. But when workmen's organizations were extended to cover the whole field of great industries, the stoppage of which paralysed other trades and inflicted great hardships on the public, the Government, representing the public, could no longer remain disinterested spectators. Small industries and district unions might engage in local disputes without greatly inconveniencing their neighbours, but the conflicts of great industries and federations of unions affected the whole country. From this time onwards all Governments were to hold a watching brief and often actively to intervene in the conflicts of capital and labour. The disputes of these years may thus be said to mark a stage in the interference of Government in what employers had hitherto claimed as their private affairs, and much legislation followed which had the acknowledged intention of satisfying the reasonable demands of labour without exposing the country to the loss and damage inflicted by great strikes.

National Insurance

In spite of the constitutional crisis the Government contrived during 1911 to pass through Parliament at least one measure of first-class importance, the National Insurance scheme for sickness and invalidity of which Mr. Lloyd George was the principal author. This measure, which organized medical attendance on the panel system and provided support in sickness for millions who otherwise had no resource but the poor-law is now universally accepted, but when first introduced it encountered a storm of opposition. It was new, it was said to be German and un-English; doctors opposed it, popular newspapers raised their voices against the " stamp-licking " which accompanied it and implored their readers to stand firm against the invasion of their liberty and their privacy which the scheme involved. The Government lost by-election after by-election as the Bill passed through its various stages in Parliament, but Mr. Lloyd George showed remarkable skill and resourcefulness in winning over the insurance societies, educating the public, and bringing the doctors to reason. The Bill passed early in December, and escaped all but minor amendments in the House of Lords. The tide turned in the following year, thanks largely to the efforts of a voluntary Insurance Committee which sent its emissaries all over the country to combat prejudice and explain the method of the new Act. By the end of the year 1912 the Government was able to report that the new scheme was working smoothly and gaining in favour.

The Irish Question

There awaited the Government, when Parliament met on February 14, 1912, the most formidable and testing of all its legislative tasks—the final attempt to settle the Irish question by the establishment of a subordinate Parliament in Dublin. All the anger and bitterness generated in the constitutional conflict of the previous year were now to be concentrated on the question of Ireland. The Unionist party was unrepentant in its opposition to Home Rule in any form, and, if anything, had rather hardened in its attitude during the twenty-six years which had elapsed since Mr. Gladstone's first effort. The Liberals were in a position in which, though they had a clear majority over the Irish, they were liable to be evicted from office, if the Irish voted against them; and their opponents alleged that they were acting under this compulsion.

The Liberals retorted that Home Rule had been their policy for a generation; that the unsolved Irish question was a standing danger to both countries and to the Empire, that the sands were running out, and that it was urgently necessary to find a solution while there was yet time. If it was true that the Government was under compulsion to satisfy its Irish supporters, it was also true that to satisfy them was in the public interest and part of a policy which they had advocated for a generation.

Asquith's Bill, which was introduced into the House of Commons on April 11, 1912, followed generally Mr. Gladstone's models. It transferred purely Irish matters to an Irish Parliament, and reserved to the Imperial Parliament all questions touching the Crown, army and navy, foreign policy, the making of peace and war, and new customs duties. The Irish Parliament was to be debarred from establishing or endowing any religion or imposing religious disabilities of any kind; and for six years the Royal Irish Constabulary was to remain under the Imperial Government. The common Treasury was still to exist, and the Irish Parliament was not to add more than 10 per cent. to income-tax, death-duties or customs duties imposed by the Imperial Parliament. Irish members were still to remain in that Parliament, but to be reduced to forty-two in number. Granted that Home Rule in any form should be given to Ireland, the measure could not be called an extreme one; on the contrary, the question was rather whether with so many reservations and with others conceded as it passed through Parliament, it could be made to work administratively.

In introducing his Bill Asquith described it as " only the first step in a larger and more comprehensive policy," which would one day give other parts of the United Kingdom the same right of dealing with their own affairs, and thus release the Imperial Parliament to fulfil its duties to the whole country and the Empire." The Bill was well received by Irish Nationalists, and a National Convention which met in Dublin on April 23 passed a resolution " welcoming it in the spirit in which it was offered," and declaring its " solemn conviction that the passage of the Bill into law would " bind the people of Ireland to the people of Great Britain by a union infinitely closer than that which now exists and by so doing add immeasurably to the strength of the Empire."

Unionist Resistance

That was less than ever the opinion of the Unionist party, which now declared its intention of carrying resistance to all lengths and at all costs. The Bill was fought at every stage in the House of Commons, which sat in continuous session throughout the winter and into the following spring. It passed its third reading on January 16, 1913, and a fortnight later met its expected fate in the House of Lords, being rejected on second reading by a majority of 257.

In the old days this would have been fatal and final, and a third Home Rule Bill would have gone the way of its pre-decessors. But the Parliament Act was now in force and the Bill would automatically become law if passed again in two successive sessions by the House of Commons, in spite of its rejection by the House of Lords. To secure the defeat of the Government or the withdrawal of the Bill before this period elapsed became now the resolute purpose of the Unionist party.

The chief hope of the Opposition and the greatest difficulty of the Government lay in the attitude of the six Protestant counties of Ulster, which declared that they would in no circumstances submit to be governed by a Parliament in Dublin. In 1886, when Mr. Gladstone's first Home Rule Bill was introduced, Lord Randolph Churchill had said that " Ulster would fight and Ulster would be right," but this had not been taken very seriously. The idea of any part of the United Kingdom resisting by force an act of the Imperial Parliament seemed fantastic to the great majority of Englishmen in those days. But in 1912 there was no shirking the fact that it had seriously to be reckoned with. Even before the Irish Bill was introduced the Ulster Unionist Council had announced its intention of setting up a " Provisional Government " for their own province if or when a Parliament in Dublin was established, and in the following months the English Unionist leaders made it known that they would support them in this project and in whatever steps might be necessary to promote it. Speaking at a Unionist demonstration on July 28, 1912,

Mr. Bonar Law said, " I can imagine no length of resistance to which Ulster will go in which I shall not be ready to support them."

" Ulster will fight "

At the end of September the Ulstermen held a mass meeting near Belfast, at which an immense number signed a " Covenant " pledging themselves to " use all means which may be necessary to defeat the present conspiracy to set up a Home Rule Parliament in Ireland." Sir Edward Carson, a distinguished Irish lawyer and former Attorney-General in a Unionist Government, was chosen as leader of the movement, and had for his aide-de-camp and " galloper," Mr. F. E. Smith, another distinguished lawyer and a future Lord Chancellor. Sir Edward said before he went to Ireland that he intended to " break every law that is possible," and Mr. Smith said that he would not shrink from the consequences of " his convictions, not though the whole fabric of the Commonwealth be convulsed." In the next few months the Covenanters set to work to arm and drill, and, though some Englishmen were still incredulous and regarded these performances as Irish opéra bouffe, there was no longer any serious doubt that the Ulstermen were preparing to resist Home Rule by force, or that in this they had the active support of the British Unionist party.

When the Home Rule Bill was being drafted there had been much discussion in the Cabinet as to whether Ulster or the six Protestant counties should not be excluded from it, but at that time it seemed the more heroic course to make at least an effort to save the ideal of a United Ireland, and only to yield if at a later stage it was judged wiser to do so. Moreover, the Government had no guarantee that conceding this point would abate the opposition to their measure as a whole, for the Ulstermen had declared their objection to Home Rule for any part of Ireland, and many English Unionists had a strong sentiment against leaving the Unionist minority in South Ireland isolated, as they would be if the North were cut off from the South. But as events were now developing this decision placed the Government in a position of great difficulty. They could not yield to these threats without great loss of credit, and they could not proceed against the ring-leaders of the threatened rebellion with any hope of getting a conviction from an Irish jury. To turn the blind eye to the proceedings in Ulster was especially the advice of the Nationalist leaders, who remained confident that the trouble would blow over, and warned the Government that British intervention or British coercion in what they deemed to be an Irish quarrel would be distasteful to all parties in Ireland.

The Curragh Incident

Seeing nothing else to do, the Government did for the next eighteen months turn the blind eye, while the Ulstermen continued to arm and drill and import arms, under the nose of authority, with the declared intention of challenging the Imperial Parliament. Whatever arguments there might have been for this inaction, the results were highly demoralizing. It was not to be supposed that while the North was thus active the South would remain quiescent, and the immunity which was given to the one could not be withheld from the other. All through 1913 the Chief Secretary reported that there was rising up in the South of Ireland, a movement in which the extreme parties—Sinn Fein, the Irish Republican Brotherhood, the Gaelic Associations and others—were joining hands to raise a force of National Volunteers to get even with Ulster and to demand something more than a subordinate Parliament from the Imperial Government. On both sides the forces of reason and moderation were being fatally undermined, and the settlement, whatever it might be, was slipping out of the hands of Government and Parliament into the hands of armed extremists on both sides. The Ulster " Provisional Government " in Belfast was now matched by a " National Provisional Committee " in Dublin, and both were actively engaged in arming and gun-running.

Inevitably in the circumstances speculation turned to what the regular army would do if it were called upon to act either to enforce Home Rule or to keep the peace between these parties. The War Office by now was a house divided against itself, one of its most eminent officials, Sir Henry Wilson, the Director of Military Operations, being in active sympathy and regular communication with the Ulster Volunteers.

In December, 1913, the Chief of the Imperial General Staff and the Adjutant-General reported that so many efforts were being made to seduce officers and men from their allegiance that there was a real danger of indiscipline in the army, and at a conference which followed the Commander-in-Chief in Ireland obtained permission to allow officers domiciled in Ulster to " disappear " without prejudice to their prospects or promotion afterwards, if the army were called upon to deal with disturbances caused by the Ulster Volunteers.

To grant this discretion for his private use the Commander-in-Chief might well have been wise in the circumstances, but unfortunately it was expanded in the next few weeks from an indulgence to Ulster officers to a test for all officers. Thus on March 20, 1914, when it had become necessary to move troops for the guarding of certain arms and munitions depots in Ulster, the Commander-in-Chief summoned his officers to the Curragh, and while informing those who were domiciled in Ulster that they might absent themselves, told the others that if they were not prepared to carry out their duty as ordered, they must say so at once and in that case would be dismissed from the service. They were given two hours to come to a decision, and when the time expired, Brigadier-General Hubert Gough and fifty-seven officers (out of a total of seventy) of the 3rd Cavalry Brigade replied that they preferred to be dismissed.

The news of this event caused alarm and dismay throughout the country. Excited debates took place in Parliament, where Liberal and Labour were unanimous in calling upon the Government to restore discipline in the army, and assert the authority of Parliament over the " mutineers." The Cabinet appears to have been very imperfectly informed of the proceedings of the Army Council, and, when he learnt the facts, Asquith decided at once that a serious mistake had been made in requiring the officers on pain of dismissal to express a judgment on the policy of the Government, and thus placing them in a painful dilemma between their military duties and what might be their political convictions. He thought it unjust to visit them with dismissal for their choice under this pressure, and altogether a misnomer to speak of their having " mutinied " when they had merely chosen one of the alternatives put to them by their superior officer. In order to clear up the situation he took the office of Secretary of State for War, and laid down the impeccable doctrine that no officer or soldier should ask questions about orders which may be given to him, or be asked questions about his attitude towards such orders, and that in particular it is the duty of every officer and soldier to obey all lawful commands " either for the safeguarding of public property or the support of the civil power in the ordinary execution of its duty, or for the protection of the lives and property of the inhabitants in the case of disturbance of the peace." On that the officers returned to duty, but the course of events behind the scenes had been one of blundering all the way, and it required all Asquith's personal authority to restore order, and to convince the House of Commons that he had not bargained with the officers for their return to duty.

The King and the Crisis

By these various events political parties between them had, in the years 1913 and 1914, brought affairs into a position in which there was no safe way out for either of them. If the Liberals persisted, Ulster threatened rebellion; if the Unionists succeeded in driving the Liberals from office and extinguishing Home Rule, the Nationalists threatened rebellion.

The King, meanwhile, was in danger of becoming for the second time in his short reign the centre of a constitutional storm. Unionists entreated him to assume the functions of which the House of Lords had been dispossessed, and either to veto the Home Rule Bill or dismiss his Ministers and dissolve Parliament. Officers in the army appealed to him to absolve them from their obedience to the Government in the name of their allegiance to the Crown. Others warned him that it would be more dangerous for the Crown to be associated with a rebellion against Parliament than to risk the displeasure of the Conservative party by remaining neutral. Through it all the King remained wise and cool, and used his influence to bring party leaders together and induce them to accept a compromise.

There was nothing which Asquith more desired, and from the summer of 1913 onwards he set himself to it with characteristic patience and pertinacity. He had always been of opinion that the exclusion of the Protestant counties of Ulster would at some stage be a practical necessity, and before the year was out, he had discovered that the Unionist leaders were ready to accept Home Rule on that basis. But considerable difficulties still remained. The objections of the Nationalists to the partition of Ireland had to be overcome; the area to be excluded had to be defined and the conditions of its exclusion—whether it was to be temporary or permanent, whether, if temporary, the excluded part was to vote itself in or vote itself out—had to be determined. Though the arming and drilling and fulminations on platforms continued, Asquith debated these subjects in private talk with Sir Edward Carson and Mr. Bonar Law behind the scenes, with the result that the controversy was fined down to a difference of half a county in the boundary of the excluded area, and the terms on which, if the excluded portion were willing, reunion might be effected later.

But these relatively small points proved exceedingly stubborn, and the conference of party-leaders which the King summoned at Buckingham Palace in July 1914, for a last effort to compose them had to report that it had failed. Then the Government decided to push forward with the Home Rule Bill, but to attach to it an amending Bill granting an option to the Ulster counties, voting as counties, to vote themselves in or vote themselves out for a period of years, at the end of which they would have had an opportunity of reconsidering their decision. The Bill was passed under the Parliament Act after the war had broken out (September, 1914), but held up under a suspensory Act which postponed its operation until the war was over. This too was the subject of a bitter debate in which the Unionists demanded that no Parliament should be set up in Ireland until after another General Election.

What would have happened if a greater issue had not intervened to sweep the Irish question off the board for the time being can only be guessed. It was Asquith's belief that, when the public realized that it had been narrowed down to the small points that were left unsettled after the Buckingham Palace conference, the general good sense would have asserted itself over the extremists who wished to fight about these. Whether that would have been so, or whether the failure of the leaders to reach a settlement whould have revived the whole issue, it is impossible to say. But certain very serious consequences followed. The idea of rebellion had taken root in all parts of Ireland, and British Governments had now to reckon not only with Ulstermen who objected to Gladstonian Home Rule but with Nationalists who demanded a great deal more. Further, the growth of the Sinn Fein party was a serious set-off to the loyal and generous support which Mr. Redmond and the leaders of the Irish Parliamentary party tendered to the Government on the outbreak of war, and led to the rebellion of 1916. Scarcely less important, the idea, which had been almost a religion among Englishmen, that acts of the Sovereign Imperial Parliament were unchallengeable, had received a serious check, and the fact that the Conservative party, which was supposed to be specially the guardian of law and order, had lent itself to a challenge, stirred uneasy thoughts in the minds of others who were less respectful of authority. It became apparent in these years that there was an unmapped boundary between the things which could and the things which could not be settled by argument and reason along which even Sovereign Parliaments had to walk warily.

The Women's Movement

A place must be found in the record of these times for the Women's Movement which came to its climax and presented the Government with a problem of great difficulty in the years before the war. Nothing in the end had more important social and political results on the life of the country. At the beginning of the present century the cause of Woman Suffrage seemed hopelessly blocked. It had been powerfully advocated by the most influential and respected women, and it had behind it a large support in Parliament and in the country. Private members' Bills proposing it had been carried on their second reading time after time in the House of Commons. But paradoxically the great obstacle to its accomplishment was that it could not be made a party question, since the dividing line between supporters and opponents cut across parties. It could therefore not be adopted as part of their policy by either the Conservative or the Liberal party, or be proposed by a Government of either without breaking Cabinets and causing dangerous schisms in the party ranks. Lacking this Ministerial support it had little or no prospect of passing into law.

Early in the twentieth century the most ardent supporters of the cause began to say that this was an intolerable position. All the ordinary methods of suasion and education had been tried but without result. Year after year the women were put off with academic debates on private members' Bills, and told by their male friends that they must wait for a more convenient season. It was time for them to act for themselves and show the male politicians that they could not be ignored.

Accordingly, Mrs. Pankhurst and her daughters and a few other kindred spirits started a militant movement which began about the year 1905 by interrupting public meetings and making demonstrations in the House of Commons. The constitutional suffragists disapproved, and the immediate result was to stiffen the backs of the male opponents. For the first time for more than twenty years women suffrage Bills were defeated in the House of Commons in 1911 and 1912. But though alienating the politicians in the House of Commons, the militant movement gave an immense advertisement to the cause in the country and large numbers of ardent and active young women flocked to Mrs. Pankhurst's standard.

Asquith, who was personally opposed to Woman Suffrage, had promised to give facilities to private members to insert amendments granting it in the male Franchise Bill which the Government was pledged to introduce, provided, of course, they could obtain a majority for them on a free vote. Beyond this he would not go, and even in going so far, as it turned out, he wrecked the Government Franchise Bill, since the Speaker ruled that the introduction of such an amendment would require the whole Bill to be withdrawn and a new Bill drafted. (January 23, 1912.) The militant agitation, meanwhile, was increasing in violence. Women mobbed and assaulted Ministers, smashed shop-windows, even set churches on fire. One woman met her death by rushing forward and seizing the reins of a horse during the race for the Derby at Epsom. When imprisoned the women went on hunger-strike, and put the Home Secretary in the painful dilemma of having either to release them or let them die in prison. Special legislation, dubbed the "Cat and Mouse Act," which enabled him to let them out and take them back again, had to be passed to meet this emergency.

Then the war came and put an end to this kind of militancy. The work done by women during the war won universal acknowledgment, and it was agreed even by opponents that this controversy must never be renewed. The Speaker's Conference on the Franchise question which sat in 1916 and 1917 proposed household franchise for women with an age limit of 30, and this was carried in the Franchise Bill of February, 1918. More than eight million women were now added to a register which contained thirteen million male voters. In 1928 Mr. Baldwin's Government wiped out the last discrimination between male and female by reducing the age limit to 21, and the register now contains an actual majority of women voters.

The franchise movement ran parallel with a general emancipation which brought an increasing number of women into professions and occupations hitherto the preserve of men; equalized the conditions of divorce between the sexes and in manners and morals obliterated many distinctions which previous generations had thought permanent and ineradicable. The effects upon the life and character of the nation may well be one of the principal studies of the historian of morals in future times.

AGADIR AND THE BALKAN WARS

AFTER the Bosnia-Herzegovina crisis ended in March, 1909, Europe enjoyed a few months of comparative tranquillity. Russia and Austria demobilized and the Tsar visited the Kaiser at Potsdam. The Balkan States were quiet for the moment; the war which had threatened between Greece and Turkey about Crete was averted by the action of the Powers to which the King of Greece for the time being submitted. French and Germans came to an agreement about Morocco. The year 1910 passed quietly and feelings seemed to be assuaged. But trouble again broke out in Morocco in February, 1911, when the French declared themselves under the necessity of advancing to Fez to secure the lives and property of French residents supposed to be threatened by the turbulent tribes. The other Powers hoped that the French move was covered by the Franco-German agreement of 1909, but this was not the view of the Germans, who claimed that the occupation of Fez would be a new fact requiring a reconsideration of the Treaty of Algeciras and entitling them at least to compensation. The French admitted the claim to compensation, and started negotiations on this basis.

The Germans demanded a large slice of the French Congo, and the French were unwilling to give so much. The negotiations dragged on for several weeks while the German claim was watered down; then, just as M. Jules Cambon, the French Ambassador in Berlin, thought he was in sight of a settlement, the Germans suddenly sent a warship, the *Panther*, to Agadir, a small port on the southern part of the Atlantic coast of Morocco, on the plea that it was necessary to protect German trade and German residents in that region. Agadir was not a commercial port and there were no German residents near it or German trade with it. The dispatch of the warship was the idea of the German Foreign Secretary, Kiderlen

Waechter, who seems to have believed that a timely display of the big stick would sharpen the negotiations and secure Germany a bigger slice of the French Congo.

German methods were often difficult to understand, and both French and British were greatly mystified and disturbed. To both, the appearance of the warship seemed like the sudden planting of a fist in the middle of peaceful negotiations; the British saw the Germans pegging out a claim to a port on the Atlantic, where they least desired them to be; the French feared that as in 1905, when they had sacrificed their Foreign Minister to German threats, they would again have to choose between humiliation and war. Sir Edward Grey told the German Ambassador that he considered the situation " new and important." The French Ambassador spoke in the same sense to the German Foreign Secretary.

The Kaiser, who appears to have accepted Kiderlen Waechter's assurance that only the dispatch of the warship was needed to bring the French to terms about the Congo, asked, " What the devil is to happen now? " Kiderlen offered to resign, but no one knew how to answer the question, and for nearly three weeks London and Paris were left waiting for the explanations which they too were seeking. Then Mr. Lloyd George, with the approval of Asquith and Grey, made a speech at the Mansion House in which he said that " if a situation were to be forced upon us in which peace could only be preserved by the surrender of the great and beneficent position Britain has won by centuries of heroism and achievement, by allowing Britain to be treated, where her interests are vitally affected, as if she were of no account in the Cabinet of Nations, then I say emphatically that peace at that price would be a humiliation intolerable for a great country like ours to endure." (July 21, 1911.)

These were far-sounding words, but more significant still, they were spoken by the man who at that time was supposed to be the leader of the Radical and pacifist party in the Cabinet. If Mr. Lloyd George spoke thus, the public both in Germany and Great Britain judged that the situation must indeed be serious. It was now extremely difficult to find a peaceful solution. Honour and prestige were engaged on both sides. The French were at Fez, the *Panther* was at Agadir; the world knew all about it, and the withdrawal of either would have been a public humiliation.

A Long-drawn Crisis

The Germans showed no signs of withdrawing, and four days after the Mansion House speech, Sir Edward Grey told Mr. Winston Churchill, the First Lord of the Admiralty, that he had received a communication from the German Ambassador " so stiff that the fleet might be attacked at any moment." The crisis continued on this edge all through August, and on the very day on which they were engaged in their final struggle with the House of Lords, British Ministers were in doubt whether they might not be at war with Germany before the week was out. The tension continued right up to the middle of October, and for all that time the naval and military forces of the three Powers stood on guard, lest the negotiations should take an unfavourable turn. In such a situation it was everything to gain time, and the British Government, while keeping outwardly a bold front, did their utmost behind the scenes to persuade the French to yield all they could to the German demand for " compensation." They did in the end yield more than was at all agreeable to them, but they got finally in return the free hand in Morocco, which was more important to them than the slice of the Congo which they gave up. The Franco-German Treaty regulating these matters was signed on November 4, and the *Panther* was withdrawn at the end of the month. The settlement came just in time to enable King George to sail to India for the great Coronation Durbar which was held at Delhi in December this year.

These events left an uneasy feeling in all countries. How often, it was asked, would Europe stand these shocks, and what seemingly trivial cause might not bring irreparable catastrophe? The Franco-German quarrel was unhealed; The British-German naval competition had become one of the major issues in the contention between the Powers; the Turkish Empire was visibly crumbling; the rivalry between Austria and Russia was unabated. The network of treaties and obligations was such that almost any Power was liable to be involved in any dispute.

Italy and Tripoli

These anxieties were amply justified, and before the Agadir crisis had passed another and, as it proved, the final chapter in the story of pre-war Europe had been opened. British Ministers, it now turned out, had been right in perceiving that the annexation of Bosnia-Herzegovina by Austria-Hungary would open a wide door to mischief, if it were allowed to go by default. From the day when Austria reaped her success all the expectant heirs of the " sick man of Europe " —big States and little States—were on the move, each fearing that the others might steal a march on it in the final scramble for the " sick man's " inheritance.

Italy was the first to act. She had an understanding with nearly all the Powers that one day she would be permitted to occupy Tripoli. She had been deeply mortified when France got in front of her and occupied Tunis with its large Italian population ; she had looked on when Britain occupied Egypt, and France added Morocco to Tunis and Algiers ; she had seen Austria annex Bosnia-Herzegovina. On each of these occasions she had deferred to the advice of friends who declared the moment to be inopportune, but in the summer of 1911 she decided that she would wait no longer. Tripoli was all that remained of the North African coast and in the scramble now impending it might slip from her grasp. So in July and August Italian newspapers wrought opinion into a high state of excitement about the misgovernment of that Turkish province and the grievances of Italian subjects domiciled there, and at the end of September she sent an ulti-matum to Turkey demanding the right to occupy it. Though she was the ally of Germany, she did not inform the German Government, and the Kaiser was very angry at her proceeding without warning to an act which involved the Triple Alliance, and threatened the policy of friendship with Turkey, which he was pursuing with great zeal at that moment. But the ties which bound Italy to her partners were becoming very frail, and she was in a position to remind them that her special interest in Tripoli was carefully guarded in the various treaties of the Triple Alliance.

The Balkan Wars

The Italian campaign was not a very glorious one, for the country was difficult and the Turks put up an unexpectedly stubborn resistance. But it played into the hands of the Balkan States, which, on the powerful initiative of the Greek patriot, Venizelos, backed by Russian influence in Serbia and Bulgaria, had composed their differences and formed a fighting alliance, which also awaited its favourable moment to fall upon the Turk. There could hardly have been a better one than when his treasury was exhausted and his forces depleted by the struggle with Italy, and before 1912 was far on, the Balkan League was straining at the leash. The Powers were seriously alarmed at the drift of events, and Russia, which was not prepared for war, saw the situation which she had helped to make slipping out of her control. Sazonoff, the Russian Prime Minister, started on a round of visits to European capitals in a last-hour effort to procure intervention to keep the peace, but he was too late, and before the Powers could act, the King of Montenegro rushed in to attack the Turks, and within a week the Balkan Allies were at the throat of their hereditary enemy.

By the end of October, the Turks had been defeated on every front, and were falling back on the Chataldja lines for the defence of Constantinople. So quick and complete a victory astonished all the onlookers and greatly mortified Austria, which regarded the Slav victory as a serious menace to her Empire. Serbia especially had long been a thorn in her flesh, and she had hoped that even if the Turks did not win, the struggle would at least be long and exhausting enough to quench the warlike ardour of this militant little people. Now she saw the Serbs victorious and exultant, claiming an outlet to the Adriatic, and signalling to their disaffected brethren within the Austrian Empire. Russia too was seriously disturbed lest Tsar Ferdinand of Bulgaria, being now so near, should push on to Constantinople and get himself crowned in St. Sophia, which was known to be his secret ambition but the last thing that the greater Tsar was willing to tolerate. Germany was only less embarrassed. She saw her Turkish policy in ruins and herself in danger of being drawn into an

THE
BALKAN STATES
1914

English Miles

0   50   100   150   200

RUSSIA

AUSTRIA-HUNGARY

Danube

Theiss

Save

Maros

Transylvania

Moldavia

Dniester

Sereth

Bessarabia

Pruth

Jassy

Galatz

Belgrade

osnia

rajevo

Drina

rze-
vina

Wallachia

Danube

Aluta

Bucharest

Giurgevo

Rustchuk

Constantsa

BLACK

MONTENEGRO

Cetinje

The
Sanjak

Novibazar

Nish

Plevna

Balkan Mts

Varna

SEA

Sofia

Eastern Roumelia

Uskub

Ishtib

Vardar

Philippopolis

Maritsa

Adrianople

Kirk Kilisse

Lule Burgas

Bosporus

Scutari

Durazzo

Monastir

Constantinople

Scutari

Rodosto

SEA OF MARMARA

Kavala

Valona

Macedonia

Salonika

Thasos

Dedeagatch

Gallipoli

Dardanelles

Janina

Larissa

Imbros

Lemnos

Asia

Patras

Athens

Corinth

Nauplia

Sparta

Lesbos

Chios

Samos

Smyrna

Minor

MEDITERRANEAN

Dodecanese
(Italian)

Rhodes

Rhodes

SEA

Crete

R.O.

MONTENEGRO

Scutari

ALBANIA

Dra

SERBIA

Morava

Danube

BULGARIA

Struma

GREECE

AEGEAN SEA

TURKEY

DOBRUJA

ROUMANIA

M
E
D
I
T
E
R
R
A
N
E
A
N

Austro-Serbian quarrel which might easily develop into a world war. Italy objected almost as much as Austria to the Serbian claim to a port on the Adriatic.

The Turks made bad worse by declining the terms offered them at the Peace Conference held in London in December, for when they resumed the war they were again disastrously beaten, and compelled now to cede Adrianople in addition to their other losses. This, however, was not the end, for no sooner had they concluded their final peace with the Turks than the Allies fell into a dispute among themselves about the division of the spoils, Bulgaria protesting that she was entitled to a far larger slice of Macedonia and better access to the Ægean than Greece and Serbia were willing to concede to her. Bulgaria had a real grievance, but she forfeited all sympathy when she fell suddenly on her Allies, and after a heavy reverse was compelled to accept peace on the intervention of Rumania. The Turks now reoccupied Adrianople, and in the Treaty of Bucharest which ended the third Balkan War the Bulgarians were required not only to surrender most of their previous gains, but to cede the Dobrudja, which was a considerable part of their territory on the Black Sea littoral, to Rumania.

The Ambassadors' Conference

The Powers having failed to stop the war did the next best thing by consenting to Sir Edward Grey's proposal of a conference to keep the peace among themselves. This conference, which consisted of the Ambassadors of the Powers in London, sat at the British Foreign Office, with Sir Edward himself presiding, from December 1912 to August 1913, and performed the very useful service of keeping the various Governments in touch while these dangerous events were proceeding. It was the most informal and the most successful of all the conferences of these years. It dealt with fluid material which changed from week to week, and sought compromises and adjustments for each emergency as it arose. Its main difficulty was to reduce the large Serbian claims to Albania and a port (Durazzo or another) on the Adriatic to what Austria would accept, and there was a critical moment when the King of Montenegro, acting in collusion with the

Serbs, seized and occupied Scutari. But Germany and Russia were both at this time anxious to keep the peace, and they worked loyally with Sir Edward Grey in bringing the Serbs to reason and requiring the Montenegrins to evacuate Scutari. Albania was made a Princedom under a German Prince, and Serbia guaranteed commercial access to the Adriatic.

These arrangements saved the peace for the time being, and Sir Edward Grey was warmly congratulated on the skill and impartiality with which he had steered this conference. When August came the clouds seemed at last to be lifted, and there was a widespread belief that the last of the great crises had come and gone. Russia was content, Germany had worked for peace, Britain and France had no interest in any of these Balkan quarrels except to keep the peace. Unfortunately these sanguine calculations left Austria-Hungary out of account. All through the months when the conference was sitting, the Austrian war-party, under the impetuous Conrad von Hötzendorff, Chief of the General Staff, had been gaining strength, and nothing but the restraining hand of Germany and the reluctance of the aged Austrian Emperor, who wished for peace in his time, had prevented it from breaking loose and declaring war. "I will not fight to keep the Serbians out of Durazzo," was the Kaiser's word to Vienna, and to that even Conrad had to defer. But the Austrians remained profoundly discontented with the course of events, and if they submitted for the time being it was with the firm resolve to seize the next favourable moment to settle accounts with Serbia.

Austrian Alarms

It cannot be said that the Austrians were without reason for their alarms. They were visibly failing to solve their internal problems. Most of their many races were seething with discontent; their parliamentary institutions were breaking down; all the solutions propounded, Federalism, Trialism [1] and the rest, had been thwarted by the opposition of one race

---

[1] Trialism, *i.e.* the constitution of a third self-governing unit composed of the Slavs of the Empire to be of equal status with Austria and Hungary was the solution specially favoured at one time by the heir to the throne, the Archduke Franz Ferdinand. Federalism required the establishment of a central Government to which all the States would have been subordinate.

or another, or of the official classes which stood stubbornly in the old ways. A Liberal policy steadily pursued might have enabled the Dual Monarchy to obtain the leadership of the Balkan peoples and to wean them from their habit of looking to Russia as their patron. But the German and Magyar aristocracies had thought of little but their own ascendancy, and blunder upon blunder had finally landed the Dual Monarchy in the position in which the existence of any success-ful and self-assertive Slav State outside its boundary acted as a magnet to the millions of discontented Slavs within. The Serbs in the autumn of 1913 had none of the craft which con-ceals a future design. They were jubilant, they talked at the top of their voices, and made no secret of their desire to re-establish the greater Serbia which must necessarily carve a large slice out of Austria-Hungary. At the same time Rumanians were talking of the "great Rumania" which would presently liberate and absorb the Rumanians under the Magyar yoke.

When the third Balkan War was over Conrad declared for what he called the "great solution"—the solution by war, which he clearly foresaw would be war not with the Balkan States only but with Russia, and probably set all Europe on fire. Some time in the summer of 1913 he appears to have converted the German Chief of Staff, General von Moltke, to this view. In his Memoirs he records conversations in which the two Chiefs of Staff confided their ideas to one another, and found that they were in agreement. Both held that the European balance of power had been profoundly disturbed and to the disadvantage of the Triple Alliance by the victory of the Balkan Allies. Rumania, hitherto a faithful adherent of the Central Powers, was now doubtful; Italy was in sharp disagreement with Austria; Serbia, greatly aggrandized, must be counted on the side of Russia; and Greece, if tested, would probably follow Serbia. The only gleam of light was Bulgaria, which would be drawn to the German side by her hatred of Serbia and Greece. This situation, said Conrad, would grow worse, not better, by waiting—waiting would give Russia time to prepare, and though weak and unprepared at the moment, Russia had incalculable resources which might make her irresistible in a few years' time. Conrad complained that many favourable moments had been lost by the reluctance of Germany to abet his plans, and Moltke agreed that waiting for Russia to complete her plans would be as dangerous for Germany as for Austria-Hungary.

The Kaiser and the " Inevitable War "

The Kaiser, who had resisted these ideas up to the end of the London Conference, began to waver soon afterwards. From this time onwards, the fear of Russia seemed most to weigh with him, and he talked gloomily of the " inevitable war between East and West," Slav and Teuton. The Austrians now plied him with the argument that the fortunes of Germany were indissolubly bound up with those of Austria-Hungary, and that Austria's favourable moment would also be Germany's last chance of settling with Russia before she became irresistible. Russia, they pointed out, had elaborate plans for strategic railways on her western frontier—plans which could only be aimed at Germany—and a new scheme which would obviate the delays in mobilization, which were now her chief weakness. To wait until these were completed would be to play into the hands of Russia. It followed on this line of reasoning that it was not Germany's interest to prevent Austria from asserting her authority over Serbia for fear a war with Russia should result, but rather to welcome the opportunity which would thus be provided for both Germany and Austria to settle accounts with Russia while she was still unprepared.

The Kaiser saw Conrad at the Austrian manoeuvres in September, and a few weeks later paid a visit to Vienna. There on October 26 he visited Berchtold, the Austrian Foreign Secretary, and, according to the latter's account, gave him carte blanche for a forward Austrian policy against Serbia. Berchtold reports him as having said, " Whatever issues from the Vienna Foreign Office shall be to me a command." Conrad and Berchtold, the Kaiser decided, should have no more reason to complain that their " favourable moments " were lost and their policy thwarted by the opposition of Berlin. The work of the London Conference was thus undone in an hour, and the tendencies making for war were re-established in a more dangerous, because underground, channel.

British Efforts for Peace

The British Government, meanwhile, being unaware of this turn of events, was taking advantage of what seemed to be the more favourable atmosphere to improve its relations with Germany. The Haldane Mission in January, 1912—the last of the many efforts to come to terms on the naval competition—had broken down on the old obstacle of the " political equivalent " demanded by the Germans, which appeared to the British Government to be nothing less than the abandonment of the French and Russian Ententes; and the Kaiser had contemptuously rejected Mr. Winston Churchill's idea of a " naval holiday," *i.e.* the cessation of ship-building for a period of a year. But British Ministers hoped that relations might still be improved, if the area of controversy were shifted, and they succeeded in removing the numerous causes of friction between Britain and Germany in their colonial and oversea relations. All through the winter months and the spring of 1914 the German Ambassador and his colleagues in London worked out the details with British Ministers, and arrived finally at a friendly settlement of the thorny question of the Bagdad Railway and various other questions touching the colonies of the two countries in Central Africa. The agreement was completed and only not published because of a difference about the form of publication which had not been settled, when the war broke out. But as between Britain and Germany alone, the atmosphere had seldom seemed more favourable than in the early months of 1914. The German Ambassador, Lichnowsky, was a warm friend of Great Britain who was visibly working for peace; British Ministers were relieved and thankful at last to have discovered ground on which they could work amicably with the Germans.

The Unrest in Europe

But the unrest in Europe continued unabated in these months, and the arms competition was at fever pitch. The Germans had not only added largely to their army, but raised a capital levy of £50,000,000 which the French interpreted as a specially ominous sign that they were on the war-path. Russia had raised a large loan, was reorganizing her Black Sea fleet, and had plans ready for the strategic railways which the Germans so greatly feared. France had raised her period of military service from two years to three, and was working overtime to effect the considerable changes in organization which this required. As between France and Germany the atmosphere was heated by the Zabern incident which displayed Prussian methods at their worst in Alsace, and as between Russia and Germany by a violent press campaign which broke out simultaneously in Berlin and St. Petersburg, and had all the appearance of being prompted by the two Governments. The visit of King George to Paris in April, 1914, was watched with suspicion in Germany, and the "naval conversations," which Sir Edward Grey permitted between British and Russian naval officers, were magnified into the story of a naval convention between the two Powers for common action in the Baltic in a coming war.

Europe in fact had become a powder magazine which might be ignited by any spark, and military advisers who were reckless of consequences, provided they saw what they thought to be a favourable moment for their campaigns, were daily gaining ground over civilian statesmen. The Russians held a war council in January, 1914, and though professing to desire the maintenance of the *status quo*, decided that they would be ready for war any time from the year 1917 onwards. Conrad and the Austrians, fortified by the promise of German support and being persuaded that Russia was unprepared, were for forcing the issue at once. On May 13 Conrad, the Austrian Chief of Staff, visited Moltke, the German Chief, and the German explained to the Austrian the Schlieffen plan for the invasion of France through Belgium. "We hope," said Moltke, "in six weeks after the beginning of operations to have finished with France or at least so far as to enable us to direct our principal forces against the East." Early in June, 1914, the Austrians prepared a memorandum for submission to their German Ally proposing that Rumania should be called upon to declare herself publicly on the side of the Triple Alliance or take the consequences, which would almost certainly be war. The memorandum was delivered a month later with its preamble unaltered, but the proposed ultimatum was directed to another Balkan State, for by this time an event had taken place which gave the Austrian war-makers a unique opportunity.

CHAPTER XVI

On Sunday, June 28, 1914, the Archduke Franz Ferdinand was murdered with his wife in the Bosnian town of Serajevo, where he had gone on an official tour of inspection. The two assassins, Princip and Cabrinovic, were young men of twenty, natives of Bosnia and therefore Austrian subjects. They belonged to a student group which was pledged to resist and avenge the severe acts of repression that had accompanied Austrian administration since the annexation, but they were undoubtedly in touch with secret and patriotic associations across the border in Serbia and had recently been in Belgrade, where they had been furnished with hand-grenades and revolvers and, thus armed, had crossed the Drina back into Bosnia.

No event could have been better calculated to kindle into flame the smouldering passions and animosities described in the previous chapter. The Archduke was not a popular figure in his own country. He had broken the Hapsburg tradition by a morganatic marriage and thereby incurred the anger of the Emperor, who was inclined to see the finger of Providence in the tragedy which had overtaken both man and wife in the Bosnian town. They received less than imperial honours at their funeral, and the people of the Dual Monarchy seemed not to be greatly afflicted by their loss. But Austrian statesmen and soldiers leapt to the opportunity which the occasion offered for forcing the issue in the Balkans and this time they carried the Emperor with them. They could now more than ever rely on the German Kaiser. The Archduke was his intimate friend; his feelings were greatly stirred by the outrage on Monarchy in the murder of an heir to the throne, and no efforts were needed to persuade him that strong and immediate action was peremptorily necessary. During the fortnight after the crime he was in a state of great agitation, and incited the Austrians to go all lengths against the Serbians.

The Austrians needed no incitement. They believed, or professed to believe, that not only the Serbian secret societies but the Serbian Government itself was privy to the crime; and changing their original plan, which had been to address an ultimatum to Rumania in the summer of this year, they now resolved to address themselves to Serbia, and this time to make a final settlement of the long account they had piled up against her. The possibility that Russia would intervene they faced with their eyes open, for the idea of trying conclusions with her also was greatly in favour with both the Austrian and the German General Staffs.

The Ultimatum to Serbia

All this for the moment was behind the scenes and outwardly there was a pause which led many people to hope that no serious consequences would follow. The Kaiser, having expressed his indignation and taken counsel with his military advisers, went on a yachting cruise, and the French President started on an official visit to Russia. The British people were immersed in their own troubled politics—the failure of the Buckingham Palace Conference, and the danger of civil war in Ireland—which seemed much more important than the murder of an archduke in Bosnia. If they had any views on that, it was simply to share the general horror at a cruel murder and to hope and expect that justice would be done after proper inquiry.

Then suddenly, shattering all these illusions, came on July 23 the Austrian ultimatum to Serbia, couched in terms so ruthless that its acceptance, demanded within twenty-four hours, was clearly not intended or expected. Its delivery had been timed for the moment when the French President was at sea on his return journey from Russia, with the evident purpose, in which it partly succeeded, of throwing French and Russian diplomacy into confusion. The advice hurriedly offered to the Serbians by the other Powers was that they should do everything possible to satisfy Austria, and their reply within the twenty-four hours was an almost total submission. The Austrian Minister in Belgrade did not even open it, but instead produced a fresh note announcing the rupture of diplomatic relations and the immediate departure of himself and his staff. Two days later (July 28) Austria declared war upon Serbia. The menace to the general peace was now clear to all the world, for it was impossible to suppose the Austrians unaware that they were throwing a challenge to Russia which it would be extremely difficult, if not impossible, for her to decline.

British Action

In these dangerous circumstances the British Government considered that the best service it could render was to endeavour to set up again the process of conciliation which had served Europe so well through the Ambassadors' Conference of the previous year. Accordingly, on the day after the Austrian ultimatum (July 24), Sir Edward Grey proposed mediation by the four disinterested Powers, Germany, France, Italy and Great Britain, and continued to urge it for the next three days. Germany, however, rejected all Sir Edward's proposals on the plea that Austria's quarrel with Serbia was a matter with which Russia had no concern, and that if Russia intervened the responsibility would be entirely hers. Lord Grey has related how he was reduced to despair by the refusal of the Germans to " press the button for peace," but the truth was that they were deeply committed to support Austria in any action she might take, and that the General Staffs of both countries had plans which they believed to be infallible ways of defeating any combination against them, if only they were permitted to act quickly, and were not tangled up in dilatory negotiations. The master-plan was that invented by a former Chief of the German Staff, Count Schlieffen—the plan for outflanking the great line of fortresses on the French eastern front by marching through Belgium and descending in a wide sweep on Paris—and it depended on getting into action before the Russians could mobilize. To Germans and Austrians, therefore, it was imperative to move swiftly from the moment that war threatened, and correspondingly to French and Russians it was a necessity to accelerate Russian mobilization so as to defeat the main assumption on which the Schlieffen plan rested.

The Soldiers in Charge

The refusal of the Germans to accept mediation meant that the soldiers and not the statesmen were in charge, and though Sir Edward Grey battled manfully to stem the military tide, the thoughts of all the other Governments were on the prospects of victory or the danger of defeat in the war which they now thought to be inevitable. Sweeping aside the objections of the Tsar, the Russian military chiefs insisted on mobilizing as the Austrians mobilized, and Russian mobilization gave the signal for German, and German for French. It was thus that the Alliance system worked and was bound to work, when the civilian Governments decided on war or despaired of peace. Each justified itself by the action of its neighbour and probable enemy, and between these various pleas it can only be said that the chief responsibility belonged to those who first set the military machine in motion.

The situation at the end of July was that the Austrians were at war with Serbia, that Russia had replied first by a partial and then by a general mobilization, that Germany had mobilized and presented an ultimatum to Russia, and that France had mobilized with the certain result of bringing a declaration of war from Germany. On July 29 the Germans had had a momentary repentance, and for a few hours appeared to give their support to a last effort by Sir Edward Grey to bring about direct negotiations between Austria and Russia. But the German and Austrian military chiefs combined to defeat this proposal, and though the Kaiser and the German Chancellor seem to have been sincere in wishing to give it a chance, they were helpless against this opposition.

The Bid for British Neutrality

On July 30 the German Chancellor, Bethmann Hollweg, made his famous bid for British neutrality—an offer " to make no territorial acquisition at the expense of France," if Britain would remain neutral. The offer did not extend to French colonies, and it left Germany free to do what she chose with Belgium. Sir Edward Grey answered briefly but decisively:

What he asks us, in effect, is to engage to stand by while French colonies are taken and France is beaten so long as Germany does not take French territory, as distinct from the colonies.

From the material point of view such a proposal is unacceptable, for France without further territory in Europe being taken from her could be so crushed as to lose her position as a great Power, and become subordinate to German policy.

Altogether apart from that, it would be a disgrace for us to make this bargain with Germany at the expense of France—a disgrace from which the good name of this country would never recover.

The Chancellor also, in effect, asks us to bargain away whatever obligation or interest we have as regards the neutrality of Belgium. We could not entertain that bargain either.

Sir Edward Grey sent this reply on his own initiative after consulting the Prime Minister, but however much his Cabinet colleagues might differ on other points, they were at one in holding that he had done rightly.

The Belgian Question

This bid for neutrality made it clear on July 30 that the Germans were contemplating war, and contemplating the invasion of Belgium. From this point onwards Belgium became the deciding issue for the British Government, the issue which was to bring Ministers to the all-but-unanimous decision that their entry into the war was an obligation of honour as well as a necessity of policy. Up to this point there had been three opinions in the Cabinet; one, held by a majority at the beginning, that the threatened war was a continental struggle in which we were under no obligation to intervene; another, that our intervention should be confined to action at sea and not extend to landing an army on the continent; a third, which was at first the opinion of only a small minority, that interest and policy would compel us to intervene to prevent the downfall of France, and its certain consequence, the establishment of a German hegemony in Europe.

On all the issues touching our relations with France or Russia, it could be argued that we were under no obligation to intervene. We had again and again explained to the French that in promising diplomatic support and consenting to " military conversations " we reserved the decision of peace and war to ourselves and to our own Parliament, if or when the time came. Our naval arrangements with the French did indeed place us under an obligation to defend the northern coasts of France, but on that the Germans had offered to meet us by refraining from attacking these coasts if we would remain neutral. The French, therefore, however much they might have felt what they would no doubt have regarded as their desertion by their British friend, would not have been in a position to reproach us with the breach of any promise or treaty obligation, provided their northern coasts were not attacked. The case of Belgium stood on a different footing. We were under treaty obligation to defend the neutrality of Belgium; we had given not merely a joint and several guarantee, but what a previous Foreign Secretary, Lord Clarendon, had described as " an individual guarantee " to defend it when menaced; and when it had last been threatened in the Franco-Prussian War of 1870, we had taken special steps to ensure that both belligerents should respect it. Thus, on Sunday, August 2, when it was no longer possible to doubt that the Germans were about to invade Belgium, an instant decision was called for from the British Government.

The British Decision

There were what one member of that Cabinet described as " heavy wrestlings " in the two meetings of that day. There were some who thought that, if the Belgians themselves did not resist, a " simple traverse " of their country would not be ground for our intervention. It was argued that we should have no right to make their country the cockpit of the European belligerents, if they themselves were consenting parties to their own violation. But this the great majority thought to be merely catching at straws, and by Sunday evening it was agreed that any ·" substantial violation " of Belgium would require British intervention. Lord Morley and Mr. John Burns thereupon resigned, and two other Ministers, Sir John Simon and Lord Beauchamp, still expressed grave doubts. When the Cabinet reassembled the next morning there could no longer be any question that the violation would be " substantial " or that the Belgians intended to resist. The King of the Belgians was now appealing for the help guaranteed by the Treaty, and not to respond would have been to repudiate the Treaty and leave him unaided to defend what we had always maintained to be a vital principle of our own European policy.

There were no more debates in the Cabinet. German action had done what in all probability nothing else could have done at that moment—resolved the doubts of Ministers and brought them to the all-but-unanimous conclusion that Britain could not shirk her part in the war. There was the same unanimity in Parliament and the country. There can seldom have been a Parliament more reluctant to break the peace than the Parliament of 1914, and in the previous week Asquith had been warned that at least half the House of Commons was resolutely opposed to participation in the war. But when Sir Edward Grey had finished the powerful and moving speech in which he set out the whole case, the only important dissent was from the leader of the Labour party; and Mr. Redmond, the leader of the Irish party, told the Government that they " might to-morrow withdraw every one of their troops from Ireland in confidence that her coasts would be defended by her own armed sons, and that for this purpose armed Nationalist Catholics in the South would be only too glad to join arms with the armed Protestant Ulstermen in the North."

Thus the die was cast and Great Britain too issued her ultimatum. At midnight on August 4 she was at war.

Asquith has been justly praised for the masterly manner in which he held his Cabinet together until the supreme moment, but even he would almost certainly have failed in the end but for the German invasion of Belgium. To millions who were unmoved by the argument from interest and policy, that seemed to be the call of duty, and the peace movement which had had powerful adherents in all parties in the previous days faded out of sight as soon as it was clear. From this moment all internal strife was hushed, and men and women of all parties and classes vowed that they were willing for any effort and any sacrifice to defeat the hated thing they called " Prussianism." In a phrase which became historic the German Chancellor, Bethmann Hollweg, complained bitterly to the British Ambassador in Berlin that Britain was going to war for a " scrap of paper." The British people saw in this " scrap of paper " a solemn promise, again and again renewed, which they were bound in honour to fulfil.

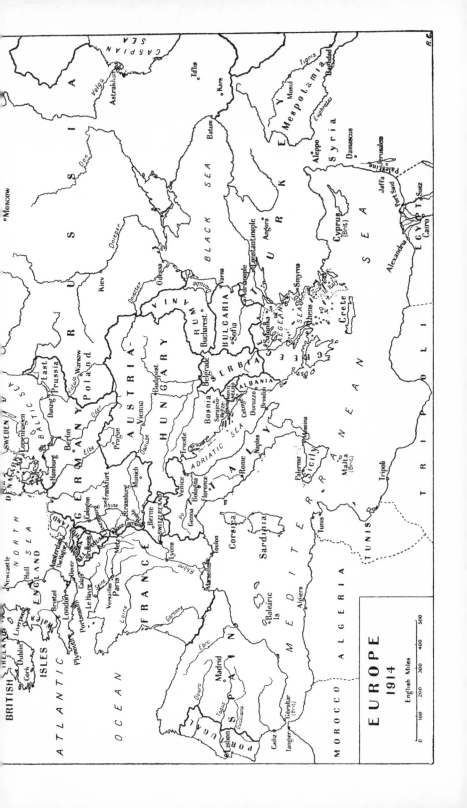

EUROPE
1914

English Miles

0   100   200   300   400   500

Questions after the Event

It has been debated in after years whether by any action the British Government could have averted the terrible calamity which was now coming upon the world, and it has been suggested that if they had said clearly at the beginning, that if Germany and Austria declared war, they would intervene on the side of France and Russia, or even if they had said, when the crisis first became acute, that they would fight to prevent the invasion of Belgium, they would have stopped the war. But even on the Belgian question the decision was only reached when it was evident that the Belgians would resist, and were looking to us for help; and in point of fact either declaration at any early stage would have broken the Government and divided the country, which looked to Ministers to exhaust all efforts for mediation and peace before committing themselves to engage in war.

Still more, no one could say at the time whether any British action of this kind would act as a deterrent to one side or an incentive to the other, and, if it had failed, it would have left Great Britain exposed to the charge of having encouraged the war-makers on the side whose causes she had espoused. In the atmosphere of July, 1914, nearly all the soldiers in both the European camps had persuaded themselves that war was inevitable, and statesmen who sought to delay action by negotiations were said to be endangering the safety of their countries which now depended on the rigid execution of military plans. The Germans were convinced that the Schlieffen plan would enable them to conquer France before Great Britain could intervene; French and Russians were convinced that the German plan could only be defeated if it were forestalled by rapid action on their part. It is improbable that any action by a Power which stood outside these military schemes would have affected the course of events. The drift to war had been checked a dozen times in the previous twenty years, but on each occasion it had become a little less probable that the peace would be saved, and finally it gained volume against which the peacemakers were powerless.

CHAPTER XVII

MONS AND MARNE

THE world will hardly contain the volumes which have been written about the Great War, and the story is still unfinished. Here it can only be dealt with in simple outline with a certain emphasis on the parts which specially concern our own country.

On August 2, 1914, the Germans occupied Luxembourg and directed their march on Belgium, thereby, as related in the previous chapter, adding Great Britain to the number of their enemies. In the next three weeks they occupied a large part of Belgium and entered Brussels on the 20th. The Belgians made a gallant resistance, which had great value in giving time for the transport of the British Expeditionary Force to France, but they were finally powerless against the big guns and greater numbers of the Germans, and were driven back into the fortress of Antwerp.

By August 20 five out of the six divisions of the British Expeditionary Force had been conveyed to France without the loss of a man or mishap to any ship. It was an extraordinary feat, only rendered possible by the elaborate forethought and preparation provided under the great scheme of army organization carried through by Lord Haldane seven years earlier. The British army was stationed to the left of the French, which was deployed along the River Sambre with its right flank on the Meuse above Namur, and the general hope and expectation was that it would advance with the French into Belgium to repel the German attack. It did advance to Mons which it reached on August 22, but then all manner of things happened which neither side had foreseen.

The Retreat from Mons

The French had underestimated the German strength and wasted a good deal of their own strength by an attack in Alsace and an offensive in the Ardennes, both of which failed. During the next ten days both French and British were in full retreat under the pressure of superior numbers, and often in danger of losing touch with each other and being defeated in detail. The retreat of the one army involved the retreat of the other, and General French, the British Commander-in-Chief, complained that he was left uninformed of the movements of his Ally. At a critical moment he reported, to the dismay of the Cabinet, that being in danger of complete isolation, he proposed to go back behind the Seine, but Lord Kitchener, who was sent to France to deal with the emergency, fortunately succeeded in bringing the French and British commanders together and restoring their communications. The retreat from Mons will always be remembered for the stubborn resistance of both armies, and splendid incidents like the rear-guard action of the British under General Smith-Dorrien at Le Cateau, but the general situation at the beginning of September was one of extreme danger, and it seemed very doubtful if Paris could be saved. The French Government, indeed, had taken the precaution of evacuating Paris and transferring the seat of Government to Bordeaux.

Fortunately for the Allies, the Germans too were making mistakes. Miscalculating in their turn the strength of British and French, they transferred two army corps from France to meet the Russian attack on East Prussia—an attack which in spite of its ultimate failure thus rendered a priceless service to the Allies. The German force was now insufficient for the original design, and General von Bülow being seriously threatened near Guise called for help from the right flank under General von Kluck, which was intended to descend on Paris from the west. Von Kluck responded, but in so doing changed the whole line of his march and now directed it to the east, instead of as originally intended, to the west of Paris, leaving the French to the west and north of him and ignoring or forgetting the British force to the south. He seems to have supposed that the British had been effectively defeated and that the French Sixth Army under Manoury, which lay on his flank and rear, was too weak to be formidable. These miscalculations were to provide General Joffre, the French Commander-in-Chief, and General Gallieni, who commanded the garrison in Paris, with just the opportunity they needed for the great counterstroke of the battle of the Marne.

The Battle of the Marne

To strike at von Kluck, to drive a wedge between his army and the other German armies, and by the same movement to threaten the other armies with envelopment and compel their retreat were now the aims of French and British, and all were accomplished in five days of hard fighting. General Joffre waited until von Kluck had crossed the Marne and was facing the British, and then gave the signal for a general offensive. Manoury with the French Sixth Army now attacked from the north and west, and von Kluck being threatened in rear and flank had to bring his troops back across the Marne and in so doing left an increasing gap between his army and the army of von Bülow on his left. The British coming up from the south advanced into this gap and reached the Marne bridges in time to relieve Manoury, who in his turn was hard pressed and in danger of being enveloped (September 8). On the right of the British the French Fifth Army under Franchet d'Esperey engaged von Bülow, and occupied Château-Thierry after heavily defeating his right, and still further to the east a newly formed French army under Foch fought desperately with von Bülow's left, which in combination with the German Third Army under von Hausen, was attempting to break through what was then the French centre, and was pushing south in the triangle between the Marne and the Aube. Foch's action has been exposed to some criticism, but he held his ground, while British and French widened the gap between von Kluck and von Bülow and carried it further west.

At this point von Moltke, the German Commander-in-Chief, watching from his rather remote head-quarters at Luxembourg, decided that the situation was becoming dangerous, and sent a Staff Officer to confer with the Army commanders and arrange for a retreat, if it should become necessary. Von Bülow had no doubt that it was necessary, if his flank was to be saved, after the British had crossed the Marne, and the order was given to von Kluck to fall back in conformity with von Bülow. The retreat of these two armies compelled the others to follow, and by the afternoon of September 9 the whole German army from Verdun to near Paris was in retreat to new positions behind the Aisne and Vesle. The Germans had made a last attempt to retrieve the position by an attack across the Moselle in which they hoped to cut off Verdun, but this too was foiled by the timely arrival of reinforcements.

In extent, in numbers engaged and duration, there had been no battle like the battle of the Marne in the previous history of the world. In one phase or another it raged over a front of 140 miles; a million men were engaged in it, and it lasted for five days. The British force was only 100,000 strong, but the " old contemptibles," as they liked to call themselves,[1] were among the best-trained troops in the field, and they played an important part at a decisive point. In the operations thus far the little British army had given their Ally just the support it needed to tip the balance in its favour and frustrate the German plan, but immensely the greater force had been French, and it was evident that, if the war continued, the British contribution in men would have to be enormously increased.

The Beginning of the Trench War

Looking back to it in the light of the long conflict which followed, we are apt to think of the battle of the Marne as only the opening of the Great War. But it was decisive in that it destroyed the idea with which Germans and Austrians entered the war. That was to defeat the French and seize Paris by a rapid outflanking movement through Belgium, and then, leaving a comparatively small force to hold Paris and contain the French, to march with the Austrians against Russia. As already related, Moltke, the Chief of the German Staff, told Conrad, the Austrian Chief, in June, 1914, that they expected to have disposed of the French in six weeks, and then to be free to throw the greater part of their forces conjointly with the Austrian against Russia. It was apparently assumed that the German descent upon Paris would be too rapid for

[1] In allusion to an alleged description of the British army by the Kaiser as Britain's "contemptible little army." The Kaiser afterwards strongly denied that he had ever used the words.

British troops to be on the spot in time to affect the result, even if Britain decided to intervene, and on this assumption it was confidently believed that the French would be defeated by the middle of September, and that Russia would not long resist the joint attack of Germans and Austrians. The war would then be over by Christmas, and Britain would be obliged to conform on pain of exposing France to destruction.

But when this plan miscarried, the Germans had no other except that of digging themselves into French territory and defying the Allies to turn them out. The Marne was a defeat but not a rout. The Germans retired from it in comparatively good order, and stationing themselves behind the Aisne and the Vesle began to construct the trench line which finally stretched from the Swiss border to the North Sea. As they dug themselves in, so did French and British on a parallel line to the west. If it was imperative to keep the Germans from Paris, it was also imperative to prevent them getting to the coast and the Channel ports, whence they might have harried with submarines, or bombarded with shells, ships bringing British troops and munitions to France, and even stopped the oversea supplies by which London and a large part of England was fed.

The battle of the Marne was no sooner over than French and British raced north again to construct their line between the Germans and the sea, and on this line round about Ypres in Belgium terrible battles were fought between British and Germans in the autumn of 1914 and the spring of 1915. In the meantime, Antwerp had fallen, though a spirited attempt to relieve it, of which Mr. Winston Churchill was the chief instigator and even the personal leader, had detained German troops which would otherwise have been available in these battles. By this time the original British army was sadly depleted, and the new army was not ready to take the field. But the line held, and after desperate fighting, the Channel ports were saved. Early in 1915 British and French on one side and Germans on the other lay dug in on the fronts which with little change were to be maintained for the next three and a half years. There now set in the grimmest war of attrition between two vast and evenly balanced armies that the world had ever witnessed.

In the early days the Allies had hoped that the Russians,

whose supply of men was supposed to be unlimited, would advance on Germany from the east, and compel the enemy to withdraw a large part of his army from France to defend his homelands. The Russians did indeed perform a signal service to the Allies by their attack on East Prussia before the battle of the Marne, but that ended in the terrible disaster which Hindenburg inflicted on them in the battle of Tannenburg, and being ill-equipped and short of rifles and munitions, they had all they could do at the beginning of the war to repel the Austrian invasion of Poland, and to maintain their own line in front of Warsaw against German attack. By keeping the German and Austrian armies engaged and exhausting their man-power, Russia was to contribute immensely to the final victory, but the expectation entertained in 1914 that she would play the crushing part of a " steam-roller " was doomed to disappointment.

Turkey Joins Germany

The war at sea opened with a mishap which was more serious in its consequences than many major disasters. This was the escape of the German ships, *Goeben* and *Breslau* which, making their way to Constantinople, gave German power in that city a visible and material ascendancy over the moral influence of the Allies. The Turks had been embittered by the commandeering for the British fleet of two battle-ships under construction for them in British shipyards, and though this act was entirely legitimate and according to the contract under which the ships were constructed, it offered easy material for the Germans to work upon. The *Goeben* and the *Breslau*, though continuing to be manned by German officers and crews, were now nominally transferred to Turkey to compensate her for the ships taken by Great Britain; and after a period of diplomatic fencing which masked the fact that the Turks were bound to the Central Powers by a secret agreement, these two ships forced the issue by shelling Russian Black Sea ports (October 28).

The addition of Turkey to their enemies greatly complicated the task of the Allies. It shut off the easiest road of communication and supply between the Western Allies and Russia; it required Great Britain to take measures for the defence of

Egypt and the Suez Canal, the safety of the Persian Gulf, and the supplies of oil from Persia. Large forces were from henceforth to be occupied in the Dardanelles, in Egypt, in Mesopotamia, and eventually in Palestine. Within a few weeks of the outbreak of war an expedition was sent from India to the head of the Persian Gulf, and occupied the mouths of the Tigris and Euphrates. This was the beginning of the Mesopotamian campaign which after many vicissitudes captured Bagdad for the Allies and ended Turkish rule in Arabia.

CHAPTER XVIII

THE WAR IN 1915

IMMENSE efforts were now being made in Great Britain and the British Empire to reinforce the little army with which the country had entered the war. The appointment of Lord Kitchener as Secretary for War had been universally applauded, and his appeal for the new voluntary army which was called by his name met with overwhelming response. There were some who questioned whether he had done right in discarding the Territorial organization, which had been provided for the expansion of the Regular Army, and creating a new army on a new basis; but there was no doubt about the magic of his name or the appeal that it made to vast numbers. There were still graver doubts about the dissipation of the General Staff through the appointment of its members to commands in France, and experience was to prove them well-founded. The Secretary of State now had upon his shoulders the immense burden of providing for the Regular Army, of raising and organizing the new armies, and of advising Ministers as the principal, if not the sole, channel of communication between them and the soldiers in the field.

Lord Kitchener worked heroically, and showed remarkable foresight in measuring the scope and duration of the war, but he had taken on himself more than one man could do, and his multifarious duties involved him in friction and controversy which might have been avoided if he had been more willing to delegate his authority. The British War Office was intended for the administration of the small Regular Army, and it was faced with altogether new problems, which could only be solved with civilian co-operation on the largest scale, when it was called upon to raise and equip the immense new armies which were now to be created.

Promises of support poured in from the Dominions which in a few days were feverishly at work preparing expeditions for the support of the mother country and the common cause. From India too came striking demonstrations of loyalty, princes and people vying with each other in offers of aid and service. By all the signs the Empire was unanimous in its decision that the war was necessary and just.

The Munitions Question

By the month of April, 1915, the British force in France, which had been barely 100,000 at the battle of the Marne, had been multiplied five times, and an immense number more were being trained at home. But it was one thing to raise the men and another to organize them as armies, and to provide them with munitions on the scale that was now demanded. Great Britain had done everything that she had contracted to do when the war broke out, provided the supreme navy to keep the seas for the Allies, and a military force which it was hoped and expected would be sufficient to give the French preponderance in the fighting on land. But she, like all the nations, was now involved in a struggle for existence waged on a scale which no one had foreseen, and demanding sacrifice and effort to which there could be no limit short of complete exhaustion. The idea in favour before the war of Britain contributing ships and fighting at sea, while France contributed men and fought on land, or of either Ally limiting its liabilities or its contributions in ships, men or money—all this and any calculations founded on it vanished in smoke in the retreat from Mons and the battle of the Marne. Before the war was six weeks old, it was evident that everything was at stake for everybody, and that no Empire would survive if it was beaten in this war.

But in rallying to this emergency Great Britain had a task of peculiar difficulty. With her small voluntary army she had none of the great arsenals and war establishments which the continental nations had provided for their conscript armies, and she was now required to improvise on an enormous scale. How great a scale was revealed in the trench fighting of the winter of 1914 and spring of 1915. In front of the trenches on both sides the opposing armies had constructed barbed-wire entanglements which had to be destroyed before either could attack the other with any chance of success. The shrapnel with which the guns had been supplied in previous wars, and especially the British guns in the South African War, proved quite unequal to this, and the demand grew for high explosives on the largest scale. There were differences of opinion on all manner of technical points—the kind of high explosives which could be safely used, the time-fuses and so forth—upon which the War Office was slow to trust civilian judgment, and accompanying these, serious questions about the organizaton of labour and the relations to the War Office of the industries which had now to be brought in.

Controversies arose between Mr. Lloyd George, who was specially zealous in demanding quick action, and Lord Kitchener, who' was unfamiliar with the ways of modern industry, and reluctant to part with War Office control. Some delay there was for these reasons, and though the War Office was able to claim that it had increased the supply of munitions nineteenfold between August, 1914, and April, 1915, this was far below the scale on which they were being consumed at the front. It is easy to say after the event that the British and French should have postponed their attacks if they were not sure that their supplies of munitions were sufficient, but everything at this stage was experimental. Sir John French was a high-spirited and confident man who believed in taking and keeping the offensive, and between March and the beginning of May, 1915, he made three successive attacks at Neuve Chapelle, Hill 60 and Festubert respectively, at the end of which he declared himself baffled for lack of munitions. Sir John now turned his guns on to the Government, whom he charged with having failed to supply him with the munitions necessary for success, though in launching these attacks he had said that munitions would be " all right."

Questions of Strategy

This had important political results which will be dealt with later, but these after all were minor incidents compared with the fate of the gallant men who were exposed to this merciless warfare. Were they just to hold their trenches, clinging grimly to the Ypres salient with its exposed flanks, sitting still while munitions on one side were countered by munitions on the other, and the scale of the conflict was

perpetually enlarged and new weapons of destruction invented?
Ignoring what were supposed to be the laws of war, the
Germans had used poison-gas at Festubert, and this from now
onwards to the end of the war was to be a device common
to all the belligerents. The old art of war, the art of rapid
movement, manœuvring, outflanking, outwitting, as practised
by the Marlboroughs and Napoleons, seemed suddenly to have
gone bankrupt, and its place to have been taken by a squalid
and bestial struggle to exhaustion between too evenly balanced
forces seeking to destroy each other with high explosives and
poison-gas.

All humane persons fought against this conclusion, and
before 1914 was over many busy brains were studying maps
to find ways round or ways out of the deadlock on the western
front. In a conflict which extended over so vast an area,
which embraced Russia, Austria, Turkey, Italy and the Balkan
States as well as France, Germany and Great Britain, there
must, it was argued, be weak spots in the enemy line if only
they could be found. Why hammer at the impenetrable
trench barrier in France and Flanders, when Austria might
be attacked, when a force might be landed in Schleswig-
Holstein, or an advance made through the Balkans, or
Turkey thrown out of action by the capture of the
Dardanelles. Mr. Lloyd George, the future Prime Minister, was
sure from the beginning that he knew of far better ways than
the concentration in France and Flanders which commended
itself to the orthodox soldiers, and he began energetically
proposing these plans from the end of the year 1914 onwards.

So far as the objects were concerned, no one could gainsay
them. Nothing was more to be desired than that some alternative should be discovered to the costly war of attrition
on the west front. But from the beginning—and to the
end — all alternative plans encountered very formidable
objections, one or other of which proved fatal to most of them,
when it came to action.

First, the enemy held what are called the interior lines,
whereas the Allies were working on the outer circle. This
enabled him to move his forces rapidly and freely from one
point to another of the great circle, and to attack any part of
the line which he thought to have been weakened by the

withdrawal of his enemy. The Allies on the other hand had to move round this circle, and if they attacked in the south and east had long and difficult communications by sea, which made it impossible for them to transport and reinforce their armies quickly or to change their direction as he changed his.

Thus, if the British army, or the greater part of it, had been removed from France to Salonica for an expedition through the Balkans, as Mr. Lloyd George proposed, it would have been possible for the Germans in a few days to concentrate all their forces on an attack upon that part of the line thus depleted, and perhaps win a decisive victory. Had there been troops and munitions to spare after making the west front secure against such an attack, there would have been an argument for using the surplus for attacking the enemy at another point, but both French and British commanders were of opinion that there was no such surplus, and that the withdrawal of any considerable part of the British army from France and Flanders would have left them dangerously exposed to a German attack.

The French were the most persistent in this argument, since it was their country which was in occupation by the enemy, and their country which would have had to bear the brunt of any miscalculations of the enemy's strength. For reasons that are still obscure they favoured the Salonica expedition at the end of the year 1915, but even then they held tenaciously to their view that the west front was the main front, and that there only would the final decision be reached. In this matter fear and sentiment came in to reinforce strategy, and the withdrawal of the British army or any considerable part of it from the west front to a distant scene of operations would have caused feeling in France which would greatly have strained and might have been fatal to the alliance.

Other practical considerations supported this conclusion. There were no suitable bases in the Eastern Mediterranean for the large armies which would have been required for most of the operations proposed. Docks, wharves, and warehouses could not be improvised; the existing roads and railways were quite inadequate, the country behind them was difficult and unhealthy. All these might seem minor obstacles to the eye of faith seeing only the great results which might be achieved by a victorious army, but they naturally weighed with practical soldiers who were responsible for the safety and health of the troops. There was also, as the war went on, an increasing difficulty in finding sea-transport for distant expeditions and ensuring its safety against the submarine menace. In the last years of the war a large part of the personnel for operations in the east was found from men already on the spot, and the supplies for them drawn from neighbouring countries.

The Dardanelles Expedition

Most of these difficulties were illustrated in the Dardanelles expedition of 1915—the one great operation away from the main theatre undertaken by Great Britain up to then. If there was to be any diversion from the central task, this one seemed to offer the greatest advantage. If successful, it would throw the Turks out of the war, open the way into the Black Sea and enable Russia to be supplied with the munitions which were her great need, save Egypt from invasion, prevent Bulgaria from entering the war, help Serbia, threaten Austria, and generally deliver a shattering blow at the enemy's power and prestige. Mr. Churchill, its zealous advocate, discoursed eloquently on these undoubted advantages and converted the Cabinet and the Committee of Imperial Defence to his views.

There was no doubt about the advantages, if the thing could be done, and there was no doubt that the best way of doing it was to attack simultaneously by land and sea, and, as far as possible, to take the enemy by surprise. But in January, 1915, when the scheme was first seriously discussed, the situation in France was such that both British and French commanders were agreed that no troops could be spared. The Russians had suffered a serious reverse in the east, and no one could say when the Germans might wheel round and attack in the west. At this point Mr. Churchill came forward with a plan for a purely naval attack on the Dardanelles, a plan which, it was said, would almost certainly succeed, but which, if it did not succeed, could be broken off without loss of prestige. This plan was accepted by the War Council as a means of going forward with the operation without drawing on the army in France. Unfortunately it did not succeed, and had to be broken off after the first day owing to the impossibility of clearing the channel of mines. This failure may not have entailed any loss of prestige, but it had the very serious result of depriving any future attack there might be of the element of surprise and rendering it much more difficult. The Turks were now warned and proceeded to fortify and entrench and bring up large forces for the defence of the Gallipoli Peninsula.

In the meantime the situation had cleared on the west front, and the French at length consented to contribute a division themselves, and to permit the 29th British Division to be diverted from the west to the Dardanelles. With this encouragement it was decided to go forward with a joint naval and military attack, and to devote the Australasian troops which had recently arrived in Egypt to that purpose. Sir Ian Hamilton who was appointed to command was soon at Lemnos, which was chosen as his head-quarters, but his first report was that " large numbers of field-guns and howitzers were available for the defence, the arrangements for which appear to have been made with German thoroughness." At the same time both he and the French commander, General d'Amade, were of opinion that no attack could be made immediately, since the troops sent from England and France had been arranged for transport only, and would need to be sent to Alexandria to be rearranged for the landing at Gallipoli.

So when finally on April 25 the attack was made, it was against an enemy who was forewarned and forearmed, and though prodigies of valour were performed by the army which effected its landing at Cape Helles, Sir Ian Hamilton had to report, when the battle was broken off, that the dominant positions were still in the hands of the Turks, and that he was faced with an entrenched force which he could not hope to overcome with the force at his disposal. The army which had been sent to outflank the trenches on the west front now found itself up against new trenches in even more difficult conditions. It could only be reinforced by a long sea journey, whereas the enemy had safe and uninterrupted land communications by which he could send more guns and munitions to his front whenever it was threatened. The peninsula was long and narrow, the few landing places small and exposed to shell-fire; the opposite shore a few miles across the Narrows was in the hands of the enemy, whose mines and guns made any attack by the fleet precarious or impossible. It is possible that perseverance and continuous reinforcements would in the end have won success, and the Cabinet decided to go on in that hope, but the great Suvla Bay attack on August 6 again just fell short of the commanding positions, and the question of reinforcing and going on again raised all the old debates about the numbers which could be safely spared from the west front. In the end, the French, by suddenly deciding on an expedition to Salonica—their one exception to their otherwise stubborn adherence to the main theatre—and requiring the British Government to provide 150,000 men for that project, compelled the evacuation of the Peninsula, for it was impossible at that moment to find troops for two great eastern expeditions, and, failing them, it was the opinion of Lord Kitchener, who had been sent out specially to report on the situation, and of all the soldiers on the spot, that there was no alternative but to wind up the expedition.

The evacuation, carried out without the loss of a man, was a triumph of skilful and secret preparation, and the culminating disaster which some had predicted on any attempt to extricate the expedition was happily averted. Though the enterprise had failed in its main object, it was by no means fruitless. By exhausting the military strength of the Turks it made Egypt secure against invasion, and paved the way for the operations which drove them out of Mesopotamia and Palestine in later phases of the war. Nowhere was greater courage shown by all the army in adverse circumstances. To Australians and New Zealanders especially, the doings of the Anzacs (Australian and New Zealand Army Corps) will always be a proud memory. Though the maximum British strength in this expedition was never more than 128,000, the casualties were 112,000 including 33,000 dead or missing.

The First Coalition Government

High hopes had been built on the Dardanelles expedition, and the disappointment which followed the comparative failure of the first effort had serious results for Asquith's Government. The differences between Mr. Churchill, the First Lord of the Admiralty, and the First Sea Lord, Lord Fisher, were by this time notorious, and the sudden resignation of the latter brought matters to a climax. The question of munitions was also at this moment at an acute stage, and the newspapers controlled by Lord Northcliffe were attacking Lord Kitchener with great violence and charging the Government with neglect and supineness. The leaders of the Opposition, Lord Lansdowne and Mr. Bonar Law, said, not unreasonably, that they would be obliged to raise the question of the Dardanelles in Parliament, unless they were satisfied that everything possible was being done to meet the emergency, and it was certain that if criticism started again on party lines it would not be limited to one subject. Asquith judged that the Opposition leaders could only be satisfied, and parliamentary and national unity preserved, if they were invited to join the Government and to share its responsibility. In fact he thought their demand reasonable and fair. The Liberal party thus stepped down from the place which it had filled for nearly ten years as the ruling power in the country, and gave way to the first War Coalition, which was formed in the last fortnight of May, 1915.

Asquith was still Prime Minister, and it was acknowledged by all that no one else had the authority or the skill in managing men which the occasion demanded. He retained the more important of his Liberal colleagues, but he now had in his Cabinet Mr. Bonar Law, Lord Lansdowne, Lord Curzon, Mr. Austen Chamberlain, Sir Edward Carson and Lord Selborne, and though Mr. Churchill remained in the Cabinet as Chancellor of the Duchy of Lancaster, Mr. Balfour succeeded him as First Lord of the Admiralty.

There was at least one serious difficulty in the formation of this Government, and that was the insistence of the Unionists on the exclusion of Lord Haldane, who had done more than any man living to organize the country for war, and to prepare the Expeditionary Force which had played a supremely important part in the first phase of the war. What is now acknowledged to have been a serious injustice can only be explained by the atmosphere of war. Lord Haldane had incurred the unfounded suspicion of being a " pro-German " by his habit of acknowledging his debt in his philosophic studies to the great German writers and thinkers, and he had

even said once that "Germany was his spiritual home."
Hence the conclusion was drawn by political opponents who
knew nothing of philosophy that he was a German at heart.
This idea was an obsession beyond argument or reason at
the time, and the Unionist leaders said that, whether true or
false, it was so widespread as to make Haldane a hindrance
rather than a help, and compelled Asquith to sacrifice his old
friend as a condition of their support. When he returned from
the final victory in 1918, Lord Haig's first act was to call at
Lord Haldane's house in London and deliver with his own hand
a bound volume of his dispatches inscribed to " the greatest
of England's War Ministers."

It cannot be said that as an instrument for conducting
war the first Coalition was an improvement on its predecessor.
It consisted of very able men, the pick of both parties, but
the new-comers necessarily required to be informed about
everything from the beginning and that caused delay at a
time when it was very necessary to act promptly. Many of its
members held strong views of their own, and were reluctant
to delegate their responsibility. The difficulty of conducting
the war through a Cabinet of twenty or more became more
and more evident, but every scheme for entrusting it to a
small executive met with formidable objections. The claimants
for a seat on such a body were many; the idea that it ought
to reflect the balance of parties persisted; the leader of the
Unionist party was from the beginning under the impression
that he had come badly out of the distribution of places and
priorities.

Asquith laboured to do impartial justice, but though the
Government was called a Coalition, the parties to it remained
parties still, and on certain critical occasions were largely
governed by what they thought would be acceptable to their
supporters. Party feeling reasserted itself in the struggle over
compulsory service, which was carried through in the teeth
of strong Labour and Radical opposition in the spring of 1916,
and on the Irish question later in the year. At the front almost
everything seemed to go wrong. Not only was the Dardanelles
Expedition a failure, but the great offensive in France planned
by General Joffre for the autumn led to immense losses with
little results. The British were held up before Loos, the French

failed to capture Vimy Ridge, and though they carried the first and second lines of German trenches in Champagne, they were checked by German reserves and failed to break through.

Italy and Bulgaria

The one gleam of light in the whole year was the entry of Italy into the war on the side of the Allies, which took place on May 23. Her declaration of war was against Austria, and not against Germany, and it was hoped that by concentrating against Austria, the weaker partner in the opposing Alliance, Italy would succeed in driving her out of the war. But the mountain barriers between the two countries made military operations extremely difficult, and when General Cadorna struck eastwards towards Trieste and attacked the Austrians on the Isonzo, he found himself held up by the trenches which his opponents had constructed to defend the flatter country between the Julian Alps and Trieste, and on the Italian front, as elsewhere, trench warfare set in.

Four months later, the secession of Bulgaria had to be set against the adhesion of Italy. Diplomacy was much blamed for this event, but from the beginning it was extremely difficult to persuade the Bulgarians even to think of fighting on the same side with Serbia, whom they held chiefly responsible for their humiliation in the Balkan War; and with Russia as well as Serbia obstinately refusing to make the concessions that they demanded, and Germany apparently winning all along the line in the east, Allied diplomacy had a very poor hand to play. Tsar Ferdinand of Bulgaria, who was a realist, appears to have concluded that even if the Allies promised what he asked, they were not likely to be in a position to fulfil their promises when the war ended—a prognostication which was not without plausible excuse in October, 1915. For the time being, the secession of Bulgaria greatly complicated the situation in the east, and led almost immediately to a joint attack on Serbia, by Germans, Austrians and Bulgarians, who overran the country and drove the Serbian army to take refuge in the mountains of Albania, whence, after grievous sufferings in the snows of winter, it was painfully extricated and brought to Corfu for rest and re-equipment.

Mesopotamia

A last mortification in the winter of 1915 and spring of 1916 was the disaster which befell the Mesopotamian expedition under General Townshend, who had been authorized to advance on Bagdad. He had come within a few miles of the city, after defeating the Turks at Ctesiphon, but was caught by Turkish reinforcements, and driven back into Kut-El-Amara, where he was besieged until the following April, when starvation compelled him to surrender. This reverse was brilliantly retrieved by another expedition under General Maude in the following year, but at the time it caused a painful impression and afterwards became the subject of inquiry by a Royal Commission which blamed the Government of India and the Indian military authorities for the inadequacy of their preparations, and commented with special severity on the lack of proper provision for the wounded.

AT the end of January, 1916, the country passed from voluntary service to conscription. The Derby scheme for recruiting launched in the previous October had failed to give the necessary numbers, and Asquith was now bound to redeem his pledge to the married men who had volunteered under that scheme that they would not be called up until the young unmarried men had been brought in. There was serious opposition both in the Cabinet and in the country; Sir John Simon resigned from the Cabinet; organized Labour, fearing that military would be followed by industrial conscription, was declared by its leaders to be against it root and branch. The Cabinet was badly shaken by the controversy; one scheme had to amended by another, Ministers had to adjourn debate in the House of Commons pending agreement with one another, the Prime Minister was said to be on the point of resigning in despair of healing the differences among his colleagues. In the end it was decided that nothing short of general and immediate compulsion for all male subjects between the ages of 18 and 41, married as well as single, would meet the case, and a Bill to that effect was carried through both Houses of Parliament and became law on May 25. The seriousness of the situation procured its acceptance by all parties in Parliament and the country.

The Irish Rebellion

Another event which seriously shook the Government and brought out the differences of opinion among its members was the Irish Rebellion which took place in Easter week this year.

When Mr. Redmond announced in the House of Commons on August 3, 1914, that the Irish party would support the Government in the war, hopes ran high that fighting together in the common cause would bring Irishmen and Englishmen together. That, unfortunately, was not to be. On September 14, when the Government proceeded to obtain the Royal assent to the Home Rule Bill while postponing its operations until the end of the war and promising an amending Bill for Ulster when the war was over, the Unionist party broke into violent protests, and the extreme Irish complained bitterly both of the postponement and of the promise to Ulster. With Mr. Redmond's aid, recruiting for the war proceeded with much success in Southern Ireland during the next few months, but enthusiasm was gradually damped down by the refusal of the War Office to make concessions to Irish sentiment, to permit Irish regiments to carry the National colours when on service, and even to allow priests to accompany them to the front. The British military authorities apparently walked in fear lest the army should be infected by Irish disaffection, and had not imagination enough to understand what their religion and their symbols meant to the Southern Irish. These were costly mistakes. There were Irishmen who held stubbornly to the old view that England's difficulties were Irish opportunities, and these too were recruiting under the auspices of Sinn Fein and the Irish Republican Brotherhood.

The Republicans were in touch with kindred spirits in America and established communications with the Germans through Sir Roger Casement, a former British Consul with a distinguished record in Africa, but now a fanatical Irish extremist. It was arranged that Casement should sail to Ireland in a German ship carrying stores and munitions in the week before Easter 1916, and there join hands with Sinn Fein and Republican volunteers for an attack on Dublin. But the plan went astray; the German ship was intercepted and scuttled by her crew to escape capture, and Casement was brought ashore in a German submarine. The party sent to meet him mistook their road and drove into the sea and were drowned, and when he landed he fell into the arms of the police, who immediately arrested him and sent him to London. The organizers of the movement then attempted to call it off, but a section of their supporters insisted on going on, and for a few days in Easter week had a large part of Dublin, including the Post Office, the Four Courts and St. Stephen's Green at their mercy. The authorities had been taken by surprise, and for these days were practically prisoners in Dublin Castle, but with the arrival of troops from England, the rebellion was easily quenched, and by the end of the week most of the ringleaders were in the hands of the Government.

Asquith, the Prime Minister, himself went over to Ireland, and did his utmost to keep the inevitable penalties within bounds. Fifteen of the leaders were tried by court martial and shot, 160 were sentenced to various terms of penal servitude, and 1800 deported to England and interned there. Asquith visited all parts of Ireland, making his own inquiries, and came home deeply impressed with the necessity of going forward immediately with Home Rule, if Mr. Redmond and the Irish Parliamentary party were to be given a chance of asserting themselves over the Sinn Feiners and the Republicans. In this he was supported by Mr. Balfour and Mr. Bonar Law, but Lord Lansdowne and other Unionists strongly dissented, and after a struggle which nearly broke the Cabinet, this project had to be abandoned. Mr. Duke, who had succeeded Mr. Birrell as Chief Secretary, proved to be a mild administrator, but the postponement of Home Rule, combined with the bitter feelings aroused by the executions after the rebellion, gave fresh power to the extremists, and from this time onwards their candidates were almost uniformly successful at by-elections.

Verdun and the Somme

The war was now entering upon its grimmest stage, and all questions of strategy were in abeyance while the Allies fought for their lives on the western front. In February came the tremendous German assault on the great fortress of Verdun, a position which the French held to be of the utmost importance, both as the eastern elbow of their line and for the immense mass of material that was accumulated there. Raising their famous battle-cry " They shall not pass," the French stood firm against wave upon wave of the oncoming Germans, but for eventual relief they looked for the promised British offensive which was due in the summer. That was launched on the Somme on July 1 and continued without

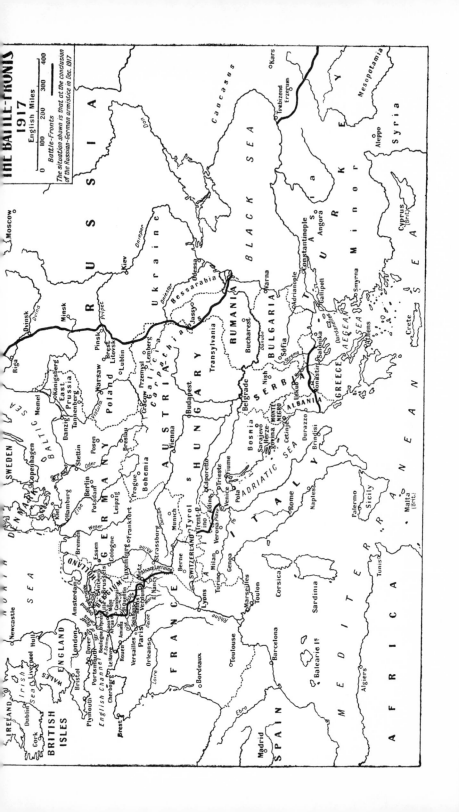

THE BATTLE-FRONTS
1917

English Miles
0   100   200   300   400

Battle-Fronts
The situation shown is that at the conclusion
of the Russian-German armistice in Dec. 1917

ceasing until the end of October, when it was brought to a standstill by the exhaustion of both sides. At the end of the year the Allies had a little more than held their own against the enemy, but the moral remained the same for French, British and Germans. In spite of immense massed attacks, enormous expenditure of ammunition, fearful casualties, unheard of acts of bravery and devotion, the defence was still proof against attack. The Germans had not broken the French and British lines; the French and British had not broken the German lines, and the hope of liberating French soil was still deferred.

Once more, many voices were heard protesting against this seemingly useless slaughter, and complaining of the resourceless strategy which could find no other way but that of battering against impenetrable barriers. Yet, if we may believe the German military historians, this phase of the war was largely decisive. "The German army had been fought to a standstill and was utterly worn out," says Ludendorff; "if the war lasted our defeat seemed inevitable." It was, in fact, as was revealed in the German inquiry into the war in the year 1919, the conviction of the German generals that the war could not be won on land, which led them at the beginning of 1917 to press upon their Government the urgent necessity of starting the "unrestricted submarine" warfare at sea, which they wrongly supposed to be an infallible short-cut to victory.

The Russians played no small part in the year 1916 in relieving their Allies from German pressure. In March they came to the rescue of Verdun by attacking in force at Lake Maroc, and though no victory could be claimed, they kept a large German force, which otherwise would have been available for operations in France, heavily engaged at a critical moment. In June the Russian General Brusiloff inflicted a tremendous defeat on the Austrians in the Bukovina, and by so doing stopped the projected Austrian attack upon Italy and compelled the Germans to withdraw troops from the Somme in order to aid their Ally. Nothing could happen anywhere over this vast field of war without having consequences and repercussions in all parts, and though Russia in the end was numbered among the vanquished, her former Allies would be very ungrateful not to bear in memory the aid which she brought them at many critical moments in their own struggle.

But the contributions which any one country, or one battle, was making to the final result was hidden from the watchers at the time, and the rising complaints and anxieties as one effort after another fell short of expectations, led in all countries to agitations and intrigues in which there were heavy casualties among Governments, Prime Ministers and generals in the field. When things went wrong in the field there was a natural demand for change, which, in the atmosphere of war, took little account of the services and merits of individuals.

Lord Kitchener, who had been the target of many criticisms and much newspaper attack in the previous twelve months, met a tragic death on June 5, in the foundering on an enemy mine of the cruiser *Hampshire*, which was taking him on a mission to Russia. Controversy was forgotten in the universal mourning and generous tributes to his memory. But discontent with the course of the war continued and came to a climax in the autumn of 1916 when disaster overtook the Rumanians, who had been encouraged by the brilliant but temporary success of the Russian offensive under Brusiloff to throw in their lot with the Allies. Unfortunately they were too late to seize the opportunity of co-operating with the Russians, and they insisted, against the advice of the Allied strategists, in invading Transylvania, thus leaving Bucharest and the southern part of their country at the mercy of the German force under Mackensen which swept through it and drove them out of the war. A similar disaster had overtaken the Serbians a year earlier, and loud murmurs went up against the supposed supineness and lack of foresight which had left to their fate the unhappy peoples who had joined their fortunes with those of the Allies. Nothing could well have been more remote from any influence which the British Government could have exerted, and that Goverment had in fact warned the Rumanians that it would be unable to help them. But the incident lent itself readily to the fierce campaign against the Prime Minister, Mr. Asquith, now being conducted by the group of newspapers which had imbibed Mr. Lloyd George's views of the right way to conduct the war, and at the end of November Asquith found himself the target of an attack conducted simultaneously from within the Cabinet and by these newspapers outside.

The Fall of Asquith

The story of his displacement has been told very candidly by some of those who played a principal part in it, and it will always remain a subject of curious study by those who are interested in the methods by which politicians waged war on one another in these years.   Mr. Lloyd George was honestly convinced that he knew how to conduct the war better than Asquith, and his object was to place himself in control of the military operations, whether as Prime Minister or as Chairman of a War Committee of the Cabinet.   What followed was a tangle of cross-purposes, in which the Prime Minister misunderstood the action of his Unionist colleagues, and they were taken by surprise by the results of their own proceedings.   Within a fortnight they had made his resignation inevitable, though they had started out with the quite different intention of curbing the activities of his principal critic and rival, Mr. Lloyd George.

In historical perspective the event stands out as one of those which are fated in war.   Asquith has been called the last of the Romans, and he held firmly to the traditions of the classical British statesmanship—especially its regard for collective responsibility, its dislike of personal advertisement and public recrimination, its high respect for Parliament and parliamentary forms.   He had stood between the soldiers and what he thought to be unfair or impatient public criticism, he had taken all the blame when things went wrong, and shared the credit with others when they went right.   He regarded it as his special task to secure national and Cabinet unity, and drew a clear distinction between the great objects of policy and strategy which were the Government's sphere and the conduct of the war which was the soldiers'.   For more than nine years he had carried the country through emergencies in home and foreign affairs which called for the utmost courage and decision, but he had concealed his own activities under a mask of seeming passivity which enabled his enemies to say that he waited on events, but which very often meant that he refused to be hustled or flurried when others were losing their composure.

These were great qualities, but in war-time, as Mr. Bonar Law said, the public expected the Prime Minister not only to be active but to seem active, to keep himself in the public eye, to impart the thrills and the sense of drama which the occasion seemed to demand.   Mr. Lloyd George had all the qualities which stir and excite; he knew how to manage crowds and newspapers, to bind spells on great audiences, to gather about him a great company of serviceable adherents.   Such a man coming on the scene in the circumstances of December, 1916, with the promise of a new kind of warfare which would avoid the losses and reverses of the previous years, had all the advantages over a man of Asquith's temperament and disposition, and an anxious multitude welcomed the grand high pressure of bustle and excitement, the wide advertisement of the activities of the Minister, the chorus of approval in the popular newspapers which followed his accession to power and the elimination of the " old gang."   The war—the country was told—was now to be conducted by a small body of competent Ministers with the Prime Minister on top directing everything; the base of the Administration was to be broadened by bringing in business men, men of " push and go " to smarten and enliven the official class; everything was to be tightened up; there was to be no more " wait and see," or hiding of lights under bushels.   Illusion and reality are so mingled in the atmosphere of war, and the necessity of producing the right impression on the public mind is so large a part of war on the " home front " that merely to have produced this impression was a contribution to war-making at that moment.

CHAPTER XX

THE part played by the British navy, though not a spectacular one, was absolutely vital to the Allied cause. It has sometimes been asked in after years whether a great fleet of capital ships which never succeeded in destroying the enemy's fleet, and which remained shut up in a distant base for the greater part of the time really served any useful purpose. The question is best answered by considering what would have happened if this fleet had not existed. In that case the enemy's fleet would have been free to bombard the British coasts, to cover a German invasion, to cut off British food-supplies, to render impossible the transport of a British army to the continent or anywhere oversea—in short, to make British co-operation in the war impossible. The knowledge that the British fleet was on guard, and the belief that it was superior, prevented or checked all these enterprises on the enemy's part and rendered possible the uninterrupted communications between Great Britain and France which continued throughout the war.

German naval strategy in the war was that of the inferior fleet, acknowledging itself to be inferior, but endeavouring to equalize the conditions and eventually to tip the balance in its favour. The Germans, therefore, hoped to wear down the British margin by mine and submarine, or by catching and destroying squadrons or units which had temporarily been detached from the main body. In this they had considerable success. Quite early in the war three armoured cruisers, the *Aboukir*, *Hogue* and *Cressy* were torpedoed off the coast of Holland; another suffered the same fate off Peterhead, and a new first-class battle-ship, the *Audacious*, fell a victim to a mine off the coast of Ireland. It is true that two could play at this game, and in a raid into the Heligoland Bight in August, 1914, Admiral Beatty sank three German cruisers and one destroyer. But the British margin was so important to the whole. Allied cause that this early experience led the British Government to prescribe a certain caution in all naval operations.

Further, the Germans had counted on the fact that the British navy had multifarious duties which required a certain scattering of forces, whereas their own, with the exception of a few raiders or raiding squadrons, could remain concentrated and available at any moment for use as a whole. Thus in the early months of the war the British had to clear the seas of German commerce-raiders which, though few in number, were capable of doing great damage. A German squadron consisting of two armoured and three light cruisers under von Spee was at large in the Pacific, and this had to be hunted down and disposed of. Von Spee caught his pursuers off guard near Coronel off the coast of Chile (October 27, 1914) and made his escape after sinking the *Good Hope* and *Monmouth* —a heavy reverse which had to be made good by detaching the much more powerful squadron under Admiral Sturdee which caught von Spee at the Falkland Islands and destroyed his squadron. Other smaller forces were engaged during the same months in hunting down the *Emden*, the *Dresden* and the *Königsberg*—raiders which had done much mischief. In the following year one big battle-ship and many less powerful ships were engaged in the Dardanelles, and all the time there were demands for convoys for transports bringing Dominion and other troops from oversea and needing protection from submarines.

With these many calls upon it the British fleet was by no means in a position to treat lightly the German effort to wear down its margin. That was conducted with considerable skill. The raids on Yarmouth, Hartlepool, Scarborough and Lowestoft—which caused great indignation at the time as aimless attacks on undefended towns—had the serious purpose of creating a demand for local protection which would have divided the British fleet and laid it open to attack in detail. If made in force, they also offered a chance of catching British ships sent hurriedly to the scene of action. To lure a portion of the British fleet into waters where submarines were lying in wait, or on to mine-fields through which an attacking force could escape but in which its pursuers would be caught was another part of the same effort and required constant vigilance on the part of British commanders.

The Battle of Jutland

All this must be borne in mind when we consider the battle of Jutland (May 31, 1916), the one occasion on which the two fleets were engaged in anything like full strength. In this battle the Germans could afford to risk all on a stroke which, if it had succeeded, would have brought them speedy victory on land as well as on sea, and, if it failed, would have left them little worse off; whereas the British were in a position in which, if they failed, all would be lost for their Allies as well as themselves. In land warfare an army might be risked, and replaced if lost; in this sea warfare, if the fleet were lost or suffered such casualties as to deprive it of its " command of the sea," the disaster would be beyond repair. Admiral Jellicoe was, accordingly, under general instructions' not to risk his fleet beyond necessity, not to expose it unnecessarily to submarines, not to engage in night attacks, unless he clearly saw his way ahead; not to be lured in pursuit of the enemy on to the hidden mine-fields with which there was every reason to suppose he would protect his retreat. These limiting conditions precluded any of the win-all-or-lose-all strokes which might have resulted in a spectacular triumph at the risk of total disaster, and threw the British Commander-in-Chief back on an able but cautious handling of his forces as the battle developed.

The battle has been described as a chance encounter, and the description is true in the sense that neither side was aware until comparatively late in the day that it was to meet the other in full strength. In conformity with their usual strategy the Germans had hoped to entice the British fleet to sea while submarines were laying in wait for it, and to bring their full force to bear on a detached part of it. The British sailed on a report from the Admiralty that the Germans were putting to sea and hoped in their turn to draw a certain number of them far enough from their base to admit of their being crushed before they could return to safety. Admiral Beatty, running south from Rosyth with his battle-cruisers, first made contact with the enemy, and then running north led the combined

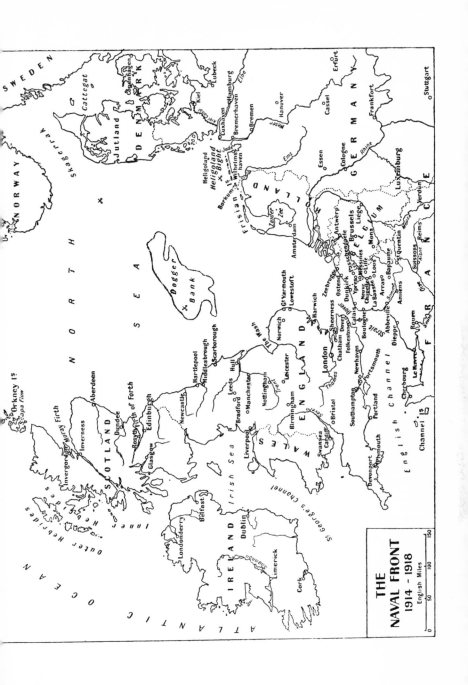

THE
NAVAL FRONT
1914 - 1918

English Miles

0   50   100   150

German High Seas Fleet into a general engagement with the combined British Grand Fleet.

The visibility was bad, and made worse by the very effective German smoke-screens. The intelligence on both sides was confused and conflicting; the wireless was often interrupted, and signals were difficult to read in the smoke of battle, and were sometimes misread. Owing to the immense range of modern guns most of the ships engaged were ten or twelve miles apart. The story of the battle is that of contacts made and lost, engagements begun and broken off, the enemy appearing and disappearing, and finally escaping in fog and darkness and getting back to port. There were great episodes and terrible disasters. Three great British battle-cruisers were blown up and went down with all hands; a German battle-ship and battle-cruiser suffered the same fate. But the stupendous encounter between massed fleets imagined by laymen never took place and never could take place in the conditions of modern warfare with its long-range guns, submarines and destroyers, necessitating constant and rapid movement and the deployment of the fleets over a great expanse of water. Critics after the event have said that, if Admiral Jellicoe had done this or that at certain moments in the battle, he would have succeeded in destroying the enemy fleet instead of merely driving it back to its ports. He would no doubt have done so, if he had possessed their knowledge of the enemy's disposition and intentions, but he was feeling his way through fog and darkness on a sea infested with mines and submarines, and he had on his shoulders a responsibility greater than any borne by any single commander in the whole war.

The Escape of the Germans

The " victory " claimed by the Germans consisted in having escaped destruction at the hands of the British fleet, and the manœuvre which enabled them to do this was undoubtedly both daring and skilful. The gunnery was about equal on both sides, but the German shells, being fitted with special delay-action fuses which caused them to penetrate before bursting and to burst inside the British ships, undoubtedly did the greater damage, and were responsible for the sinking with all hands which caused the British loss of life to be greater than the German. It was also conjectured that the two most serious British disasters, the loss of the battle-cruisers *Indefatigable* and *Queen Mary*, were due to the imperfect protection of their magazines from shell-fire.

Whether the German fleet could have come out again after the battle of Jutland, and whether, if it had, it could have done anything to affect the course of events has been much debated in after years, but the decision of the German Admiralty at the time was that it could not. Captain Persius, the well-known German naval commander, said in discussing the question soon after the war was over: " Our fleet losses were severe, and on June 1, 1916, it was clear to every thinking person that this battle [*i.e.* the battle of Jutland] must and would be the last one. Authoritative quarters said so openly." This conclusion was, in fact, one of the main reasons which led the Germans to decide that their principal naval effort must in future be under the water and not on it. The worst result for the Germans, in the meantime, was that the British fleet remained free to continue the blockade of Germany. That silent pressure was being more and more felt with every month and in the spring of the following year the entry of the United States into the war removed the last obstacle to making it complete. There was now no powerful neutral to claim the freedom of the seas, or assert its right to trade with either or both belligerents. There was on the contrary, a large accession of naval strength to tighten the steel belt with which Germany was ringed in.

The Unrestricted Submarine

After the war the Germans testified that their military power was exhausted when the battle of the Somme was ended, and that they no longer expected to win a victory on land. As they looked at their position at the end of the year 1916, it seemed to be one of the gravest peril. They had failed to break the naval supremacy of Great Britain, and they saw no way of overcoming French and British resistance in France and Flanders. But they had in reserve what they believed to be an infallible short cut to victory, namely the " unrestricted submarine " warfare which they were preparing for the early months of 1917. The ordinary and humane rules of naval warfare, which permitted the search and seizure of merchant ships suspected of carrying contraband, but insisted that their crews and passengers should be conveyed to safety, were now to be completely abandoned, and submarines were to be instructed to " sink without trace " and without search all ships, enemy or neutral, which they might suppose to be carrying munitions or supplies to their enemy, in short, almost all merchant ships on the sea.

In his evidence before the German Committee of Inquiry held in November, 1919, Herr von Bethmann Hollweg gave a poignant account of his mental agonies and wrestlings before he gave way to the unanimous assurances of the naval and military staffs that England would be brought to her knees within three months by this method of warfare. He knew that the ruthless sinking of merchant ships, neutral as well as enemy, without mercy for their crews or passengers, would be abhorrent to neutral opinion, and he foresaw that it would almost certainly bring the United States into the war against Germany. But admirals and generals insisted that there was no other way if Germany was to be saved, and were quite confident that the war would be over by the starvation of England before the Americans could land in Europe, even if it was possible to transport them in the teeth of the submarine. Bethmann Hollweg described himself as doubting to the end, but unable to accept the fearful responsibility of resisting what the high technical authorities declared to be the one and only way—and that a quite certain way—of saving the country.

This passionate belief in the submarine is the key to the attitude of the Germans in the peace *pourparlers* of December, 1916. On December 12, after the fall of Bucharest, they themselves proposed the opening of peace discussions, and President Wilson seized the opportunity to ask the belligerents to define their terms. The terms which the Germans conveyed to him included the practical annexation of Belgium, " rectifications of frontiers " at the expense of France, and the payment of an indemnity for the release of French territory—terms which could only be justified on the assumption that they had won or would certainly win the war, and not at all on the estimate of their military chiefs that their power was exhausted or all but exhausted on land. The discussions of December were in fact little more than a manœuvring for position on both sides, the Allies being in no mood to abate their war-aims and the Germans being mainly concerned to impress neutrals with the idea that they had sought in vain to make peace before being driven to the desperate expedient of the " unrestricted submarine."

America Comes In

That was begun at the end of February, and in a few weeks the sinking of American ships, which by design or accident coincided with an attempt to instigate Mexico to take action against the United States, ended President Wilson's hesitation and brought America into the war (April 6, 1917). The following weeks were perhaps the period of gravest anxiety for the British people in the whole war, and there were moments when the German Admiralty seemed to have been not so far wrong in its calculations. In the month of April the Allies lost 900,000 tons of shipping—60 per cent. of it British—and it was only too clear by the end of the month that a continuance of this rate of loss must starve the British people and prevent them from supporting their armies in the field. Happily it did not continue. In May it declined to 550,000 tons, and by November it had fallen to 250,000. All manner of devices were tried—mines, nets, depth-charges, hydrophones, camouflage, air-scouting—but safety was found eventually through the convoy system, by which merchant ships were grouped together and escorted by destroyers. This had been objected to on the ground that destroyers were insufficient in number and that merchant captains could not be expected to learn the complicated manœuvres of zig-zagging in squadrons. But the entry of the United States into the war increased the numbers of available destroyers, and the merchant captains after a little training proved remarkably efficient in these complicated tactics.

The Defeat of the Submarine

The British people tightened their belts, submitted to drastic rationing of their food-supplies, and worked feverishly to replace the lost ships. All this helped, but what saved them finally was the skill and daring of their seamen both in the navy and in the merchant service. There was none of the demoralization on which the Germans had relied to paralyse the British sea-service. Men who had been torpedoed twice and three times put to sea again undaunted, bringing an inbred and unrivalled sea-sense to bear on the new and perilous conditions. Cunning was matched with cunning; camou-flaged " Q-boats " brought swift destruction on unsuspecting submarines. The struggle was grim and tense and long drawn out. The country held its breath as the figures of sinkings mounted up, and scarcely dared to think of the future if they went on. But before the end of the year the victory had definitely been won, and experts went so far as to say that in view of the defensive measures now evolved, the fear of blockade by submarine might finally be ruled out. To the defensive was now added an offensive campaign, which took a steadily rising toll of the enemy's submarines. In May, 14 were lost out of a total of 125 in commission, and before the end of the year no fewer than 199 were numbered among the missing or lost, of which 175 fell to the British navy. There was at the time little pity for the victims, who were deemed to have met a justly deserved fate in an illegal and inhuman warfare. But they too were acting under orders in the service of their country, and the story on their side was one of daring effort and grim endurance under nerve-racking strain. The strain in the end went far to break the nerve of the German navy, and contributed not a little to the mutiny which was one of the preludes to the final defeat.

Zeebrugge

It may be added here that the naval event most remembered in the last year of the war (1918) was the attack on Zeebrugge, one of the German submarine bases on the Belgian coast. It was an affair of terrible gallantry in which a small squadron of old cruisers, backed by destroyers and motor-boats, risked every-thing to storm the Mole and destroy the viaduct which con-nected it with the shore. In this it was entirely successful at a cost of 197 killed and 440 wounded and missing. Desperate fighting and hand to hand encounters attended this operation, and the individual exploits may be judged from the fact that no fewer than nine V.C.s were awarded to those who took part in it.

The War from the Air

Of all the terrible novelties of the war, the development of air power was perhaps the most sinister. The skill and daring of the pilots, and the acts of individual and solitary heroism that they performed can never be rated too highly, or the prospect which lies before us if their art is developed, be too clearly understood. It is generally believed that the work of aircraft in the Great War was only a pale shadow of what it may be in another war if there is one, but it was enough to cause profound changes in strategy and tactics and to bring a new terror to the civilian populations. It was now possible for every commander to know what was going on on the other side of the hill, and for his artillery to direct its gun-fire by wireless messages from airmen observing the positions of the enemy and the effect of the shells. Under skies swarming with air-scouts it became extremely difficult to conceal any considerable concentration of troops or their preparation for attack, and the element of surprise, which was thought to be a chief part of the art of war, was in consequence largely eliminated from the great offensives. In the last years of the war expedients were gradually devised for screening the movement of troops from observation by airmen, but to the end, the immense scale of the attacks and the long preparation needed for them rendered deception of this kind extremely difficult. Whenever, as in the Palestine campaign, an army well provided with aircraft was pitted against an enemy who had few or none, it was found that the former had an immense advantage.

The Germans set the example of bombing civilian populations from the air by sending their "Taubers" over Paris in October, 1914, and on the following Christmas Eve dropped their first bomb on British soil. In 1915 and 1916 their main attacks on England were the raids of Zeppelins—the great lighter-than-air ships—which under the famous commander, Mathy, inflicted considerable damage and loss of life. London was their principal target, but Hull, Lowestoft, Yarmouth, Chatham, Dover and Woolwich also suffered heavily, and each raid left its trail of dead and wounded, including many women and children. Before the end of 1916 aeroplanes armed with explosive bullets which ignited their gas-bags began to get the better of the Zeppelins, and several were brought down in flames. The Germans now changed the form of attack and employed aeroplanes instead of airships, and for some months there seemed to be no effective defence against their raids. A bomb dropped in Folkestone fell in a crowded street killing 33 people, mostly women, and during June and July 150 people were killed and 500 injured and many buildings destroyed or damaged in raids on London. The attacks continued by day and by night up to the summer of 1918, London being visited as often as three days in the week during one period of the spring of that year. Terrible scenes, which might have filled the newspapers with horrors, if the war-time censorship had not forbidden publication, accompanied some of these raids. Bombs fell upon shelters where people were crowded together, killing them in scores, set fire to workshops where girls were at work, crashed into playgrounds where little children were at play. To many the warning guns, the hour of suspense filled with the sounds of the battle in the air, and the relief of the " all-clear " call are still their most vivid memories of the war.

The total casualties in England were 1400 killed and 3400 wounded—a negligible number compared with the death-roll of the battlefield, and of no importance for its supposed object of affecting the morale of the civil population. The result was, on the contrary, like that of the " unrestricted submarine," to add to the exasperation which, when the war ended, made a wise peace so much the more difficult. It must be added that when the end came none of the belligerents had a clear conscience, for in 1917 and 1918 British and French air-squadrons practised " reprisals " on German towns with equally cruel results to the civil population. New long-range guns added to the terror and on Good Friday, 1918, a shell from " Big Bertha," the 70-mile range German gun, hit the church of St. Gervais, killing and wounding many of the worshippers. In its last stage, the Great War became a great savagery, and men were speaking below their breath of horrors unimaginable to be let loose if it continued for another year.

The Nivelle Plan

THE defeat of the submarine was for Great Britain the great event, and the chief achievement of the new Government in the year 1917. If the British people had been balked of a spectacular triumph over the enemy, they had at the end of this year the satisfaction of knowing that their sea-power and the valour of their seamen had once more proved invulnerable. There was little else for congratulation in this year. The " change in the direction of the war " which Mr. Lloyd George desired proved as impossible under him as under his predecessor. True to his idea of shifting large forces from the western to the eastern or southern front, Mr. Lloyd George warmly supported the project of an attack on Vienna via Laibach put forward by the Italians at a conference in Rome early in January 1917. But the French were no more inclined than before to run the risk of an enemy attack in force on the lines in France after they had been depleted for this enterprise, and countered the Italian proposal by a new scheme of attack in the main theatre proposed by General Nivelle, who had greatly distinguished himself at Verdun in the previous autumn, a scheme said to be based on novel principles which contained all the elements of success. The British Cabinet were converted to General Nivelle's ideas and backed them to the extent of placing their own Commander-in-Chief, General Haig, in a subordinate position to the French general, who for a short space became *Generalissimo* of both British and French armies.

The scheme, nevertheless, miscarried, and threw all the intended operations for the year 1917 out of gear. General Joffre, who was superseded as French Commander-in-Chief by General Nivelle at the end of 1916, had intended to resume the offensive on the Somme at the earliest moment in 1917, and in the change-over from this plan to the Nivelle plan, the Germans slipped away from the Somme, straightening out the Lens-Noyon-Rheims salient and entrenching themselves on a new line called afterwards the Hindenburg line. As they went back, they devastated the country and sowed it with land-mines and explosives, which made the task of pursuing them difficult or impossible. This unforeseen manœuvre dislocated a large part of Nivelle's plan and his main attack (on the Craonne plateau) east and west of Rheims on April 16 was a disastrous failure. The disappointment of the hopes built on this scheme led to a corresponding reaction, and mutinies followed in important sections of the French army. The coolness and good sense with which these were handled by General Pétain saved a perilous situation, but inevitably the brunt of the fighting fell on the British for the remainder of this year.

Passchendaele

They had played the part assigned to them in the Nivelle scheme by capturing Vimy Ridge on April 9, and with little intermission continued their offensive against the Germans until the month of November. Early in June the Second Army under General Plumer gained Messines Ridge after an elaborate tunnelling and mining operation culminating in the simultaneous explosion of a score of immense mines. At the end of July there began at Ypres what came to be known as the Passchendaele offensive which had the double object of freeing the Belgian ports and relieving the pressure on the French. No operation undertaken by the British army has been more criticized, and the material for a fair judgment is by no means complete. There is no question that it failed in the first of its objectives, and the degree in which its pursuance was necessary for the relief of the French can only be ascertained when all the records of this period have been published. Undoubtedly it was General Haig's view that not to let go of the enemy was an imperative necessity during these months, and, unfavourable as the ground proved to be, he held it to be impossible to change suddenly or quickly to a more promising scene of attack.

The military situation had seldom looked blacker for the

Allies than in these months. Added to the troubles in the French army was the collapse of Russia, which continued progressively from March to October and came as an unexpected boon to the Germans, giving them a new hope of victory on land and enabling them to release powerful forces from the East for use in the West. On the other side, the entry of the United States into the war promised large reinforcements for the future, but not in time to meet the immediate emergency. With the Germans reinforced, the French crippled, and the Americans still in the stage of training, the business of hammering the Germans and keeping them occupied while the French recuperated, fell on the British, and it was insistently argued that they must not let go.

Whatever may be the ultimate verdict, the Passchendaele offensive remains one of the ghastliest memories of the war. It is a story of heroic fighting against desperate odds, vain attempts to advance over shell-scarred and water-logged ground, in an autumn of heavy storms and blinding rain, a story of fearful casualties and painful death in this veritable Slough of Despond. The realities of war as they were progressively revealed in the clench between the vast, heavily entrenched, evenly balanced armies may be said to have come to their climax at Passchendaele.

The Tanks

Small wonder if again many minds were at work considering if there were not better ways of vanquishing the enemy than this interminable war of attrition and the hurling of human beings against barbed wire and machine-guns. Nivelle supposed himself to have devised a new tactic which would infallibly " break through " with a minimum loss of life, but unhappily he proved to be mistaken. Gas had been tried and proved a double-edged weapon, inflicting new forms of agony and chronic disease, and full of menace for the future, but not seriously affecting the result in the forms in which it had been used up to this time. Mining had been elaborately developed on certain sectors, especially in the Argonne, and had been used with great effect in the attack on Messines Ridge. But it required elaborate preparation, extending possibly over months, and assumed a stationary enemy pinned to one position who would be taken by surprise. The problem was pondered by all the belligerents in the first three years of the war, and British inventors may claim to have been first in the field with the "tank."—a species of land battle-cruiser, armoured and gunned, carrying its own crew, and able with its caterpillar wheels to surmount trenches and flatten out barbed wire. Like all novelties, it met with scepticism and obstruction from orthodox authorities, and there has been much controversy in subsequent years as to whether it was not too long delayed, and whether, when used, it was rightly used or used prematurely and ineffectively. This is the history of all new inventions, and the tank won its way to acceptance by the ordinary route of disbelief, hesitating experiment, trial, error and acceptance. Those who failed to see its value must bear the blame, and those who believed in it and persisted in their belief against opposition, obstruction and personal rebuffs, deserve the corresponding measure of praise.

Sixty tanks were brought into action at the end of the Somme battle, but with no great success. The numbers were insufficient and the appropriate tactics and handling had not yet been devised. The Commander-in-Chief, General Haig, was much criticized afterwards for having disclosed them prematurely, but the Germans appear, like most of the older British generals, to have regarded them as freaks, and to have paid no serious attention to them. The experience was valuable and enabled a much more skilful and successful use to be made of an improved type at Cambrai in November, 1917. Here 200 tanks were brought into action, and effected a real surprise in a brilliantly planned raid. Unfortunately there were no reserves available to exploit this success, and much of the ground gained was lost in a German counter-attack. But the tank was vindicated, and the experience at Cambrai helped materially to the development which made it invaluable in the following year.

The Collapse of Russia

The collapse of Russia, which was the other chief event of the year 1917, was both political and military. She had made her last great effort in the summer of 1916, when Brusiloff swept over the Bukovina, and a large part of Galicia, and captured 250,000 Austrian prisoners. It was an enormous and far-resounding success, and by drawing Germans from the western front for the relief of Austria brought timely succour to the Allies at a critical moment of their fortunes. But the Russians had suffered immensely, and from this time onwards their bolt was shot. They had enormous reserves of man-power on paper, but the numbers they could arm and feed were strictly limited, and the paucity and inadequacy of their transport and strategic railways greatly hampered their movements. Before the end of 1916 they were short of everything, rations, rifles, guns, munitions, aircraft; their men were going into the trenches armed only with sticks, trusting to pick up rifles from dead comrades; orders were confused, discipline was lax, desertions were increasing. There were rumours of corruption and even of treachery among officers; the Government was in a state of distraction. Competent Ministers were arbitrarily dismissed and their places filled with incompetent reactionaries—it was generally supposed at the whim or bidding of the Tsarina and her spiritual adviser, Rasputin. The Tsar had left the capital ostensibly to live the " simple life " among the troops, but, as many alleged, to avoid the burden of decision, and the friction of contact with his Ministers.

The Duma—the shadow of a Parliament which had been permitted in Russia—urged the necessity of reform, and called for the establishment of National Councils to bridge the widening gulf between the autocracy and the people, but the Government ignored this advice, and clung to its belief that the rising discontent could be quelled with machine-guns. On March 9, 1917, Petrograd was in revolution—for the moment a bloodless revolution—and the Tsarist Government collapsed without firing a shot. Five days later the Tsar abdicated, and a Provisional Government was formed, consisting in the main of moderate reformers or " Menshevists " under Prince Lyov as Prime Minister, with the Liberal Milukov as Foreign Secretary, and Kerensky as Minister for War. This Government was bent on continuing the war, and Kerensky who was a powerful orator went to the front and rallied the troops to a last effort in the south-west. This had a momentary success in the battles of Brezezany and Zborow, but it hastened the exhaustion which was to make persistence in the war impossible.

In the meantime the new Liberal Government was being undermined by the growth of the Soviet movement, which, beginning with hastily formed councils of workmen and soldiers, gradually disintegrated the army and drew the populace to its side for the full Revolution which was to end the war and establish Communism in Russia. The Germans, who were well informed of the trend of events, had played a crafty stroke by arranging that Lenin, who was well known as a revolutionary extremist, should be conveyed in a sealed wagon from Switzerland, where he was in exile, through German territory to Petrograd, where he at once made himself the leader and brain of the revolutionary party.

The Triumph of Lenin and Its Results

The Provisional Government struck at the extremists and drove Lenin and other revolutionary leaders temporarily into hiding. Kerensky had now become Prime Minister, and for a few months he kept the revolutionaries in check, and struggled to continue the war, but in November soldiers, sailors, and workmen stormed the Government buildings in Petrograd, and compelled the Government to take flight. Lenin, who had come out of his hiding, now seized the reins, and, as President of the " Council of People's Commissars," became the supreme power in the country. The story of the Revolution must be continued in its proper place, but these events were decisive for Russia's part in the war. Not only was her army exhausted and demoralized, but peace was the necessary policy of the men now in power. They believed that the war was a struggle of capitalists in which the workers had no concern except to extricate themselves as quickly as possible, with the maximum of damage to all the Governments at war. They believed—or professed to believe—that if the Russian workers refused to continue fighting, the workers of Germany, France, Britain, Italy and America would follow their example, and overthrow any capitalist Government which refused to make peace. They found themselves in the end solitary and helpless against Germany, which compelled them in the following year to accept the kind of peace which they had by no means contemplated—the harsh peace of Brest-Litovsk under which the Germans occupied the Ukraine, deprived Russia of her Baltic Provinces and left Petrograd at the mercy of any invader from the borders of Finland and Esthonia.

It may be argued that these events were in the long-run a disaster for Germany, since they encouraged her to continue the struggle with the western Allies beyond the point at which a moderate peace was possible. But for the moment the collapse of Russia came as a gift from the gods providing men and munitions for a last great fling against the Allies in the west. The first-fruits were an attack on the Italians at Caporetto in the Province of Venezia (October 24, 1917), where a German and Austrian force broke through and won an immense, if temporary, success. The Italian commander, General Cadorna, only saved his army by retreating precipitately to the line of the Piave with the loss of 250,000 prisoners and for a few days it seemed as if the whole plain of North Italy might be overrun, and great cities like Venice, Verona, and even Milan fall into the hands of the enemy. But the Italians rallied; the British and French rushed troops to their aid, and the enemy had no sufficient force in reserve to exploit an advantage which had greatly exceeded his expectations. The Italians stood firm on the line of the Piave until the coming of winter ended these operations.

Peace Efforts in 1917

Something has been said about the peace-terms which the Germans proposed in December 1916 as a preliminary to their submarine war and a word may be added here about other peace efforts in the year 1917.

The aged Austrian Emperor, Franz Joseph, died in November, 1916, and was succeeded by his grandson, Charles, a young man of 29 who had had little experience of affairs to qualify him for the terrible position he was now called upon to occupy. But he showed a certain independence from the beginning, and was with great difficulty persuaded to consent to the adoption of the unrestricted submarine warfare upon which the Germans decided in January of the following year. He believed a peace of victory to be impossible, and, backed by his Foreign Minister, Count Czernin, offered a strong opposition to a measure which he believed would be fatal to a peace by agreement. In this he was overborne, but he persisted in his efforts to bring the war to an end, and in April Count Czernin prepared a memorandum for the German Emperor, in which the idea was broached that Germany should restore Alsace-Lorraine to France and take " Congress Poland " with the addition of Galicia as compensation for herself. April, unfortunately, was the month in which German hopes of a speedy victory by the submarine ran highest, and the Germans, so far from being willing to restore Alsace-Lorraine, were now meditating new acquisitions such as the annexation of the Briey and Longwy coal basins, at the expense of France, and the practical annexation of Belgium. In dealing with the Germans the Emperor Charles appears very speedily to have dropped his idea of restoring Alsace-Lorraine, and instead to have sat down with them to a far-reaching scheme for the division of the spoils of the expected victory.

But Charles and Czernin continued to prepare for a less favourable result, and (apparently without informing their Ally) pursued a negotiation of their own with the French through the Emperor's brother-in-law, Prince Sixtus of Parma. The Emperor entrusted a letter to his brother-in-law to be shown to M. Poincaré, in which he declared his readiness to support the claims of France to Alsace-Lorraine in Berlin, and to work for the restoration of Belgium and Serbia as sovereign States. M. Poincaré was not impressed; he saw in this letter evidence of the desperate plight of Austria rather than an honest desire to make peace; and Baron Sonnino, the Italian Foreign Minister, to whom it was communicated, strongly objected that no concessions were made to Italy in the proposed terms of peace.

Prince Sixtus's mission thus broke down, and a subsequent meeting in Switzerland, to which the French Government was privy, between the French General Staff-Major, Count Armand, and a relative of his in the Austrian Diplomatic Service came to nothing because the terms proposed were unacceptable to Germany. German hopes, which had waned when the unrestricted submarine fell short of expectations, had by this time been rekindled by the collapse of Russia. Nevertheless there was evidence of a certain war-weariness in the German public, which was suffering greatly from the blockade, and a motion proposed by Erzberger, the leader of the Centre party, favouring a " peace by understanding " without annexations or economic disabilities, was adopted by a majority in the Reichstag on July 19.

The long and short of it was that the Governments were inclined for peace or the reverse in proportion as they thought they were losing or winning the war. " The de'il was sick, the de'il a saint would be; the de'il was well, the de'il a saint was he." At the beginning of 1917 the Germans were confessing to themselves that their chance of winning the war on land was slight, but their belief in the unrestricted submarine was unbounded, and their terms were accordingly for a conqueror's peace. By July this belief was shaken, and they were willing that the ground should be explored, but before the end of the year the collapse of Russia had released large forces for a final stroke in the west, and they were less than ever inclined for the only peace—the peace ceding Alsace-Lorraine—which the French would have accepted. On the other side the Allies were now confident that, if they could conquer the submarine, the entry of America into the war would give them the ultimate victory; and though they had little cause for rejoicing in the military events of the year 1917, they were buoyed up by a new sense of strength in reserve, as the strength of the enemy was declining. Between the two, Lord Lansdowne, pleading for a moderate peace in his famous letter published in the *Daily Telegraph* in October, 1917, had little chance of a hearing and was fortunate in being the bearer of a great and respected name, which saved him from a worse reproach than that of being a " defeatist." Undoubtedly he showed great courage in publishing this letter, and a subsequent generation which realizes the havoc that was being wrought by the prolongation of this terrible war may well hold him in honour, but at this time the minimum terms of both belligerents were such that neither could accept what the other demanded except under the compulsion of defeat. So it was to be till the end.

CHAPTER XXII

THE VICTORY OF THE ALLIES

THE last weeks of the year 1917 witnessed a brilliant if minor success for the Allies in the capture of Jerusalem by a British force under General (afterwards Lord) Allenby. In February, 1915, the Turks had made an effort, which was easily repulsed, to invade Egypt by the Suez Canal, but this raid—for it was little more—had proved that it was possible for large bodies of troops with properly organized transport to cross the desert, and it had therefore been necessary to retain a considerable body of troops in Egypt, when the withdrawal from Gallipoli set the Turks free for enterprises elsewhere. It was now decided that the best way of defending Egypt was to clear the Turks out of the Sinai Peninsula, and thereafter to advance into Palestine. The first part of this task was accomplished before the end of 1916, by which time the British had advanced across the desert to El Arish and Rafah in the south-west of Palestine, laying a railway as they went. An attack on Gaza in March, 1917, which was to have inauguarated the second part was unsuccessful, but Sir Archibald Murray was able to take up a position near by, and advance his railhead to within striking distance of that place. In July it became known that General Falkenhayn, in command of the Turkish army at Aleppo, was planning to drive the British force back into the desert as a preliminary to an attempt to recapture Bagdad. The British General Staff thereupon decided to anticipate Falkenhayn by striking at Jerusalem and thus securing their own position and diverting the Turkish force intended for Bagdad. The plan adopted was that of a surprise attack on the Turkish left at Beersheba, combined with a holding attack on the Turks at Gaza; and being carried out with great skill and daring, it resulted in the capture of both places and the retreat of the whole Turkish army. From Beersheba to Jerusalem the British force had to fight its way through difficult mountain passes against stubborn resistance, but the final attack on Jerusalem on December 8 was completely successful, and General Allenby made an official entry into the city on December 11. He had rightly insisted that if he was to undertake this difficult operation, he should be provided with sufficient troops and the necessary equipment and transport, but, even so, success could not have been achieved without the most careful preparation beforehand or the most skilful leadership in action.

The Supreme War Council

This success had a heartening effect on the public, and it had positive results in securing Egypt from invasion and disposing of the threat to Mesopotamia. There were nevertheless not a few military critics who doubted the wisdom of any diversion from the main task of securing the west front which, after the Russian collapse, more and more lay under the threat of a great German offensive with the aid of the forces set free from the east. The situation in the west was complicated by lack of unity among the Allies and by strong differences of opinion between the soldiers in command, and even between the Governments and the soldiers. After the Italian disaster at Caporetto, a body called the " Supreme War Council " was set up at Versailles, but the soldiers who sat on it objected to being merely advisers without executive authority, and before long it became necessary to appoint an executive committee of soldiers with General Foch as chairman, whose special function it was to form and direct a joint body of reserves. But this arrangement too was far from solving the problem of prompt joint action in emergency. Both British and French commanders complained that while they remained in control of the chief part of their armies, the highly important part of their duties, which consisted in the handling of reserves, and upon which all else might depend, had been taken from them and relegated to a committee removed from the scene of operations and very unlikely to act promptly in an emergency. These objections proved well founded in the event, but it was only by the process of trial and error that the Allies were led finally and under sheer necessity to accept the solution of a *Generalissimo* controlling reserves and, for the time being, directing all operations.

More serious still, there was a sharp division of opinion about the general conduct of the war during the early months of 1918. Mr. Lloyd George and the British Cabinet held it to be proved by experience that the lines on the western front were impregnable against attack even by superior numbers, and were in favour of holding these lines defensively during 1918 and postponing any decisive campaign until 1919, when the Americans would be present in force, and of employing any available troops meanwhile in a further campaign in Palestine or elsewhere in the East. Friction had developed between the Home Government and General Haig about the Passchendaele offensive, which he considered imperative to keep the Germans occupied, and which some Ministers regarded as a needless sacrifice of life. Relations between the Government and the general were strained, and they were indisposed to provide him with more troops for use in further operations of the same kind. The word went out that the western front was " over-insured " and that any surplus forces would be better employed elsewhere.

The Great German Offensive

The result of this confusion of plans and ideas was that the early months of 1918 passed without any provision being made to reinforce the western front. In the meantime, Sir Douglas Haig had been required to extend the British line as far south as the Oise, thus taking in another sixteen lines of peculiarly vulnerable front. In ordinary seasons this section had behind it an almost impassable region of bog and swamp, and had in consequence been very lightly fortified, but in March, 1918, the ground was hard and dry, and to fortify it adequately in the short time available was impossible. Having this additional responsibility without reinforcement, the British commander felt obliged to say that he could not spare the thirty divisions for reserves required as the British contribution by the Versailles Committee, but this further dislocated the joint plans for the defence.

For the Germans, seeking a point of entry for their new offensive, these circumstances were an all but open invitation to choose the new British sector opposite St. Quentin. The ground was ill-fortified and thinly held, it was the junction between the British and French armies, exactly the spot where a break-through offered the possibility of dividing British and French, capturing the great railway centre of Amiens, severing the vital north and south communications of the Allies and opening the road to the Channel ports. Ludendorff was clever enough to keep the French doubting to the last moment whether his main attack would not be on the Champagne front, but it was upon this British sector, as Sir Douglas Haig had predicted, that the full weight of the German offensive fell on the disastrous 21st of March. Aided by an untimely fog the Germans swept over the Fifth Army, and in two days' fighting advanced about ten miles, creating a scene of chaos and confusion along the line of advance. The casualties were enormous (14,000 officers and 286,000 other ranks); 65,000 prisoners and 769 guns as well as an immense amount of war material fell into the enemy's hands. It was the blackest day of the war for the British army. But great as the German success was, it fell short of its objectives, and when the fighting died down, there were already shrewd critics who said that the enemy had shot his bolt and failed. The British rallied quickly from the shock, and for the enemy to bring up fresh troops over the devastated ground became increasingly difficult. On March 28 the British Third Army repulsed the German attack, and from that moment recovery began.

Unity of Command

Under stress of these events unity of command was at last achieved, and at a conference at Doullens Foch was appointed " to co-ordinate the operations of the Allied armies on the western front." Experience had proved that the handling of reserves must be entrusted to one supreme commander, and their masterly use during the next few weeks went far to retrieve the position. The next most dangerous move was a German attack in Flanders which also had a great immediate success, but again was stopped short of its objective, the important railway junction of Hazebrouck, the capture of which would have been only less, if at all less, serious than that of Amiens. Another German attack on the Ypres salient captured the Hill of Kemmel, but the timely arrival of French reinforcements stopped any further advance in this direction, and the other important ridges remained in the hands of the Allies.

The very diversity of these attacks contributed to their failure in the aggregate. Measured by previous achievements on the western front they had had enormous success, but in each case the initial rush had fallen short of the vital objectives, and forces had been dissipated which, if concentrated on one effort might have gained a decisive victory. Before the end of March Ludendorff had changed his plan, and instead of continuing his drive on Amiens was attacking simultaneously in Flanders and south of the Somme, and being checked by French reinforcements. At the end of May he launched another attack on the French on the heights above the River Aisne, and again had a spectacular success, sweeping over the Chemin des Dames and reaching the Marne, within forty miles of Paris. But here again he found himself stopped short of any vital objective by the arrival of American reinforcements, which in a most gallant action brought him to a standstill near Château-Thierry.

The Germans, being left in a narrow salient by this last offensive, tried to improve their position by striking out to the west towards Compiègne, but were quickly checked. Then on July 15 they had a last fling east of Rheims which ended in a crushing defeat. A day or two later the French launched a counter-attack on the Marne, and had a success so complete that it compelled Ludendorff, who had gone to Flanders to prepare a new offensive in that region, to cancel his plans and withdraw troops from the north to secure the situation on the Marne. Before the end of July the initiative had passed from Ludendorff to Foch.

There had been no more dangerous period for the Allies, and it may be said that the war was won by the fortitude with which first of all the soldiers in the field, and next to them both the French and British publics, stood the strain of the immense losses and racking anxiety of these months. The Governments rose to the occasion—Clemenceau in France and Lloyd George in Great Britain; the fighting army was reinforced in every possible way, 140,000 men being sent out from

England, and troops recalled from Palestine and other eastern fronts. Before the end of July the British divisions broken up after the March offensive had been reconstituted, and American troops were arriving at the rate of 300,000 a month, and being pushed into the battle line. The Germans, who were fighting against time in the hope of crushing the Allies before these reinforcements could appear on the scene, now began to see their position as highly critical.

The British Attack

The Allies pressed their advantage, and on August 8 Haig launched a great attack on the Amiens front, and in two days advanced twelve miles on a front of eighteen miles. This was a masterly operation planned in profound secrecy, and falling upon the enemy with complete surprise. A swarm of tanks, 360 heavy and 100 "whippets," swept over the ground, carrying all before them and clearing the way for the advance of the infantry. Amiens and the vital railway communications were thus freed from the German threat, but the moral results of this victory were even greater than the material. "We are at the end of our resources," said the Kaiser when the news reached him, "the war must be ended." Ludendorff was of the same opinion, and he too said that "the war would have to be ended." Looking back in after days he gave it as his considered opinion that August 8 was "the blackest day for the German army in the history of the war."

This was no mere temporary loss of nerve. August 8 brought home to the Germans that they had lost the race against time. If at the moment of their maximum strength they had been unable to dispose of their enemy, and if, in spite of the blows rained upon him, this enemy was capable of returning to the attack with this energy and power, what would the prospect be when he was reinforced by the new and ardent American troops who were now pouring into France in vast numbers? Much has been said in after years about the weakness of German politicians and the effect of enemy propaganda on the morale of the German people, but the simple fact that none but the gloomiest answer was possible to this question counted for more than all else, when the great German offensive of the spring of 1918 had definitely failed.

As with the French in the previous year, the disappointment was in proportion to the hopes, but whereas the French had before them the hope of recovery if they held on, the Germans had no such hope. Their reserves were exhausted, the one chance offered them of rounding on the Allies with the troops set free by the Russian collapse had miscarried, the unlimited submarine campaign had failed, the entry of America into the war was tightening the blockade which was exhausting the civil population. Ludendorff was assuredly right in his estimate of the situation after the British attack, and the facts were too evident for them to be long hidden from the army or the civil population, or Germany's Allies in the East. When the tide turned on the western front it was no longer possible for the Germans to send relief to Turks and Bulgarians, and simultaneously, with their advance in France and Flanders, the Allies renewed their attacks on both. In September and October Allenby routed and destroyed the Turkish army in Palestine and advancing to Damascus and Aleppo joined hands with Colonel Lawrence, whose leadership of the Arabs was one of the most gallant and picturesque incidents of the war in the East. At the same time General Guillaumat advanced into Bulgaria from the Salonica front, and the Bulgarian Government, judging its case to be hopeless, signed an unconditional armistice on September 25. In this war all the combatants on either side stood or fell together, and all hung on the fate of the principal armies in the main theatre.

The Germans in Retreat

At a Crown Council held at Spa a few days after the British attack, Ludendorff declared that it was no longer possible for Germany to gain her war aims, and that " a peace by arrangement " should be sought at the first favourable opportunity. A peace by arrangement for a cause which is visibly failing is, unfortunately, the least probable of all endings to a great war. The Allies, conscious of their own strength, were now more than ever determined to go to the end—*jusqu'au bout*. Within a few days the French followed up the British victory by capturing the massif of Lassignes and the heights above Soissons, and during the last weeks of August the British recaptured the whole area of the Somme battle-fields, and two-thirds of the ground gained by the Germans in their spring offensive. At the end of August another British attack forced a general retreat on the Flanders front. Blows now fell thickly on all parts of the front, and on September 12 General Pershing with nine American divisions drove the enemy from the St. Mihiel salient, south of Verdun.

But as they went back the Germans were still fighting bravely and offering a stubborn resistance, and on the northern part of the field the Allies still had in front of them the formidable task of breaking the famous Hindenburg line—the heavily fortified trench system running from St. Quentin northwards, established by the Germans after their withdrawal from the Somme in February 1917. This task fell mainly to the British and entailed much heavy fighting, which lasted for the greater part of the month of September. Success was achieved by a series of simultaneous and convergent attacks along the whole battle-front, in which French and Americans engaged the enemy west of the Meuse and in the Argonne, and a mixed force of British, Belgians and French under King Albert attacked in Flanders, while the British stormed the Hindenburg line in the centre. The battle in its various phases lasted for nine days and at the end of it the greatest of the German defences was broken and the enemy in full retreat. The fighting was more prolonged on the Meuse and in the Argonne, where the Germans opposed an obstinate and gallant defence to the French-American attack, but on November 1 a general offensive broke through the enemy line at all points, and the rest was pursuit over open country all along the line from the Dutch frontier to the heights above the Meuse. The Flanders offensive, meanwhile, had driven the enemy from the coast and over the river Lys and compelled him to evacuate Lille. The next moves—planned by Foch—were to have been a further attack in Flanders on November 11 and an offensive into Lorraine by French and Americans on November 14 but on November 11 the enemy asked for an armistice and the war was over.

The story of the last days is voluminous and intricate and abounds in incidents to the honour of all the armies, French, British, American, Belgian, and among the British the splendid

Dominion troops, Australian, Canadian, New Zealanders, not least. For four years and four months the great German war-machine had withstood all assaults and maintained a war on three fronts with amazing endurance and resourcefulness. But when it broke, it broke catastrophically. In the last stage all was confusion. Supplies failed, transport broke down, rebellion threatened in the rear and revolution was on foot at home. On November 10 the Kaiser had been forced to abdicate and had taken refuge in Holland; between soldiers and civilians, an all but starving people were in a state of distraction.

There were some insatiable fighters who were still in favour of going on and pursuing the Germans into their own country. Their militarist spirit, it was said, would only be completely subdued if they were compelled to take their own medicine and see their villages and cities devastated by a foreign enemy. Humanity forbade. The Allied Governments and their commanders in the field were agreed that it would be a crime to sacrifice more life when their war-aims had been accomplished, and the enemy had submitted. The news that fighting had ceased was an enormous relief not only to the soldiers but to sane people everywhere. No more victories, no more defeats, no more casualty lists, no more waiting in terror for the postman's knock, or the ring of the telegraph boy. It seemed at that moment as if the world had suddenly come out of the valley of death into the sunshine. To the multitude in the defeated countries peace, even at this price, was a blessed relief.

The British casualties alone were 947,000 dead or missing, including 141,000 Dominion and Colonial, and 61,000 Indian ; and more than two million wounded and disabled. The cost of the war was £8,417,000,000, of which £6,775,000,000 was added to the National Debt, bringing the total up to £7,480,000,000. The British people had submitted to heavier taxation than any other during the war, but there remained this immense burden for the future to carry.

THE RETURN TO POLITICS

BEFORE the war was over Mr. Lloyd George and Mr. Bonar Law, the leaders of the Coalition, had decided to hold a general election in Great Britain, as soon as the end came.   They thought it necessary for the Government to renew its mandate before it proceeded to the Peace settlement, and they felt that there could be no better opportunity of obtaining the exceptional and overwhelming vote of confidence which the occasion was said to demand than if they presented themselves at this moment as the authors of victory, and used their influence with their respective parties to secure the return of candidates who could be certified as reliable and patriotic.

In this they judged rightly.   It was certain that the Conservative party would follow their official leaders, and that the Liberal party would be divided and helpless, if in face of the joint appeal it tried to run independent candidates.   But there was one considerable difficulty.   With few exceptions all members of the outgoing Parliament, whether Liberal or Conservative, had treated the Government with forbearance and supported it in all measures necessary for the conduct of the war.   It thus seemed to follow that, if an election were held as a popular demonstration at this moment, the great majority of sitting members would be returned unopposed. That at least was the expectation of both Liberal and Labour members, with the exception of those who had opposed the war.

The Division of Seats

On the other hand, it was scarcely to be expected that the Conservative party which, as a party, had been out of office for nearly thirteen years, would consent merely to the reelection of the Parliament elected in 1910, in which they were in a minority of more than 100.   It, therefore, became necessary to displace a sufficient number of Liberal and Labour candidates to give the Conservative party the number of seats which it considered to be its due; and a dividing line had accordingly to be drawn between Liberals whom the leaders thought worthy to sit in the " Victory Parliament " and others whom they deemed unworthy. The Prime Minister decided that the test should be the solitary division in which any considerable body of Liberals had voted against the Government—that on Mr. Asquith's motion to substitute a Select Committee of the House of Commons for the two judges proposed by the Government to inquire into General Maurice's allegations [1]— and that all who had given this vote should, if possible, be excluded from the next Parliament and their seats given to Conservatives.

This method, an extremely simple one, proved highly effective. Having drawn up their list of favoured candidates, Mr. Lloyd George and Mr. Bonar Law gave them a certificate of character, popularly known as " the coupon," appealed to their respective parties to join forces in supporting them, and denounced the others as untrustworthy men, men—Mr. Lloyd George said—who had engaged in a conspiracy to overthrow the Government and injure the national cause at a most critical moment in the war. A great many electors disapproved of this method of electioneering, but, feeling it impossible on the eve of the Peace Conference to do anything which might weaken the hands of the Government, gave their votes reluctantly for its nominees. In the result the independent Liberal party was all but wiped out—their number after the election being only 33—and in the new House the Government had no fewer than 526 supporters, giving it a working majority of 420. The Labour party was a little more fortunate than the Liberal, and came back 63 in number.

---

[1] Major-General Sir F. Maurice, until recently Director of Military Operations, sacrificed his military career by writing a letter to the Press (May 6, 1918) challenging statements made in the House of Commons by the Prime Minister and Mr Bonar Law about the strength of the British army on the western front at the time of the German offensive in March 1918. Mr. Bonar Law thereupon said that since this letter " affected the honour of Ministers " the Government would invite two judges to inquire into the statements contained in it. Mr. Asquith, who objected to judges being involved in political issues, proposed that the inquiry should be conducted by a Select Committee of the House of Commons. When the question was debated (May 9) the Prime Minister withdrew the offer of inquiry, but Asquith persisted in his a motion for Select Committee, and it was supported by 106 Liberal members.

The Eclipse of Liberalism

The victims and " conspirators " included Asquith, who had borne the chief responsibility during the first two and a half years of the war, and been Prime Minister for a longer period continuously than any other man since Lord Liverpool. Ruthlessness was the watchword, and there could be no exceptions. Asquith returned to Parliament as member for Paisley early in 1920 after a vigorous election campaign in which he had expounded a comprehensive Liberal policy. Meanwhile, the Liberal party had been broken beyond repair, and scores of able and experienced men found themselves excluded from Parliament, and with little prospect of returning there. The official Opposition was now Labour in virtue of its superior numbers. This had far-reaching results on domestic politics in the coming years.

No Government appealing to the country for a vote of confidence at such a time could have failed to obtain a commanding majority. But the appeal of the Government for an overwhelming majority—a majority which would wipe out opposition—led to excited and embittered electioneering in which the Government more and more presented itself as battling with opponents who desired to " spare the Germans." On the day after the Armistice, when the Prime Minister had summoned his Liberal followers to Downing Street, he had spoken to them of a peace " based on the fundamental principles of righteousness," and of the need of putting away " base, sordid, squalid ideas of vengeance and of avarice." Before the election was over he had promised to prosecute the ex-Kaiser, to punish German officers, to expel or exclude Germans from Great Britain, to " exact the last penny we can get out of Germany to the limit of her capacity." [1]

It was with these pledges that Mr. Lloyd George and his colleagues went to the Peace Conference that was now to follow.

[1] This capacity was currently believed to be 24,000 millions. In stating this figure Mr. Lloyd George added that " having consulted the financial advisers he could not honestly encourage the hope that we should get so much." " If Germany has a greater capacity she must pay up to the very last penny."

CHAPTER XXIV

In October, 1918, when they were evidently facing defeat, the Germans intimated that they were ready for an armistice on the understanding that President Wilson's " Fourteen Points "[1] should be the basis of the Peace settlement. These " Fourteen Points " had been formulated by the American President in a speech to Congress on January 8, 1918, but they had not been endorsed by the Allies, some of whom, and especially Great Britain, objected to the " absolute freedom of navigation alike in peace and in war," which figured among the fourteen. The Allies were persuaded, however, to accept them as the " basis " of the coming peace subject to reservations on this point, and upon the right of the victors to exact reparations from the defeated; and when the Germans surrendered on November 11 they claimed to have done so on an assurance that the Peace terms would be in accordance with President Wilson's principles.

This was the beginning of misunderstanding. The language in which the points were formulated was by no means precise, and the undiluted nationalism of certain of the " points " could with difficulty be squared with the internationalism of the others, or with the merciful treatment of the enemy which

[1] The Fourteen Points covered the evacuation of all Allied territory, the restoration of Alsace-Lorraine to France; a " readjustment " of Italian frontiers; " autonomous development " for the peoples of Austria-Hungary, and for the non-Turkish nationalities under Turkish rule; the establishment of an independent Polish State; and an " impartial adjustment of all Colonial claims " in which the interests of the populations concerned were to have equal weight with those of the Governments claiming sovereignty over them. In addition they stipulated for " open covenants of peace " and the abolition of " private international understandings of any kind "; " absolute freedom of navigation alike in peace and in war, except as the seas may be closed in whole or in part by international action for the enforcement of international covenants "; the " removal, so far as possible, of all economic barriers and the establishment of equality of trade conditions " among the nations accepting and guaranteeing the peace; the reduction of armaments to " the lowest point consistent with domestic safety "; and the establishment of a League of Nations.

was supposed to be one of President Wilson's principal aims. A formal case can be made to prove that the subsequent peace was item by item on the " basis " of the Fourteen Points, but it cannot reasonably be said that the spirit in which the Allies interpreted them at the Versailles Conference was the spirit in which President Wilson had explained them in January of the previous year.

The Bitterness of Opinion

Much had happened in the last stages of the war to embitter opinion. The German retreat from the Somme had been attended with devastation unprecedented in what was called civilized warfare, and over a great belt of territory extending from the Alps to the sea ruin and desolation marked the course of the defeated enemy's advance and his retreat. The French vowed that he should pay, and many British, remembering the ravages of the " unrestricted submarine " and the thousands of non-combatants, including women and children, who had been " sunk without trace," or bombed from the air, said that the payment should be to the uttermost farthing. Ruthlessness had been the enemy's watchword, and millions in the Allied countries now said that he should be repaid in his own coin. Electioneering had further inflamed these passions, and not a few of the statesmen who went to Paris in January, 1919, to settle the peace terms went pledged to a multitude, whom they had excited with their rhetoric, to let no " misplaced leniency " or sentiment prevent them from doing stern justice.

This was not an atmosphere in which wise or durable settlements of infinitely complicated questions were likely to be reached. The impulse which had carried the Allies to victory took them far past the winning post, and the statesmen who had ridden the winning steeds now had the difficult task of pulling them in. What lay before them was little less than the creation of a new world. Four great Empires, German, Russian, Austrian and Turkish, lay in ruins, and any interpretation of the peace " basis " required the restoration of much territory that they had acquired by conquest, and the institution of a large number of new self-governing units in areas which they had previously administered. In the ordinary course of history this might have been the work of generations, even of centuries; it now had to be accomplished within a few weeks in the atmosphere of war, with the defeated countries ruled out of the negotiations and the victorious left to judge in their own cause as well as in that of their opponents.

In the days before railways and telegraphs a little group of statesmen might assemble in congress at Vienna or Verona, and settle the affairs of Europe at their discretion, and be sure that the small constituencies to which they were responsible would ratify their decision. In 1933 a vast army of newspaper correspondents watched every stage of the proceedings, and every statesman had behind him millions of eager supporters watching jealously lest he should abate an iota of their demands. Spectacular publicity attended the proceedings from beginning to end. A great company of secretaries, typists, experts, and propagandists came with each delegation, and a multitude of causes clamouring to be heard, had their agents in Paris. The mass of material accumulated and the innumerable questions thrown on the vast dump-heap of Paris in these weeks would have tested human capacity at its coolest and wisest, and at that moment cool dissection and analysis, coherent and orderly treatment of the whole, were least to be expected.

Before judgment is passed, certain things must be remembered. The statesmen at Paris did not, as commonly asserted, break the Austrian Empire in pieces; it was broken beyond repair before they met, and their task was merely to make some orderly pattern out of the fragments. Nor did they create or re-create Poland, which automatically came to life on the defeat of Germany, Austria and Russia. In these and many other respects they were dealing with material given to them in a shape already fixed. The great open questions were the reparations to be exacted from Germany, the amount of territory to be taken from her either permanently or temporarily over and above the restoration of Alsace-Lorraine, the demands of Italy for additional territory, the demand of Poland for access to the sea, the future of Turkey, and, above all, the constitution of the League of Nations, which was President Wilson's chief contribution to the peace, and the main hope of the liberal settlement which he sincerely desired.

Reparations

Mistakes were inevitable, but in the light of experience it is difficult to find excuse for some that were made at Paris in these months. The handling of reparations was disastrous. Experts issued warnings that except by borrowing Germany could pay no more year by year than her " exportable surplus," *i.e.* the balance which remained over after she had paid for her necessary imports, and that this had been a comparatively small sum even in the years of German prosperity. But the public mind was in a state of great confusion between the immovable wealth of the country—docks, mines, railways, public utilities, etc.—which undoubtedly was large, and the transferable wealth—that which could be conveyed in the form of goods and services to her creditors—which was comparatively small. A committee, which included the Governor of the Bank of England and an eminent judge, certified that the figure of £24,000,000,000 mentioned at the British elections was in fact what she was capable of paying; and though this estimate was reduced by more than half in the subsequent weeks the differences of opinion were so great that the total liability had to be left blank when the Conference ended.[1] This was the beginning of a long struggle to obtain the impossible which was to have disastrous results, both economic and political, during the next twelve years.

Territorial Settlements

The territorial settlements were spread over a large number of treaties : the Treaty of Versailles with Germany, the Treaty of St. Germain with Austria, the Treaty of Trianon with Hungary, the Treaty of Neuilly with Bulgaria, the Treaty of

[1] In 1921 the total was fixed at about £6,000,000,000 (the Paris schedules), and it was further reduced to about £2,000,000,000 by the Committee presided over respectively by General Dawes and Mr. Owen D. Young in 1924 and 1926. In 1932 at the Lausanne Conference the allies accepted with unimportant reservations the refusal of Germany to make further payments. By this time it had become clear that the necessary " exportable surplus " was not available, and that the greater part of Germany's payments had been effected by borrowings from the United States, which stopped after the slump of 1929.

Sèvres with Turkey. Some of these were not concluded or ratified until many months after the Conference, and the Treaty of Sèvres was repudiated by the Turkish Nationalists as soon as they came into power. Many of the " Mandates," *i.e.* authority to administer territories taken from or ceded by the enemy States, were conferred not by the Peace Conference but by the Allied Ministers who sat as a " Supreme Council " when it was over. It was this " Supreme Council " which gave the mandates for Syria and the Lebanon to France, and for Mesopotamia and Palestine to Great Britain. The same authority awarded Eupen and Malmedy to Belgium and gave Poland a twenty-five year mandate for Galicia.

Many of the boundaries were left by the Peace Conference for the States chiefly concerned to settle between themselves, a process which took two years or longer. Rumania, Czechoslovakia and Jugoslavia settled their respective boundaries in a treaty concluded on August 20, 1921, and in November of the same year Italy concluded a treaty with Jugoslavia by which she obtained Istria for herself and ceded Dalmatia to the Jugoslavs, leaving Fiume for the time being an independent port.

It is impossible to deal with all these arrangements in detail, but the points of greatest importance at the Paris Conference may be noted.

France, Germany and the U.S.A.

The claims of the French raised the central political issue. In the name of security they demanded—in addition to the restitution of Alsace-Lorraine and the disarmament of Germany —the cession of the Rhineland with the Rhine as the future frontier between France and Germany. This led to an exhausting struggle between Clemenceau and Marshal Foch on the one side and President Wilson and Mr. Lloyd George on the other. The French argued that in no other way could they be safe against a future attack by Germany ; the President and Mr. Lloyd George replied that the annexation of this indisputably German territory by France would violate every principle they had professed, and quite surely sow the seed of a future war of revenge. The contention on this subject came near to breaking the conference, and it was settled by a compromise which proved later to have been far from a happy one. The French were permitted to remain in occupation of the Rhineland for fifteen years, and in place of permanent occupation were promised, or led to expect, a joint military guarantee by Great Britain and the United States against " unprovoked aggression." That was always conditional on ratification by the American Congress, and, in the following year when Congress declined to ratify, it fell through, and the French were left saying that they had been misled into withdrawing their full demand by a promise which was afterwards repudiated. It could scarcely be said, however, that they came badly out of the settlement. Not only had they recovered Alsace-Lorraine but as compensation for the destruction during the war of the coal-mines in the north of France they were given an absolute property in the coal-mines of the Saar, and the right to occupy that district for fifteen years. They also added largely to their African Colonial Empire, and, as already recorded, obtained the mandates for Syria and the Lebanon.

The League of Nations and President Wilson

All over central and south-east Europe the map was redrawn, and there came into being the new States of Czechoslovakia and Yugoslavia and the nominally independent State of Albania. Italy, too, though she professed to be greatly dissatisfied with the portions assigned to her, obtained large concessions of territory, and added a considerable number of Slavs in Istria and Germans in the Tyrol to her population. Her claim to Fiume—which in subsequent years after violent struggles she has practically established—was publicly denounced by President Wilson. This all but caused the withdrawal of Italy from the conference. Wilson by this time was struggling against heavy odds to save his Fourteen Points in the welter of conflicting claims and racial quarrels. As time went on he was more and more at a disadvantage. He was a sick man, he had not the knowledge necessary for battle with the European experts; his hand was weakened by the reaction against him which was too evidently going forward in his own country, and which made it more and more doubtful whether what he was proposing in Paris would be ratified by Congress when he returned home. He fought gallantly for his "points," and endeavoured to persuade himself that the concessions that were wrung from him left their principle intact, but what carried him through was his indomitable belief in the League of Nations and his strong conviction that if only it could be established on a firm foundation it would prove a remedy for all that was harsh, unjust or unworkable in the Treaty.

This was the faith in which many others who thought large parts of the Treaty of Versailles to be harsh and unjust were led finally to accept it. The Treaty with the League was said to be like Ithuriel's spear which healed the wounds that it inflicted. Here, for the first time, was an International authority, with permanent machinery for the supervision of world affairs, enabling statesmen to co-operate in remedying injustice and keeping the peace, instead of falling apart into hostile camps and engaging in a sinister secret diplomacy. But in 1919 the nations were not prepared to take more than one step forward. They would not resign their separate sovereignties into the hands of any super-national authority. They would not arm the League with a military force which would enable it to act independently of them. They insisted that in all the greater emergencies it should act only on a unanimous decision of the statesmen composing its Council —a provision which reserved their right to dissent and break away.

These were serious qualifications and reservations, but the League nevertheless gave peace-keeping a new status in the world, and offered the one hope that the nations would not relapse into the system of hostile alliances and competing armaments which had led to the catastrophe. The nations were at least under a solemn covenant not to go to war until after they had submitted their quarrels to the judgment of the League, and they had bound themselves to act together against breakers of the peace. They had also made provision for the periodical meeting of their statesmen to consult together and keep watch over the course of international affairs.

But the League suffered heavy blows soon after its birth. To realize President Wilson's ideals, it should have included

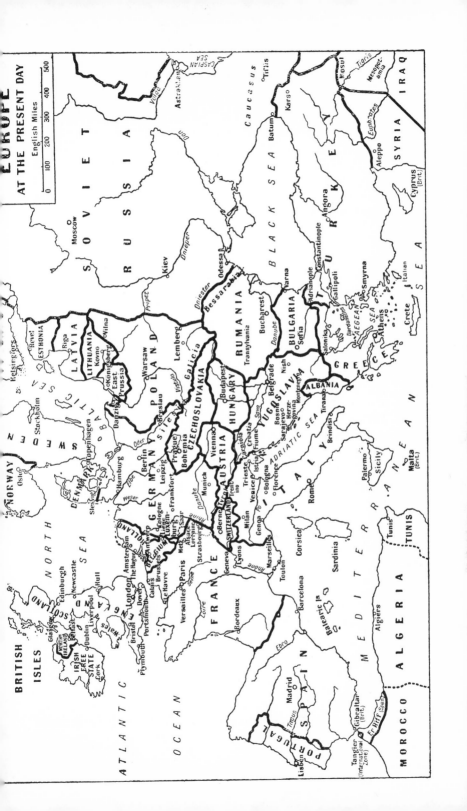

EUROPE
AT THE PRESENT DAY

English Miles

0 100 200 300 400 500

all the nations, but, when consulted, his own people would have nothing to do with it, and refused either to join the League or to ratify the Treaty which inaugurated it, thus, as was said at the time, leaving an American foundling on the European doorstep. It was, moreover, for the time being a League dominated by the victorious nations, some of whom appeared to regard it from the beginning as the special guardian of the Treaty which embodied the conqueror's terms. With the United States outside, with Germany excluded, with Russia in revolution and actually in a state of war with some of the Allies, and with its own members suspiciously on guard less their sovereignty should be invaded, the League as launched in 1919 fell short of the idea of its founders, and has been exposed to much criticism in after days because its action reflected its constitution. It was hoped that the accession of Germany, which took place in 1926, would correct its bias and extend its range, but Herr Hitler's secession clouded that prospect, and it remains still mainly an organ of opinion, dependent on the opinion behind it, and not an executive authority imposing its will on the nations.

Other Changes

Other territorial changes can only be glanced at. Belgium obtained the two Walloon cantons of Eupen and Malmedy; Denmark recovered the northern part of Schleswig; Danzig was made a free port to be administered by the League of Nations. Some of these changes raised great difficulties and created new problems which still need the most careful handling if they are not to be the cause of dangerous quarrels in the future. It was natural that the Poles should seek an outlet to the sea, but the " Polish corridor " which provides the way to Danzig through previous German territory, and creates a Polish belt between East Prussia and the rest of Germany, was bound to be an offence to the Germans, and leaves a grievance for which it is difficult to find the remedy. Austria was left in a parlous plight—a little country with an enormous capital, the relic of a vanished Empire bequeathed to a little and mainly agricultural people.

Many German subjects were passed over to Poland and Lithuania under the treaties, and the southern half of Upper

Silesia—a region predominantly German—was assigned to Poland two years later by the League of Nations after a plebiscite which only doubtfully justified this assignment. The adjustment of boundaries to racial affinities, as contemplated in the Fourteen Points, everywhere proved extremely difficult. Hungary under the Treaty of Trianon lost over 3,000,000 Magyars, of whom half went to Rumania, and the other half were divided between Czechoslovakia and Jugoslavia. With the transfer of Bessarabia a large number of Russian subjects were incorporated in Rumania. There are many other instances, and together they constitute a " minorities problem " of great importance to the peace of Europe.

The Disarmament of Germany

Germany was required to surrender her navy, and when her officers sank it on a prearranged signal on approaching Scapa Flow (June 21, 1919) the result was so welcome that the British Admiralty was (quite untruly) suspected of having connived at this act in order to avoid the inconvenient problem of distributing the ships among the Allies. For her future requirements Germany was limited to six battle-ships of 10,000 tons, and a few light cruisers, destroyers and torpedo-boats, and absolutely forbidden to build or maintain submarines. Her army was limited to 100,000 long-service men; she was required to abolish conscription, to surrender all existing munitions, to dismantle her forts and great guns, and to submit to the " demilitarization " of an area extending 50 kilometres east of the Rhine. She finally lost all her colonies, most of which were assigned as " mandated " territories to Great Britain and the Dominions, and to France, Belgium and Japan. She had also to make large deliveries in kind, merchant ships, coal, cattle, etc., and, as already stated, to compensate for the damage done to French coal-mines by giving France a long lease of the Saar and property in perpetuity in the coal-mines in that region.

Another provision in the Treaty exposed all the property of her private citizens in former enemy countries to be impounded for reparations by the Governments of those countries, leaving these citizens to recover from their own Government if they could. This set a novel and dangerous precedent, which caused great hardship and injustice even though mitigated by allowance for special cases.

The War-Guilt Clause

The clause which most rankled in the minds of the Germans was the famous " War-Guilt " clause which opens the " Reparations chapter." It runs:

> The Allied and Associated Governments affirm and Germany accepts the responsibility of Germany and her Allies for causing all the loss and damage to which the Allied and Associated Governments and their nationals have been subjected as a consequence of the war imposed on them by the aggression of Germany and her Allies.

In this clause not only did the Allied and Associated Governments affirm their own belief that the sole responsibility for the war and all the loss and damage caused by it rested on Germany and her Allies—which at the time might have been excused as an expression of their own opinions—but they required and in the end compelled the Germans to affirm this theory of their own guilt. There are very few in any country who do not regret that this clause ever found a place in the Treaty, and regret it the more because formally expunging it would have the appearance of acquitting the Germans of all responsibility. As it stands it usurps the judgment of history on a long series of complicated events for which no one nation or government can be held solely responsible, and expresses a partisan opinion which gains no additional weight because the enemy was compelled to put his signature to it. There was felt even at the time to be a certain moral cruelty in forcing him to make a formal and valueless confession of guilt at this his darkest hour, and it is now wise to assume that the closing of the " Reparations chapter " of which it was the exordium has automatically removed it from the record. The way will then be clear for the unprejudiced historic judgment.

The last scene was on June 28, 1919, the anniversary of the murders of Serajevo, in the " Hall of Mirrors," where forty-eight years earlier the Germans had celebrated their triumph over the French and the foundation of the new German Empire. With their country blockaded and their army defeated and disorganized, they could now do nothing but sign what their enemy put before them. The chief of their delegates, Count Brockdorff-Rantzau, had made his protest and resigned rather than submit to this ordeal, but this merely passed on the odious necessary task to another. It was a conqueror's peace and nothing remained for the conquered but submission.

THE POST-WAR COALITION

It had been said since the eighteenth century that " England hates Coalitions," but England with the assistance of Scotland and Wales had perpetuated the War Coalition after the war ended, and established it in power with an immense majority. Before its course was run this Government was to develop many of the weaknesses which had given its bad name to that form of government in time of peace. Some of these were its misfortunes rather than its fault. It had been born in the atmosphere of war and was required to deal with the new and extremely difficult questions of the return to peace. In the Cabinet the Liberal and Conservative elements were evenly balanced; in the House of Commons the Conservative majority was preponderant, and consisted largely of men who expected and demanded the impossible. The Prime Minister held a position of great power and influence, but he was mainly occupied with international affairs, and seldom appeared in Parliament. The House of Commons, nevertheless, kept a jealous eye upon his proceedings, and a rumour that he was being too conciliatory to the former enemy at the Peace Conference brought him a peremptory summons from 200 members to return and demonstrate that the imputation was groundless.

The war-time habit of conducting government through little groups of Ministers persisted, and though there was nominally a Cabinet, it seldom met as a whole, and it was difficult to say which members of the Government might be charged with what is commonly called Cabinet responsibility. Foreign affairs were mostly conducted by the group of Allied statesmen who called themselves the " Supreme Council," and met frequently in Paris to administer the Peace treaties and questions of policy arising out of them. This was necessary in the circumstances, but it reduced the British

Parliament for the time being to the position of a spectator of events which for the most part it was unable to control.

No Government in such circumstances could be more than transitional. The demobilization of the enormous army which had to be brought back from France and the other theatres of war taxed the energies of all departments, and was not fully accomplished before 1921. The traditional objection of the British people to compulsory military service reasserted itself strongly as soon as the war was over, and much impatience was expressed at the inevitable delays in the return to civil life. Many rash promises of favours to be bestowed on the returning soldiers had been made at the moment of victory, and disappointment set in when it was discovered that an impoverished country had not the means of fulfilling them. There was a brief interval of prosperity while immediate necessities and shortages were made good, but it was soon followed by the inevitable reaction when the great load of war debt—nearly £8,000,000,000—began to be felt and the crushing taxation which it necessitated produced its effects upon industry. Unemployment set in and rapidly increased as the same causes operated in other countries and were aggravated by the attempts to recover reparations from Germany.

Great fortunes had been made during the war in spite of the efforts of the Government to abate " profiteering " by excess profits taxation, and the contrast between the wealth of those who had stayed at home and made money during the war, and the lot of others who had fought, suffered and returned to poverty and unemployment, became the theme of many orators and led to a demand for a capital levy, which was resisted on the ground that it was impracticable rather than that it was undesirable. The Government made great efforts to reduce expenditure, and appointed a committee, of which Sir Eric Geddes was chairman, to swing the axe on the swollen officialdom which was a legacy from the war, but the pinch of poverty was now being severely felt, and nothing could stay the reaction from the exaggerated mood of December, 1918.

The general unrest found expression in a series of industrial struggles of which the London railway strike in February, 1919, and the coal crisis which followed shortly after it were the most threatening. In the latter, trouble was averted for the time being by the appointment of a Royal Commission, with Mr. Justice Sankey as chairman, which recommended an increase of 2s. a day in wages and the institution of the seven-hour day. A majority of this Commission went on to recommend the nationalization of the mines, and six years later it was one of the chief complaints of the miners that they had returned to work in 1919 in the belief that the Government was pledged to carry out this recommendation, and that it had failed to do so. It was never probable that a Government which was dependent on a Conservative majority in the House of Commons would be in a position to nationalize a great industry. The majority proved strong enough to impose its view on the Goverment on many occasions, and before the Parliament was over it insisted on the repeal of the land taxes instituted in the Budget of 1909, with which the name of the Prime Minister was specially associated.

The Irish Question

The multitude of subjects which required to be dealt with in the first years after the war must have been distracting to any Government, and though the Coalition Government tried heroically to deal with them all, it could seldom concentrate on any. There was an unfinished war in Russia where the Allies were spending immense sums of money in attempts to support the White-Russian counter-revolutionaries against the Bolshevists, and a continuous and dangerous struggle between Turks and Greeks, the latter of whom had imprudently been encouraged by the Allies to invade the Turkish homelands of Asia Minor. There were incessant conferences in London, Paris, Cannes, and Genoa, at which Mr. Lloyd George and his experts fought gallantly, but with scant success, against French opposition to mitigate the economic consequences of the Treaty of Versailles, and to restore the broken roads of international trade between the former belligerents. Nearer home there was the question of Ireland, which after the failure of British parties to come to terms on the basis of a subordinate Parliament in Dublin was entering upon its final stage. The story of that must be taken up from the point at which it was left after the Rebellion of 1916.

In March, 1917, while the war was still on, Mr. Lloyd George made a last endeavour to bring British and Irish parties together by proposing an all-party convention, including Sinn Fein, to draft proposals for a settlement. But the Sinn Feiners refused to come in, and the Ulster Unionists stipulated that their delegates should agree to nothing which had not been submitted to and endorsed by the Ulster Unionist Council. This from the beginning rendered impossible the " substantial agreement " which the Government required as a basis of legislation, and though the conference worked diligently and reported in the following April, it could offer no hope of reconciling the warring factions. The Government now abandoned these efforts at conciliation, and announced their intention of applying compulsory military service to Ireland. This, though never enforced, gave a further impetus to Sinn Fein, and Mr. John Redmond's death on March 6, 1917— following a few months after the death of his brother, Major Willie Redmond, in action in France—was to all intents and purposes the end of the Irish Parliamentary party. Mr. Redmond had done his utmost to restore peace both during and after the Dublin Rebellion, which he boldly denounced as a crime, but he protested strongly against the later developments of Government policy, and one of his last appearances in Parliament was to move a resolution declaring this policy to be contrary to the principles for which the Allies were fighting in Europe.

Sinn Fein and " Black and Tans "

The world peace brought no peace to Ireland, but rather an aggravation of her troubles. Sinn Fein now carried all before it, and chose as its leader and President Mr. Eamon de Valera, one of the ringleaders of the Irish Rebellion, whose daring and adventurous career specially appealed to it. Mr. de Valera had been sentenced to death after the rebellion, had his sentence commuted to imprisonment for life, and obtained his release in the general amnesty of 1917. In the following May he was re-arrested, and eight months later (February, 1919) succeeded in escaping from Lincoln jail and making his way to America, where he raised large sums of money and carried on a powerful propaganda for the Irish Republican cause. At the general election of December, 1918, the Sinn Feiners secured 73 of the 86 seats in Nationalist Ireland, but instead of taking their seats in the Imperial Parliament, these newly elected members constituted themselves an Irish Assembly (Dail Eireann), set up departments for administration and elected Mr. de Valera in his absence President of the Irish Republic. A desperate struggle now set in between the Irish Republicans and the Government, and in the next eighteen months, shootings, burnings, lootings and outrages of all kinds, involving many innocent people, were practised on both sides and in all parts of Ireland, including the Northern counties.

The Government had great provocation, especially in the murders of the twenty-one officers who were shot in cold blood in their lodgings on November 21, 1920, but its policy of " reprisals " practised by the " Black and Tans," an auxiliary force which seemed to pay as little regard to the law as the rebels, shocked the public conscience and gave rise to an increasing volume of protest. Mr. Asquith and Lord Grey, with the great majority of English Liberals behind them, denounced what they called a " competition in crime," and predicted widespread demoralization if the Government permitted the law to be " reduced to the level of the criminal." The Archbishop of Canterbury spoke of " casting out Satan by Beelzebub." The dictators of Europe were to better the example of the " Black and Tans " in subsequent years, but in 1920 Europeans were not habituated to the practice of these methods by their rulers, and expressed horror and disapproval at their adoption by Great Britain. Worst of all, fuel was being provided for an anti-British campaign in America which seriously threatened good relations with the United States.

Mr. Lloyd George, the Prime Minister, protested that he was battling with a murderous conspiracy and using the only weapons at his disposal, but it was clear that if these were the only weapons, the British people, with their ingrained sense of legality, would not long persist in using them. The situation was now highly confused. While pursuing its reprisals the Government had obtained the consent of its Unionist supporters to go forward with the Parliamentary Home Rule which they had rejected when the Irish accepted it, but which all schools of Nationalists now rejected as utterly inadequate. By a queer turn of the wheel the Ulster Unionists who had been life-long and bitter opponents of Parliamentary Home Rule were the first to accept it; and on June 22, 1921, the King visited Belfast to inaugurate the Northern Parliament and made a touching speech pleading for harmony and good-will in all parts of Ireland. The Government now had to make a definite choice between a regular military reconquest of Southern Ireland and coming to terms with the insurgents. The third course of " official reprisals " plainly could not be persisted in against the rising tide of disapproval and protest. Conquest was possible, but it offered no final solution and would pile up odium and cost. Settlement on the other hand was difficult, for when Mr. Asquith had declared Dominion Home Rule to be inevitable, the Government had pronounced it to be " unthinkable," and it was certain that even the moderate Nationalists would accept nothing less.

Dominion Home Rule

Given that the Government was not prepared to undertake reconquest, Dominion Home Rule was in truth inevitable, and negotiations began on that basis in July, 1921, and were continued until December 6, when an Irish Treaty was signed in London, conferring Dominion status on the twenty-six Southern Counties, and confirming the Northern Counties in their decision to remain under Parliamentary Home Rule, as defined in the Act of 1920. There were many anxious moments before this conclusion was reached, the Government requiring military, naval and fiscal reservations in the interests of the Empire, the Irish holding out for the completest in-dependence possible within the Commonwealth of Nations.

In the end Mr. Arthur Griffith, the founder of the Sinn Fein movement, and Mr. Michael Collins, one of the most dashing of the Irish insurgents, played an honourable and conciliatory part in which they were met more than half-way by leading members of the Government who in former days had been prominent in opposing Home Rule. Mr. de Valera, however, proved irreconcilable, and when Dail Eireann accepted the treaty (January 7, 1922) he ceased to be President and was succeeded by Mr. Arthur Griffith ,Mr. Michael Collins becoming head of the Provisional Government appointed to carry out the treaty. On January 22, Mr. Collins took over Dublin Castle and the whole apparatus of internal government for the twenty-six counties, and the Irish Free State came into existence. For the next year the new State was fighting for its life against its own irreconcilables. In August Mr. Arthur Griffith died suddenly, Mr. Michael Collins was shot, and Mr. Cosgrave, until then an almost unknown figure, became Chairman of the Provisional Government. Under his quiet and conciliatory dispensation order was restored, and Ireland enjoyed nearly ten years of prosperous and efficient administration, during which her old feud with Great Britain seemed at length to be healed. Then Mr. de Valera came to life again and a new chapter was opened.

The Washington Conference

On November 12, 1921, the first of many Disarmament Conferences assembled at Washington on the invitation of President Harding, who had been elected as successor to President Wilson at the Presidential election of 1920. Mr. Hughes, the American Secretary of State, was chairman of the conference, and Mr. Balfour, the leading British and M. Briand the leading French, delegates. The principal result, which was quickly arrived at, was an agreement to suspend the construction of battle-ships for a minimum of ten years with the exception of replacements limited to 500,000 tons for Great Britain and the United States, 300,000 tons for Japan and 175,000 tons for France and Italy. This was a most welcome achievement, which averted a new naval competition that might otherwise have followed between Great Britain and the United States.

In other respects the conference was disappointing. The French would not listen to the British proposal to abolish submarines, though they accepted certain limitations on their action in war and as a condition of accepting the limitation on capital ships, they held out for a much larger allowance of auxiliary ships than either British or Americans had contemplated. M. Briand's refusal to entertain any suggestion for the reduction of the French army also rendered the conference abortive so far as land armaments were concerned.

But in one other respect at least the conference was extremely important; it terminated the British-Japanese Alliance and substituted for it a treaty between the United States, Great Britain, France and Japan by which each of these Powers undertook to respect the rights of the others, to have recourse to mediation in case of controversy, and to consult together if they were threatened by other Powers. The conference also discussed at length the affairs of China, and drew up a " Nine-Power Treaty " pledging the signatories to respect the independence and integrity of China, to maintain the principle of equal opportunity for commerce and industry to all nations, and not to seek special rights or privileges. A special agreement between Japan and China provided for the evacuation of Shantung by the former. It must be added that many of these arrangements suffered a severe strain in the conflict between Japan and China in subsequent years.

CHAPTER XXVI

EGYPT AND INDIA

It was not only in Ireland that Nationalist passions and demands were causing trouble in these years. The war was scarcely over when Mr. Lloyd George's Government found itself faced with problems of great difficulty and complexity in more distant parts of the Empire.

When the Peace settlement was concluded, Great Britain had to all appearances greatly extended her power in the East. But the appearance scarcely corresponded with the reality. She had, indeed, obtained the mandates for Palestine and for Iraq (as Mesopotamia was now called), but in both there were heavy liabilities. In Palestine she was pledged by the Balfour declaration made during the war to help the Jews to set up their " national home " in that country, and somehow to reconcile that object with the welfare and contentment of the Arabs who are the great majority of its population. In Iraq she had to restore order and establish a stable government —tasks which, though conscientiously and successfully performed by exceptionally able administrators, were to cost the British taxpayer considerable sums of money. But above all she was faced with new and extremely difficult problems in eastern countries which she already possessed or administered.

Some of these were to develop gradually, but the war was no sooner over than trouble threatened immediately in Egypt. In December, 1914, it had been found necessary to depose the Khedive Abbas Hilmi, who had prolonged a visit to Constantinople after Turkey had declared war, and was necessarily under suspicion of wavering in his loyalty to Great Britain. Since the Turkish Sultan was still nominally suzerain of Egypt, his entry into the war on the side of the Central Powers had the legal effect of converting the Egyptian subjects into " enemy aliens," and it became necessary to take steps to regularize their position. The Turkish suzerainty was accordingly abolished, a British "Protectorate" proclaimed and Prince Husein Kamel, the uncle of Abbas Hilmi, who accepted the succession, given the title of Sultan of Egypt. Husein proved a wise and capable ruler, and he greatly helped to carry the country without serious trouble through the first three years of the war, and to reconcile the Egyptian people to the use made of their country and the requisitions of services and material for war purposes in these years.

Husein died in October, 1917, and was succeeded by Prince Fuad (the sixth son of the famous Ismail), who had been educated in Italy, and had less influence and authority over the Egyptian people. Discontent now began to grow up from various causes—especially the requisitions of their beasts and personal services for the Palestine expedition among the peasantry, and the multiplication of British officials, who were said to be taking the bread out of Egyptian mouths. By this time the whole East was in a ferment, and President Wilson's loud affirmation of the principle of self-determination combined with the announcement of the Allies that their purpose was to enfranchise the oppressed subjects of the Turks in Syria, Mesopotamia and Arabia gave a strong stimulus to the agitation of Egyptian Nationalists, who more and more demanded that they too should share in the general emancipation.

In proclaiming the " Protectorate," the British Government had promised that the whole question of the future status of the country should be reconsidered when the war was over. Unfortunately when that time came, British Ministers had a great many other things to do, and they not only refused to receive the Nationalist leader, Zaghlul, and rejected his programme of " complete independence," but begged the two Ministers, Adly and Rushdy, who had proposed to come to London to lay their more moderate views before the Government, to defer their visit to a more convenient season. The Ministers thereupon resigned, and a dangerous Nationalist agitation followed in the course of which Zaghlul was arrested and deported to Malta. Disturbances then broke out in all parts of the country; British soldiers and civilians were attacked at Tanta and in the Delta provinces; foreigners were blockaded in Upper Egypt, and a British Inspector of Prisons and two officers and five other ranks were murdered by a fanatical mob at Dairut station. Railway lines were torn up, telegraph wires cut, and for a few days Cairo was isolated. Lord Allenby, the Commander-in-Chief, had been on his way to Europe when the trouble broke out, but he was directed to return at once and take up the duties of Acting High Commissioner. Before the end of March he had restored order over the greater part of the country, but it still remained in a ferment of unrest, and the Nationalists persisted in their demands.

The Milner Mission

Lord Allenby had been wisely moderate in the measures that he took, both to suppress the rebellion and punish the ring-leaders, and he advised a policy of conciliation. The Government thereupon decided to send out a special Mission under Lord Milner, who was then Colonial Secretary, and earlier in his career had acted as Financial Adviser to the Government of Egypt. The object of this Mission was to redeem the promise given during the war to review the whole question of the future government of the country when peace was restored. Unfortunately, there was further delay, and the Mission, though appointed in April, did not reach Cairo before November. In the interval Nationalist agitation had again boiled up and Zaghlul decreed that the Mission should be strictly boycotted by all members of his party.

The Mission, nevertheless, persisted, and though it was the subject of many hostile and some dangerous demonstrations, it explored all departments of the Government, and obtained the views of many moderate and even of some extreme Nation-alists. Its general conclusion was that the Nationalist movement was genuine and widespread, that there was no chance of per-suading Egyptians generally to accept the status of a " Pro-tectorate," and that it would be wise and right to give them the long-promised opportunity of managing their own affairs with due safeguards for essential British interests. On its return to England, it established communications with Zaghlul, who was now willing to come to London with a delegation and confer with the Mission. An agreed settlement was all but arrived at and the Mission presented its report to the Govern-ment which laid it before Parliament on December 20, 1920.

This report proposed that a treaty should be concluded between Great Britain and Egypt in which the former recognized the independence of Egypt and the latter accepted certain reservations such as the maintenance in the country of a British force to guard the Suez Canal and imperial communications, the control of foreign policy by Great Britain, the appointment of financial and judicial advisers, the British guardianship of foreign interests and right to intervene if legislation should operate unfairly against foreigners.

Egyptian Independence

The Mission had hoped that Lord Milner would be commissioned by the Government to return to Egypt to negotiate such a treaty in the following year. But the Government had not appreciated the profound changes which had taken place in the East during and since the war, and could not make up its mind to concede as much as the report proposed. On the other side the extreme Nationalists demanded more than the report, and while the Government delayed, renewed their agitation in Egypt. In the summer of 1921 the Egyptian Prime Minister, Adly Pasha, came to London with two of his colleagues, Rushdy Pasha and Sidky Pasha, and endeavoured to negotiate directly with the Government, but their effort proved abortive, and they returned in the winter empty-handed. This further inflamed Nationalist feeling, and agitation again rose to the boiling-point. Disturbances which took place in Cairo were firmly suppressed, but the High Commissioner, with the support of British officials in Egypt, now applied strong pressure to the Government to adopt a conciliatory policy. This view prevailed, and on February 28, 1922, a declaration was sent to the Sultan recognizing Egypt as a " Sovereign Independent State," subject to four reservations: (a) the security of the communications of the British Empire in Egypt; (b) the defence of Egypt against foreign aggression; (c) the protection of foreign residents and other minorities in Egypt; and (d) the Sudan.

This was not a satisfactory solution. A treaty would have bound the Egyptians to accept the reservations; the proclamation left them free to say that they had not been consulted and were not bound by the conditions which Great Britain imposed.

The moderates were in favour of accepting what they could get and making the best of it, but the extremists continued their protest and now put up the forefront of their demands—the "restoration" of the Sudan—a subject on which their leaders had accepted without demur the intimation of the Milner Mission that no change would be proposed. Many months of confused politics followed, culminating in the cruel murder of Sir Lee Stack, the Governor-General of the Sudan, while on a visit to Cairo (November 19, 1924). Parliamentary government was now suspended, and for the next few years the country was governed by virtual dictators, while the British Government kept guard. Various efforts were made during this period to restore Parliamentary government and conclude the desired treaty with the British Government, and one, when Mr. Henderson was Foreign Minister, came within an inch of success, and was only defeated at the last moment by failure to reach agreement on the Sudan. In later years Egypt has been governed internally by the King and Egyptian Ministers who have succeeded in suppressing the Nationalist or Wafdist Opposition, though that Opposition still claims to represent the great majority of the Egyptian people.

India

Nowhere in the East did the war cause deeper and more lasting unrest than in the great British dependency of India.

Before the war a cautious step towards associating Indians with the government of India had been taken in the reforms which Lord Morley and Lord Minto, the one as Secretary of State and the other as Viceroy, were joint authors. These provided for an electoral element in the Indian legislatures, and for the appointment of Indians to the Executive in Calcutta and to the India Council in London. They were admittedly only a beginning, and even before the war hopes had been held out that they would be extended, if justified by experience.

During the war India made what was universally acknowledged to be a magnificent contribution to the British and Allied cause. She raised and sent oversea 800,000 combatants, made a free gift of £100,000,000 to the Home Government towards the cost of the war and added £153,000,000 to her own debt. The ruling princes also had been lavish in their gifts and in their professions of loyalty. In acknowledgment of this display of loyalty and goodwill the Imperial Government greatly enlarged its promise to extend self-government in India.

On August 20, 1917, Mr. E. S. Montagu, who was now Secretary for India, announced in the House of Commons that " the policy of His Majesty's Government is that of increasing the association of Indians in every branch of the administration and the gradual development of self-governing institutions with a view to the progressive realization of responsible government in India as an integral part of the British Empire." The promise was no doubt qualified by the word " gradual," and Mr. Montagu had been careful to add that it must be realized in " successive stages," and that " the British Government and the Government of India must be the judges of the time and measure of each advance," but the phrase " responsible government in India as an integral part of the British Empire " was taken to mean Dominion Home Rule and this became from that time onwards the goal of even moderate Indian Nationalists.

Amritsar

Reaction followed swiftly in India, as elsewhere, when the war was over. The extreme Nationalists started a violent campaign; the Government replied by introducing the " Rowlatt Bill," which gave it special powers for dealing with seditious crime. Mr. Gandhi, chiefl᾿ known till then as a much revered social and religiou͜ ᾿eforiner, retaliated with a passive resistance movement, and violent disturbances broke out in the Punjab. On April 13, 1919, occurred the " tragedy of Amritsar "—tragedy on any interpretation of it—when General Dyer, being called upon by the civil authorities to restore order, gave an order to fire on an unlawful assembly in the Jalianwala Bagh of that city, with the result that 400 persons were killed and nearly 1000 more wounded. Certain incidents which attended this act of repression—the unfortunate delay in attending to the wounded and the issue of an order directing Indians to " crawl " past the spot—added to the anger and excitement which the news of it caused in all parts of India. The Government of India appointed a Committee of Inquiry (the Hunter Committee) which condemned General Dyer, and it was decided that he should receive no further employment in India.

But by this time the controversy had spread to England and though the House of Commons by a large majority endorsed this action, the House of Lords passed a resolution deploring the treatment of General Dyer as unjust and " dangerous to the preservation of order in the face of rebellion," and a Conservative newspaper raised a large sum of money as a testimonial to him. Further fuel was added to these flames by the observation of a judge in the course of a libel action which raised a different issue that " the time and method of General Dyer's punishment, if he were wrong, were most unfortunate."

Diarchy

This was a bad atmosphere for the initiation of the constitutional changes now proposed. Amritsar continued for years to haunt the minds of both Indians and British, and did more than anything else to range British parties between conciliation and coercion, " die-hardism " and Liberal reforms. In July, 1919, after examination by a joint Select Committee of both Houses, Parliament accepted the Montagu-Chelmsford scheme setting up the system which came to be known as " diarchy " in the Provincial Councils of India, and providing for Indian elected members in the Central Assembly. Under this system certain subjects, such as law and order, justice, police, land and finance were reserved to the Governor and his officials on the Provincial Councils, and other subjects, such as education, excise, public health, etc., were " transferred " to Indian Ministers responsible for the Indian electorate. It was accepted as an instalment by Indian Nationalists, who made no secret of their intention to agitate for more at the end of the ten-year period expiring in 1929, when, as provided by Parliament, the scheme would come up for revision. In a few provinces in which the Governors practically wiped out the distinction between Indian Ministers and officials and brought both into consultation on equal terms, it worked well, but in many others friction between the two developed from the beginning, the Indian Ministers complaining that they were blocked by the official members and denied the money necessary to carry out their policies.

The division of responsibility thus tended more and more to

foster irresponsibility among the elected members, who proposed measures which they knew would be vetoed, but which served the purposes of agitation; and in the meantime the year 1929 became marked in the Indian calendar as a year of destiny —the year upon which effort and agitation should be concentrated. One of the main weaknesses of the Montagu-Chelmsford scheme was in fact that it was thus marked provisional, and that all India treated it as such, and began preparing for the next move as soon as it was instituted. This prevented any gradual adaptation to circumstances in the light of experience and doomed India to advance by jumps after periods of agitation.

Gandhi's Agitation

In spite of its defects the Montagu-Chelmsford scheme helped to carry India through a difficult period of religious and political unrest. The anti-Turkish policy of the Imperial Government had given great offence to Indian Mohammedans, which was not allayed when the Secretary for India, Mr. Montagu, was compelled to resign his office for having, without the consent of the Cabinet, published a dispatch from Lord Reading in which the Government was urged to soften the terms imposed on the Turks in the Treaty of Sèvres (March, 1922). The "Khalifate" movement, in sympathy with the Sultan in his supposed capacity of "Khalif" or spiritual head of the Mohammedan peoples, grew to considerable proportions in the three years after the war, and was adroitly used by Mr. Gandhi to join up Mohammedans with his Hindus in his "civil disobedience" campaign. But Indian Moslem sympathy cooled rapidly when the Turkish Ghazi, Mustafa Kemal, threw off the Khalifate, and the Government of India soon found itself more embarrassed by the renewal of quarrels between Hindu and Mohammedan than by their combined opposition.

In the meantime Mr. Gandhi's disturbing personality caused nearly as much confusion among Indian Nationalists as perplexity to the Government. In March, 1922, he had courted arrest and imprisonment and, in his absence, a large section of his party broke away from his policy of boycotting the Assembly and Councils, and constituted themselves a regular opposition in the Assembly, using it as a platform for their agitation and showing considerable skill in the use of parliamentary forms. Lord Reading's viceroyalty (1921–26) was occupied in dealing with these phases, and he so handled them that it passed without the serious trouble that had been expected at the beginning of this period. He had shown conciliation whenever possible, but had dealt firmly with the murderous conspiracies which then, as later, defaced Indian politics. In 1929 the Simon Commission went out to India and after two visits presented the monumental report which provided the material for the Round-Table Conference and the Joint-Committee of Parliament appointed to deal with the question of Indian reform.

Such is the background against which the modern problem of Indian government has to be considered. The profound changes which have come over the East since the war are not easily realized by those whose experience belongs to the previous years, but in general it may be said that the spectacle of Europe in convulsions had largely shattered the faith of Eastern man in the virtues of Western civilization, and that the wide advertisement given to the idea of self-determination as one of the objects of the war had caught his imagination. That they were as good as Europeans and as much entitled as Europeans to govern themselves became now the creed of multitudes in the East. In India, Gandhi succeeded by his religious and emotional appeals in spreading politics from the small literate class to the masses of villagers, and the Amritsar tragedy played powerfully into his hands in that effort. But he had promising material to work upon, for, when the war ended, the old spirit of submission to patriarchal government by efficient rulers from the West was rapidly waning and giving place to a widespread discontent with alien rule.

India, like Ireland and Egypt, raises the question of conciliation or coercion, but in an exceptionally difficult form. India is not one race or one nation, but many races and many nations, and so far as she has unity, that unity has been imposed upon her during the chief part of her history by alien rulers. How she can remain united and be protected from foreign invaders without British rule is a question which is as yet without an answer, and how that rule can be made tolerable to the Indian people and not too burdensome to the British is a question which it is very difficult to answer. Suppression is costly and odious, and, though modern weapons make it easier than formerly as an immediate policy, it is not likely to be persisted in for any length of time by the British people. In the long-run the Government of the 350 millions of the people of India requires Indian co-operation. The few thousand British administrators would be powerless to govern these millions if they were unable to recruit soldiers, police and the immense majority of officials from the Indian people. That is everywhere the limit of Western man's rule in the East, and all wise policy has to bear it in mind.

WAR AND REVOLUTION

THE story as it develops in these years takes us all over the world, and though each part must be told separately, it is important to remember once more that all were proceeding simultaneously and contributing to the aggregate with which statesmen had to deal. In this aggregate nothing was more important than what was happening to Russia, one of the original members of the victorious Alliance, and the great absentee in the final scene at Versailles.

To be clear about that, we must go back to the point reached in a previous chapter when she was thrown out of the war by exhaustion and revolution. Lenin, as already recorded, came to power in October, 1917, not, as is often alleged, by overthrowing the Tsardom, but by displacing the Liberal, if *bourgeois*, Administration of Kerensky, which had superseded the Tsardom. Having obtained power, he proceeded at once to decree the full Communist policy of nationalizing the banks and the land, placing the workers in control of the factories, depriving the non-working class of political rights, arming the working and disarming the "possessing classes," disestablishing the Church and secularizing the schools. To make peace themselves and to call on the workers of the other countries to compel their Governments to make peace was the next step of the new Soviet Government. In their own case they reckoned without the Germans, who compelled them after helpless protest to accept the humiliating peace of Brest-Litovsk, which deprived them of the Ukraine and the Baltic Provinces and left Petrograd, or Leningrad, as it was now called, at the mercy of invaders (March 3, 1918). The Soviet Government now moved to Moscow and passed wholly into the hands of the Bolshevists, the small but compact party of Communists which professed the complete Marxian doctrine. For defence against its enemies it created the "O.G.P.U." or

" extraordinary Commission " to suppress disturbances, and organized a body of " Red Guards " out of the remnant of the army. In the meantime the dispossessed classes were streaming out of the country, some joining the Germans, others appealing to the Allies to help them to overthrow the Bolshevists and recover their property.

The Allies for the time being had their hands full, but a body of Czechoslovakian prisoners in Russia, which was being organized to fight against the Germans when the revolution broke out, advanced westward under French instructions and took Samara (June 8, 1918). At the same time the Germans advanced eastward through the Ukraine. The position was now highly confused, and the Bolshevists saw themselves being hemmed in and cut off from a large part of Russia and their principal sources of supply. Fierce internal struggles were still going on between different schools of revolutionaries, and at the beginning of July the German Ambassador, Mirbach, was assassinated in Moscow. By this time " White " Russians had joined hands with the Czechoslovakians, and the two together were reported to be advancing on Ekaterinburg where the Tsar and his family had been interned after the Bolshevists seized power. On the plea or pretext that they would otherwise fall into the hands of the enemy the local Soviet cruelly murdered the whole family on the night of July 16 in the basement of the house in which they were held prisoners, and their action was approved by the Central Executive Committee in Moscow. A fortnight later the Czechs took Ekaterinburg, and another Allied force occupied Archangel and began to advance south.

Intervention and Its Results

History was now repeating itself, and foreign intervention was to have the same effect on revolutionary Russia as on revolutionary France a hundred and thirty years earlier. It inflamed passion, led to savage reprisals, rallied to the revolutionaries large numbers who till then had been hostile or neutral. On August 30, in Moscow, a woman shot at and badly wounded Lenin, who for some days lay between life and death. On the same day a prominent Communist leader was killed in Leningrad. From this moment the terror was unloosed, and in Leningrad alone 500 were executed as a reprisal.

How many were shot, hanged or died of frost and starvation in the wilds of Russia can never be exactly ascertained. The O.G.P.U. alone numbered its victims by the thousand and ten thousand, and an immense number perished without trace at the hands of self-appointed executioners.

By the end of 1918 the Allies had their hands free, and had taken the place of the Germans in the occupied parts of Russia. Expeditions were now being organized by Russian counter-revolutionaries, who were convinced that with a very little help in men and money they could overthrow the Bolshevists. In the south was Denikin, in the east Admiral Kolchak, and within striking distance and, at one time even in sight, of Petrograd, Yudenitch. All had with them a stiffening of Allied troops and military advisers, and an unlimited supply of money and munitions. But with them also were large numbers of " White " Russians panting for vengeance, whose proceedings, as they advanced, led the Russian peasants to believe that as little mercy was to be expected by the proletariat from the counter-revolution as by the possessing classes from the revolution. Between the two terrors they preferred the Red, and the interventionists found their armies melting away, and their position, which on all military grounds ought to have been a strong one, becoming more and more precarious against the hostility of the people they had come to save. By this time public opinion everywhere was setting against the prolongation of any sort of war, and loud protests were raised against the pouring out of money for the support of counter-revolutionary adventurers whose claim to be saving their country was so evidently rejected by the people most concerned. In most countries the workers, who at first had shared the common horror at Bolshevist atrocities, had come to interpret these proceedings as reflecting a general hostility of Capital to Labour, and this was for many years to come to make sympathy with the Soviets a test of fidelity to the Labour cause. By the spring of 1920 the struggle was over, the Allies withdrawing from what had proved an impolitic and unprofitable enterprise, and the " White " Russians taking refuge in other European countries.

The Polish-Russian War

The French were not content with this result. They still dreamed of re-establishing a Russia which would give them the same support as they had had from the old regime before the war, and with their backing and assistance the Poles now pushed forward, and on May 8, 1920, took Kiev. This was but a brief success. The Russians rallied, drove them back and were soon at the gates of Warsaw. The French, thereupon, came to the assistance of the Poles, providing them with officers and munitions, and in their turn the Russians were driven back, but once more rallied and fought their enemies. The Peace of Riga in October ended this aimless campaign, and the Soviet, having at the same time made peace with Latvia, Esthonia and Lithuania and reoccupied the Crimea, turned now to face the desperate economic confusion and state of famine which were the cumulative results of war, revolution, years of drought, and hasty attempts to enforce their Communist theories. In destroying the " Capitalist system " they had destroyed most of its values and were now to discover that there was very little which could be transferred from the rich to the poor. For good or ill the new Communist society had to be built anew from the foundations.

It is pleasant to be able to record that the sufferings of Russia in these years struck a chord of sympathy and pity in the hearts even of those who detested Bolshevism. Assistance was organized for the starving districts by the American Relief Administration under Mr. Hoover, which secured a grant from the U.S. Government, by Nansen and his Relief Committee and numerous charitable agencies. There was at this time an opportunity of peaceful economic arrangements being made between Soviet Russia, which stood in desperate need of imported manufactures and credit, and foreign countries which might have profited by supplying both. But the Russians believed Communism to be good not only for themselves but for other people, and their loud advertisement of their desire for a world revolution and their undisguised efforts to stir up strife in neighbouring countries as a means to that end chilled and frightened the commercial world, which saw its own cherished institutions seriously threatened if the

Russians were helped to make a success of their revolutionary experiment. At the same time the anti-religious campaign which the Bolshevists were now deliberately pursuing as part of their educational system alienated a vast number more, who viewed their proceedings with the same horror that their forefathers had felt at the enthronement of the goddess of Reason after the French Revolution. These emotions were not favourable to any judicious estimate of the causes which had led to the Russian upheaval, or to any wise and cool way of dealing with it. More and more in these months the gulf was widening between Soviet Russia and Western Europe.

Germany After the War

Events in Germany during this period were no less important for the future of Europe. The end of the war left the country in a chaotic and dangerous condition, and when the Kaiser abdicated on November 9, 1918, Prince Max of Baden, the last of the Chancellors under the Imperial regime, handed over the reins to Ebert, the leader of the moderate Socialists, and retired. The separate States now began to proclaim the Republic, and to form more or less revolutionary Governments. In Berlin the Socialists under Ebert had to defend themselves against the Communists—the so-called Spartacists —who were working for a Soviet dictatorship. An armed rebellion of the latter was forcibly repressed, and their leaders, Liebknecht and Rosa Luxemburg, were arrested and killed by their guards. The insistence of the Allies in maintaining their blockade until the peace was signed aggravated these troubles, and prolonged the sufferings of the German people. On January 19, 1919, a Constitutional Assembly was elected, and, sitting at Weimar, formulated the new Constitution which was proclaimed on August 11, 1919.

In the meantime there had been serious trouble in many of the States, especially Bavaria, where the Minister President, Kurt Eisner, was murdered by a Nationalist officer, and a Soviet Republic established itself in the struggle which followed, and had a brief reign. The necessity of signing the Treaty of Versailles shook the Government to its foundations, and the majority of Socialists and Centre party, who courageously undertook that responsibility, were subject to fierce attacks and personal assaults by Nationalists, alleging that they played a traitor's part. Erzberger, the leader of the Centre party, was assassinated in 1921, and Rathenau, the famous industrialist and philosophic writer, who had joined the Cabinet as Foreign Secretary, suffered the same fate in the following year. No two men had done Germany greater service in her blackest hour.

Trouble continued all through the early months of 1920. In January came the "Kapp Putsch," in which the afterwards famous Herr Hitler took part, an effort of the Monarchists under the officers of the old army, to upset the newly established Republic. It was easily suppressed, but it angered the workers, who retaliated with strikes and violent movements, which in their turn had to be suppressed. By June order was sufficiently restored to enable the elections for the first Reichstag to be held, and after it the moderate parties held together sufficiently to enable government to be carried on, first under Herr Fehrenbach and then under Herr Wirth, against the opposition of the extreme right and extreme left. But the difficulties were enormous, and the situation was greatly complicated by the occupation of the Rhineland and the demands of the Allies for Reparations. All these troubles came to their climax in the French occupation of the Ruhr in January, 1923, and the catastrophic fall of the mark which followed it. Three men chiefly—Marx, Stresemann and Luther—carried Germany through this dangerous period, and in March, 1925, Stresemann's policy of coming to terms with France and joining the League of Nations gave her a breathing-space, and ensured some years of relative quiet under Stresemann and Brüning. But the extreme parties were not appeased, and they continued their warfare below the surface until it was ready to break out in a new form. The failure of the Allies to disarm, while they insisted on the disarmament of Germany, combined with their efforts to force payment of Reparations, the wounds to German pride inflicted by the employment of black troops by the French and other incidents in the occupied territory, created a fund of ill-will and resentment which was to bear fruit later.

CHAPTER XXVIII

THE FALL OF THE COALITION

WE must now return to Great Britain where the accumulation of problems, home and foreign, and the differences of opinion to which they gave rise were placing a heavy strain on the Coalition Government. In the end the fate of that Government was largely bound up with what was happening between Greeks and Turks in Asia Minor and the Near East.

The Allied delegates in Paris had been too much occupied with other matters to settle the affairs of Turkey in the year 1919, and in order to tide over the time and perhaps also to block the secret Italian ambition to a portion of Asia Minor, they invited the Greeks to occupy Smyrna, and covered their landing with an Allied force. (May 15, 1919.) This, it was supposed, would keep the Turks in check both in Asia Minor and in Eastern Thrace, where there were no Allied forces available, until the terms of peace could be finally settled.

The Greek landing had unfortunately the very opposite effect. It was accompanied by atrocities for which the Allies were held responsible, and was followed by a great revival of Turkish nationalism under the leadership of Mustafa Kemal, who appealed to his countrymen to stand together against any encroachment upon their " homelands," and procured the election of a Chamber pledged to that purpose. The Allies then occupied Constantinople, deported a certain number of prominent Nationalists to Malta, and prompted the Sultan to denounce the Nationalist movement; whereupon Mustafa Kemal retired to Asia Minor and set up an independent Nationalist Government at Angora. The next move of the Allies was to draw up the Treaty of Sèvres which, while recognizing Turkish sovereignty in Asia Minor, arranged for Greek, French and Italian "spheres of interest" in that region, and gave Eastern Thrace, including the Gallipoli Peninsula, to Greece—all of them provisions which the Turkish Nationalists were by this time sworn to resist. The military situation was now becoming dangerous, for the new Turkish forces threatened the isolated Allied detachments in the neighbourhood of Constantinople —the French in Cilicia, the British at Ismid, etc. Once more the Allies looked to Greece and accepted a proposal by M. Venizelos to open a Greek offensive.

Greeks and Turks

This had at first some success (June and July, 1920), and for a few weeks the Greeks appeared to be in secure possession of Eastern Thrace and a considerable slice of Anatolia. But Kemal was rallying his forces and biding his time. He was also working in concert with the Bolshevists, who had expelled General Wrangel from the Crimea and were prepared to help any movement against the Allies. The latter by this time were beginning to repent of their backing of the Greeks, and were soon at sixes and sevens among themselves. Venizelos, their friend, had been thrown from power at the Greek elections in November, 1920; King Constantine, whom they regarded with suspicion, had been recalled. The French had no mind for a new campaign against the Turks, and though the British Government seemed still inclined to back the Greeks, the British public were as reluctant as the French to engage in a new war in the East.

An effort was made to build a bridge towards the Nationalists at a conference held in London in February and March, 1921, but Kemal, who had not been consulted, rejected its proposals and now set himself seriously to drive the Greeks out of Asia Minor. Within a few weeks their debacle was complete, and the Turks demanded the immediate evacuation of Asia Minor. In proportion as the Turks advanced, the Allies retired, and on August 10 " the Supreme Council " proclaimed the neutrality of the Allied Governments in what they now described as a " private war " between Greeks and Turks, though reserving several zones on either side of the Bosphorus and Dardanelles upon which the belligerents were warned that they must not enter. A little later, a French emissary, M. Franklin Bouillon, went to Angora, and concluded a separate treaty between France and the Turkish Nationalists. The Greeks, left to themselves, fell into confusion. King

Constantine, who had gone to Smyrna to lead the Greek forces and had hoped to be crowned Emperor in Constantinople, left the country and died a few months later in Sicily. Eight of his Ministers were tried by court martial and shot. M. Venizelos fortunately survived these events, and saved what he could out of the wreck when peace was made with the Turks in the Treaty of Lausanne in July, 1923.

The Chanak Crisis

In the meantime the Greek disaster and their own dissensions left the Allies in an extremely embarrassed position. Thinking themselves secure in Constantinople, they had rejected a proposal from the Turkish Nationalists for the neutralization of the Straits under the control of the League of Nations, and now were in a position in which they could only secure this desirable result by coercing the Turks. Mr. Lloyd George, who had been prominent in encouraging the Greeks, felt himself honourably bound to face this necessity. On September 16, 1922, he issued a manifesto to the press, declaring it to be the opinion of the British Government that it would be a calamity of the first order, threatening all that had been won in the war politically and economically in the Near East, to permit the Turks to encroach upon the neutral zones and dominate the Bosphorus and Dardanelles, and announcing that the British Dominions, Jugoslavia and Rumania had been asked to provide troops if the use of force became necessary for maintaining the freedom of the Straits. This incensed the Turks, who immediately made preparations to attack the Allied detachments at Chanak on the Asiatic side of the Straits, and angered the French and Italian Governments, which ordered the immediate withdrawal of their troops, thus leaving the British to face a superior Turkish force single-handed.

Only the skilful diplomacy of General Harington, the British Commander-in-Chief of the Allied forces in the Constantinople area, kept the peace, while the Allies considered what to do next. After a hurried consultation between Lord Curzon and M. Poincaré, they decided to invite the Turks to a Peace Conference on the basis of recognizing Turkish sovereignty not only in Asia Minor, but in Thrace up to the River Maritza. An armistice was signed on these terms and accepted by the Greeks on October 14. The Angora Government was now in full control, and its next step was to depose the Sultan and make an end of the old regime and the historic Ottoman Empire.

By the Treaty of Lausanne in the following year (1923) the Turks obtained practically the whole of their demands, including the recovery of Smyrna, Constantinople and Eastern Thrace. Their capital was now permanently Angora— in the " homelands " of Anatolia and a full day's journey from the sea—where they hoped to be free from the pressure which the European Governments had applied to the old regime from the Bosphorus and the Sea of Marmora. In regard to the Straits, it was agreed (on paper) that there should be " demilitarized zones " on either shore, and the Allies undertook to resist by force any violation of the freedom of navigation and any threat to the security of the zones, the Turks in return allowing a limited right of passage to warships. The " Commission of the Straits " set up in the Treaty of Sèvres was maintained as a Conservancy Board, but with diminished powers and under Turkish Presidency. It was a sign for the future that the Soviet Government did its utmost to prevent agreement even on these lines, and entered a formal protest against this part of the Lausanne Convention. The eternal question of the Straits evidently was not settled, and Trotsky, the Bolshevist, said as vehemently as in former days did Isvolsky the Tsarist, " We need Constantinople and the Straits."

The Chanak crisis was the final blow to Mr. Lloyd George's Government. Discontents had been accumulating for many months. The " die-hard " section of the Tory party were in smothered rebellion against what they described as the " Irish surrender "; taxpayers were groaning at the scale of expenditure and the continuance in peace of costly departments set up for war purposes; scandal had been caused by the indiscriminate distribution of honours, and the money transactions which accompanied it. Above all, there seemed to be chaos in policy; experiments first in one direction and then in another, according as the opinions of one group or another prevailed in the governing circle, had apparently taken the place of consistency and continuity. In foreign affairs the

Prime Minister's secretariat and the Foreign Office seemed to be working on the same ground, sometimes with conflicting ideas, and seldom in contact with one another. The Turkish affair brought all these discontents to the surface, and led to anxious questions about the impetuous handling which had landed the country in so mortifying a position, and left it to face a seemingly imminent war in isolation from its Allies. In a very short time it was evident that the Prime Minister's call to arms would meet with but a feeble response. The Dominions held back; the great mass of the home public were indisposed to enter upon a new war for any cause, and not a few sympathized with the Turks in rallying to the defence of their " homelands " against the Greek invasion.

The Conservative Revolt

A sigh of relief went up when the crisis passed, but by this time the majority of its Conservative supporters had made up their minds to bring the Coalition to an end, and proceeded to give effect to their views at a party meeting held under Mr. Austen Chamberlain's chairmanship at the Carlton Club on October 19, 1922. Very important members of the party, including Mr. Chamberlain and Mr. Balfour, were for going on and appealing to the country, when the time came, as a Coalition under Mr. Lloyd George's leadership. But by a majority of 187 to 87 the rank and file rejected this proposal, and decided on an immediate rupture with Mr. Lloyd George and the Liberal wing of the Coalition. In this they were mainly influenced by Mr. Bonar Law, who had retired on account of ill-health in March of the previous year, but returned for this occasion, and by Mr. Stanley Baldwin, President of the Board of Trade, who had only lately become a Cabinet Minister. Mr. Baldwin directly arraigned the Prime Minister, and declared his belief that if " the present association with him were prolonged," the disintegrating process in the Tory party which was already far advanced would " go on inevitably until the old Conservative party was smashed to atoms and lost in ruins." He was prepared, he said, to go into the wilderness rather than continue the connexion.

This speech sealed the fate of the Coalition. Mr. Lloyd George resigned, taking with him for the time being Mr.

Austen Chamberlain, Mr. Balfour and Lord Birkenhead, and Mr. Bonar Law became Prime Minister, the first Conservative to hold that post for sixteen years. Mr. Baldwin became Chancellor of the Exchequer, and Lord Curzon remained Foreign Secretary. Parliament was dissolved early in November, and at the general election which followed the Conservative party obtained a majority of 72 over all other parties. Labour came back 144 strong, the anti-Coalition Liberals 60, and the Coalition Liberals 55. Electioneering was greatly confused. The Conservative leaders were attacking a Government of which they had been members until a few weeks previously, and for a greater part of whose proceedings they were directly responsible. Independent Liberals were attacking the same Government from a different angle; Labour was attacking both Liberals and Conservatives; Mr. Lloyd George was defending his Administration against all three. Between these parties the only thing certain was that the electors were determined to make an end of the Coalition, and in the confusion of the other parties, they chose the Conservatives as the only available alternative. But it was a somewhat ironical result which enabled the Conservative party to reap the fruit of the reaction from a Government which they had been chiefly instrumental in forming, and of which up to the last moment its leaders had been the chief supporters.

POST-WAR PROBLEMS

THE story of Mr. Bonar Law's short Administration is largely that of difficulties and entanglements arising out of the attempt to make Germany pay reparations. Having failed to agree about the amount to be demanded, the Allies had left an enormous unknown liability hanging over Germany when the Peace Conference ended. Within a few months it became evident that the immense sums which most of them had in mind could by no possible means be recovered, and at conferences held in Paris and London at the end of 1920 and beginning of 1921 the amount was fixed at £6,000,000,000, a sum which, though compared with previous expectations looked moderate, was still vastly in excess of the German capacity to pay.

Reparations and the Ruhr

In the following year (1922) the Germans paid the first instalment of a milliard gold marks (about £50,000,000) mainly with borrowed money, but in December they announced that the utmost they would be able to pay in the following April was 200 million gold marks (£20,000,000). The Allies now granted short moratoriums, but after the failure of an inter-Allied conference in Paris at the beginning of January, 1923, the French parted company with the British, and began to threaten the seizure of what were called " productive guarantees," *i.e.* to occupy territory containing great industries which it was supposed could be worked for their benefit. Mr. Bonar Law's Government resisted this, deeming it futile as a means of recovering debts and likely to be disastrous in its political consequences, but M. Poincaré, the French Prime Minister, insisted, and on January 11 French and Belgian troops marched into the great industrial district of the Ruhr. The result was what Mr. Bonar Law had predicted. The inhabitants of the Ruhr set up a passive resistance which not only rendered the profitable working of the industries for the benefit of the Allies impossible, but made the occupation expensive and even dangerous to the invaders. In the meantime, the German Government, having now to support the population of the Ruhr instead of drawing a handsome revenue from it, was driven to inflation—an expedient welcomed by a good many Germans as a way of escaping reparations. After five months of the occupation the mark had become valueless, and Germany was evidently bankrupt. Within a comparatively short time financial disorder followed in France, and the franc fell to a tenth of its par level.

A temporary way out, enabling M. Herriot, who succeeded M. Poincaré as French Prime Minister in May, 1924, to evacuate the Ruhr, was found by the Dawes Committee (under the presidency of the American, General Dawes), which suggested new ways of payment on a lower scale. These were revised a little later by another committee under another American president, Mr. Owen D. Young, which proposed a still lower scale. The demands of the Allies had now been brought down to about 2000 millions and the corresponding annuities and sinking-funds. But all these proposals came up against fatal obstacles on the question of transfer. The money might be raised in Germany—it was plausibly argued that the Germans were asked to pay no more than the Allies were raising to finance their war-loans—but " money " could only be transferred in the form of goods, gold and services ; and the Allies were all the time raising their tariffs against German goods and services, and the use of gold for reparations threatened to exhaust the stock needed for ordinary trade purposes and to bring disorder to international commerce. Some of these consequences were evaded for a time by German borrowings which made the " transfer " a merely book transaction in which debts were balanced against loans, but the end was inevitable when borrowing became impossible.

The Debt to the U.S.A.

The lesson was only to be learnt by hard experience bringing financial crises and industrial depression all over the world, and in 1923 only a small part of it had been learnt. After the failure of the Ruhr expedition, Mr. Bonar Law had the satisfaction, for what it was worth, of saying to the French, " I told you so," but he had had in the meantime to face the stubborn question of the British debt to the United States, which raised the same economic questions on a smaller scale as the German debt to the Allies. When the war ended the European Allies were in debt to the United States to the amount of £2,200,000,000, of which about £1,000,000,000 was owing by Great Britain, who had raised this sum not on her own account but mainly for the Allies, whose credit in the United States had become exhausted in the last eighteen months of the war. The Americans held much the same view about the debt due to them as the Allies did about the reparations which they demanded from Germany. They saw no difficulty in the transfer of these vast sums from one country to another; and when the Allies suggested that their payments to the United States should be conditional on the Germans paying them, they declined to admit that there was any connexion between the two things. The Allies had " hired the money " and they must pay it back; it was no concern of America's whether Germany paid them or not; one bankruptcy would not justify another.

Some Allied spokesmen pleaded that the debt represented money spent in the common cause, that America had come late into the war, that when in the war she had the same interest in defeating Germany as the Allies, and that having contributed fewer men and incurred fewer losses, she should be willing to make this contribution in money. But in 1922 when this argument was raised, American ardour about the war had greatly cooled, and she replied shortly that she had done enough for the Allies in helping them to win the war, and that she saw no reason why she should make this vast money contribution as well. A more practical plea was that the prices paid for her goods were on the high level of prices paid in war-time and that she had recovered a large part of her loans almost immediately in the form of excess profits taxation. This she admitted as a reason for fining down the nominal loans to a considerable extent, but not as a reason for wiping them out.

Thus when Mr. Baldwin went to Washington in December, 1922, to effect a settlement on behalf of Mr. Bonar Law's Government he found the atmosphere far from favourable, and the proposal he brought back for payments of interest and sinking-fund spread over sixty-two years and rising finally to £37,000,000 a year caused something like dismay to his colleagues, and it is said that Mr. Bonar Law had serious thought of resigning rather than accept it. There has been much controversy in subsequent years as to whether more skilful or persistent bargaining could have obtained better terms, but a settlement of some kind was considered imperative in the interests of British credit, and it remains doubtful whether anything less would have avoided the delay and recrimination which was thought most undesirable at the time.

The Balfour Note

In the meantime British policy had been defined in the Balfour Note (August 1, 1922) which laid down (1) that the British Government would have been willing to forgo all claims for German Reparations or the repayment of debts due to Britain from the Allies, if this were part of a universal settlement; but (2) failing such a settlement she would be content with a total sum from her Allies and Germany sufficient to cover her own payments to the United States, though this was only a quarter of the nominal amount due to her. This reaffirmed the view of the connexion between reparations and debts, which the Americans repudiated, and placed them in the uncomfortable position of seeming to stand between the European nations and an act of generosity which Great Britain was otherwise ready to confer on them. Unless the British taxpayer was to bear everybody's burdens, this was the least that could be said, but it was unpopular everywhere. The French, who never had the intention of paying either Great Britain or the United States unless the Germans provided the means, were annoyed with the British Government for negotiating a separate settlement with the United States, instead of standing with them to resist the American claim; and the Americans objected that they were being held up to odium as the Shylocks of the world. In the subsequent years the United States made settlements with the other European countries on far easier terms than with Great Britain, but the French never departed from their firm resolve to pay nothing, either to the United States or Great Britain, unless they were paid by the Germans.

The Economic Consequences

These settlements or attempted settlements were effected by Governments and Ministers with little regard to the economic consequences predicted by experts, who urged in vain that the necessity imposed upon the debtor Governments to buy the currencies necessary to pay these enormous debts would bring confusion to international trade. These consequences were postponed so long as the creditor countries continued to lend the debtor countries as much as they required to be paid, but when lending ceased after the American crisis of 1929, their full effect was quickly seen. The two principal creditor countries, France the principal creditor of Germany, the United States the principal creditor of all the rest, having high tariffs which precluded the entry of their debtors' goods, quickly drew to themselves the major part of the world's stock of gold, and made it impossible for Great Britain and other countries to " remain on the gold standard," *i.e.* to pay gold, as they had contracted to do, when those who had entrusted them with their money for commercial purposes demanded it. The widespread confusion and depression which followed convinced the European nations that it was as much in the interests of creditors as of debtors that these debts should be cancelled, and that, with various face-saving devices, was agreed at the Conference of Lausanne in 1931. But the American public remained unconvinced, and continued to insist on payment.

Great Britain and the Dominions

One of the most important events of the year 1923 was the Imperial Conference, which opened up the large number of important questions which, after further conferences in 1926 and 1930, were settled by " the Statute of Westminster " in 1931.

It has been recorded that the Dominions gave but a cold response to Mr. Lloyd George's appeal to them in 1922 to supply forces, if armed intervention should be necessary with the Turks at the time of the Chanak crisis. The view of most, but of the Canadians especially, was that, not having been consulted about the policy, they could not be expected to pledge themselves blindly to lend military support; and at the conference of 1923 the doctrine, already embodied in the Irish Free State Constitution, was laid down that, except in case of invasion, a Dominion could not be involved actively in war without the assent of its own Parliament. It was further agreed that, while powers to negotiate and sign treaties should be granted by the Crown, *i.e.* in practice by the Imperial Government, and ratification advised by the same authority, negotiations in any matter specially affecting a Dominion should be undertaken by the Government primarily concerned, and that it should be the business of this Government to bring into the negotiations any other Government whose interests might be affected. The Canadians made the point at issue specially clear by announcing that though they had no objection to the Treaty of Lausanne recently concluded with the Turks, they could not accept responsibility for it, since they had not been consulted, and must leave the obligations under it to the British Government.

If the Empire was really a " Commonwealth of free nations " these were logical and inevitable developments, but they made large inroads into the belief, commonly accepted till then, that the Imperial Government was responsible for foreign policy, and that the Dominions would follow wherever it led. They also raised puzzling and difficult questions for international lawyers, such as whether it would be possible, if Great Britain were at war, for a Dominion to remain neutral and at peace. The answer to this from the world generally was in the negative. If Great Britain were at war, all members of the British Commonwealth would automatically be in a state of war, and, if they wished to remain neutral, would have to secede from the Commonwealth. That Commonwealth, it was said, could not have the benefits both of war and peace, and its members be free to choose either as they found convenient. Nor, said some British critics, could they expect the protection of the British fleet and the British forces if they were free at short notice to repudiate the British connexion.

But it is the virtue of British institutions that they are seldom or never pushed to their logical conclusions when these lead to a deadlock, and the conclusions of the conference were accepted broadly as laying down the principle that the

Dominions expected to be consulted by the British Government about any policy which might involve them or the Commonwealth in war. In the famous Balfour memorandum of the year 1926 adopted in the preamble of the Statute of Westminster, which gave legal form to these developments, it is laid down that the " Dominions are autonomous Committees within the British Empire, equal in status, in no way subordinate to one another in their domestic or external affairs though united by a common allegiance to the Crown, and freely associated as members of the British Commonwealth of Nations." It remains for time and usage to decide how the principle of independent autonomy " in domestic or external affairs " is to be reconciled with an association and an allegiance to the Crown which seem to imply common guidance and policy; or what meaning is to be given to the expression " Crown," and by what Minister or Government the Crown is to be advised in affairs on which the Dominions may be divided. In these as in many other questions raised by British law and practice, the solution can only come by the exercise of good sense and mutual forbearance and constant consultation between the autonomous units.

The Death of Mr. Bonar Law and Succession of Mr. Baldwin

Towards the end of May, 1923, Mr. Bonar Law, who for some months had been seriously ill, resigned, and five months later he died. He had been Prime Minister for less than seven months, and found little of the " tranquillity and stability " which had been his watchwords in appealing to the country in the previous November. He will be remembered chiefly as a highly accomplished parliamentarian who was greatly trusted by the Conservative party which he had led in an aggressive spirit before the war, and extricated with success from a Coalition which was fatal to the Liberal party. He did much difficult service during the war, and if circumstances prevented his name from being associated with any important legislation, he will hold a prominent place in the party and parliamentary history of these years.

The succession was for some time in doubt, and the general expectation was that it would fall to Lord Curzon, who had a long and distinguished record behind him. He had been

Viceroy of India and Foreign Secretary; he was unrivalled in his own party as a debater and platform orator; no one except Lord Balfour, who had deliberately stood aloof since the fall of the Coalition, had claims equal to his. He had nevertheless certain defects of temper and disposition which caused his colleagues to mistrust his judgment and to fear friction if he held the highest office; and taking refuge in the plea that it was no longer desirable that a peer should be Prime Minister they notified their preference for Mr. Stanley Baldwin, whom the King summoned to form the new Government. Mr. Baldwin had many of the qualities that Lord Curzon lacked, and it was hoped that under his leadership the Government would live out its ordinary term, pursuing the tranquillity and stability which Mr. Bonar Law had promised at the previous election.

The Suicide of the Government

These hopes were doomed to disappointment. Towards the end of October, 1923, Mr. Baldwin made a speech at Plymouth which, whether intentionally or not, brought both Government and Parliament to an abrupt end. He said he saw no means of grappling with unemployment, which since the beginning of the year had been increasing rapidly, except by the protection of manufactured goods. That was impossible in the existing Parliament, since the Conservative leaders, in appealing to the country at the previous election, had pledged themselves not to introduce Protection, but it was equally impossible that after the Prime Minister had made this announcement the Government should continue to sit through a period of rising unemployment cut off from the remedy which he had declared to be indispensable. There was no way back from this speech, and no way forward except by appealing to the country to give the Government a mandate to apply this remedy.

With his usual straightforwardness Mr. Baldwin decided to take the plunge, and on November 26 Parliament was dissolved, and an election held on the issue of Protection and Free Trade—Protection being limited to manufactured goods and qualified by a specific promise not to tax wheat or meat. The electors decided, as always up to this time they had decided, when the direct issue had been placed before them, that they would not have Protection, and when the polling was over, there was a Free Trade majority of over 90 in the new House.

Dictatorships in Europe

We may pause at this point to note the growth of the movement which in the next ten years was to extinguish liberty and democracy and to destroy parliamentary government in many European countries. Fear of Russian Communism, and the example afforded by Russian methods contributed in equal parts to this movement.

Through all her later history Russia has been doomed to play the part of bogy to her neighbours. She played it under the Tsardom for a large part of the nineteenth century to Great Britain, and for ten years before the war to Germany. It was the " Russian peril " which kept the British people alert right up to the time of the Anglo-Russian Convention of 1906; it was the " Russian peril " which weighed most with the German Kaiser in giving his countenance to the war-makers in 1913 and 1914. It was once more the " Russian peril," transformed into a " Red peril," which alarmed the governing classes in Western Europe when the Bolshevists had established themselves in Moscow.

The Bolshevists themselves invited this result by openly announcing their intention to undermine and subvert the capitalist institutions of their neighbours, and by working energetically to that end through their organ " the Third International." How far the various Communist movements in Europe were actually promoted by the Soviet Government will only be ascertained when more is known of the secret organizations of this period. But both the success of the Communists in establishing their dictatorship in Russia, and the spread of Communism elsewhere created widespread alarm which in many countries made a favourable atmosphere for the critics and opponents of parliamentary institutions.

Bolshevism thus became the parent of Fascism in Italy, Hungary and eventually Germany. There was much trouble in Italy after the war—trouble caused by disappointed Nationalists who considered that their country had been betrayed by incompetent Ministers at the Peace Conference, and by unemployed or discontented workmen who joined the Communists, seized factories and committed acts of sabotage. The Government claimed to have restored order, but this was not the view of Signor Mussolini, an able and ambitious man (himself an ex-Socialist), who saw his opportunity in the general unrest to sweep the politicians away, and install a new type of government. Bolshevism, in his view, had to be fought with its own weapons; the slow and confused movements of Parliaments and electorates were altogether unequal to an emergency which demanded quick and ruthless action. He therefore proceeded to organize young men into bands of " black-shirts " who took the law into their own hands and waged a private war with Communists and syndicalists. There was much savagery and many casualties on both sides, but more important in its permanent results was the helplessness of the lawful Government which, having remained a spectator of this feud, fell an easy victim when Mussolini marched on Rome at the head of his black-shirts (October, 1922). Within a few months he had made a clean sweep of parliamentary institutions and set up a Fascist dictatorship which, while inverting the objects, employed many of the methods of Communism. Both the Russian and the Italian dictators derided Liberalism, extinguished the liberties of the press, proclaimed their own supporters to be the only party in the State, killed, deported or imprisoned their opponents, and forbade all trade unions or organizations of workmen, except under the control of the State. A special method of the Italians was to dose their opponents with castor oil, which added a touch of ignominy to their fate.

There was no doubt that Mussolini succeeded in disciplining the Italian people. He cleaned up the streets, made the railways run to time, abolished beggars, suppressed secret societies, instituted useful public works, and made a brave outward show, which had led many visitors to the country to testify to the virtues of Fascism. Whether he has increased the wealth and happiness of his country, or reconciled its people with the submission which his system requires, are questions which can scarcely be answered in the absence of a free press and other free institutions, which would enable their opinions to be made known. In judging these systems there is a fundamental cleavage between those who think that liberty and the free play of the individual mind are the special characteristics of a civilized state, and those who regard obedience to authority as the principal human virtue.

A revival of the extremer forms of the doctrine which holds the State to be " an object in itself" justifying all means for the promotion of its interests and exacting complete obedience in its service, must be counted one of the results of a war which for a long period brought immense numbers under military discipline and familiarized them with the methods necessary to enforce it. In many countries it was found easier to suspend free institutions for the duration of the war than to bring them back to life when the war was over. That was especially the case in countries like Italy and Germany, where parliamentary institutions, as understood in Great Britain, had no roots in the past, or Russia, which but for the brief and troubled experiment of the Duma, passed from one tyranny to another. The Nazi movement in Germany stands outside the period of this book, but that too, with special German or Prussian characteristics, was part of the general reaction from Russian Communism.

CHAPTER XXX

WHEN the election of November, 1923, was over, it was plain that Mr. Baldwin's Government could not go on, but for some time it was very uncertain what Government could take its place. The Free Trade majority was composed of 191 Labour and 158 Liberal members. The Coalition and Independent Liberals had reunited to defend Free Trade, and Mr. Asquith, who had come back to Parliament as member for Paisley, had issued a joint manifesto with Mr. Lloyd George on the eve of the election. But the Labour party had in recent years made a special point of its complete independence of the Liberal party, and had proclaimed a Socialist doctrine which in many respects was in conflict with Liberal ideas. The question now was whether it would waive or postpone these points of conflict and seek common ground on which it could form a Government and carry on with the support of Liberals.

There was great alarm in certain circles at the prospect of the Labour party coming to power, and during the interval after the election Mr. Asquith was approached from many quarters and promised Conservative support if he would form a Government and avert this supposed disaster. But he felt strongly that it would be contrary to the public interest and against the spirit of the Constitution for the two older parties to join together to deprive the third party of an opportunity which rightly belonged to it in virtue of its numbers, and which could only be questioned because it was a Labour or Socialist party. He felt also that he would be in a false position if he took office dependent on Conservative support, and Mr. Baldwin in a still falser one if, after having assured the country that he could not carry on without Protection, he were to continue in office with Liberal support after having been denied the use of that remedy.

Mr. Ramsay MacDonald's First Government

Thus, on January 22, 1924, when Mr. Baldwin resigned, it fell to Mr. Ramsay MacDonald, the leader of the Labour party, to form the new Government. In addition to the well-known Labour or Socialist leaders, Mr. Clynes, Mr. Henderson, Mr. J. H. Thomas, Mr. Snowden and Mr. Sidney Webb, his Cabinet included several former Liberals, such as Lord Haldane, Sir C. P. Trevelyan, Mr. Josiah Wedgwood, Mr. Noel Buxton, one former Conservative, Lord Parmoor, an ex-Viceroy of India, Lord Chelmsford, and a soldier hitherto unknown to politics, Brigadier-General Birdwood Thomson. The composition of the Government looked reassuring, and it was hoped that the Liberal element in it would help to the mutual understanding with the Liberal party which was plainly necessary if it were to remain in office.

These hopes were disappointed. No working arrangement was established between the Government and its Liberal supporters or the Whips' departments of the two parties. Friction which might have been prevented by consultation between them developed early in the House of Commons, and was aggravated in the constituencies, where the Labour party refused to withdraw opposition to candidates and members upon whose support they were relying in the House of Commons. It soon became clear that the same parties could not long continue to support each other in Parliament, if they were fighting each other in the country. Ardent Socialists who had expected a new era to dawn when a Labour Government came into power could not understand the limit which was placed on its activities by the fact that it was in a minority in Parliament. Liberals complained that they were reduced to "hewers of wood and drawers of water" for a Government in which they had no voice, and which was proving even less progressive than they wished it to be.

Not much could have been expected of the most advanced Government in the short time that Mr. Ramsay MacDonald's had at its disposal, and its most important legislation was Mr. Wheatley's Housing Act, which provided for the building of 2,500,000 houses spread over a period of fifty years, houses to be let at rents within working-class means. This was much criticized at the time, but it proved in after years to be a useful contribution to the housing question. In most other respects discontent with the Government increased as the months passed and came to a climax in the autumn, when it was defeated by 364 to 198 on a Liberal amendment to a Conservative vote of censure.

The objection taken was rather to the method than to the policy of the Government. In the last weeks it had shown a wavering mind which suggested to the House of Commons, always sensitive on this point—that it was liable to the control of influences outside Parliament and unknown to it. In June the Prime Minister announced that on no account would Great Britain guarantee a loan to Soviet Russia, and in August he told the House that negotiations for a treaty with Russia had broken down on the question of compensation to the owners of nationalized property. A day later, after the intervention of certain members of his party, he said that a treaty had been drafted which, on the fulfilment of certain conditions, would propose a guaranteed loan. At the beginning of August, proceedings were taken in Court against a Communist named Campbell; a week later they were withdrawn in circumstances which suggested that the same pressure had been applied. The Liberal party was willing to accept a Select Committee of Inquiry into this matter in lieu of the Vote of Censure which the Conservative party proposed, but when the Government rejected this, both parties combined to vote against them, whereupon Mr. MacDonald decided to appeal to the country.

The Red Letter Election

The chief incident of the election which followed was the publication of the famous Zinovieff letter—a letter addressed to the British Communist party by the " Presidium " of the " Communist International "—a body which beyond all doubt was then an organ of the Russian Government. The recipients of this letter, which bore the date of September 15, were urged to " stir up the masses of the British proletariat," to organize mutiny in the army and navy, to foment rebellion in Ireland and the Colonies, to enlist " military specialists " holding Socialist opinions to prepare for "an outbreak of active strife," and "to keep close observation over the leaders of the Labour party, because these may easily be found in the leading strings of the *Bourgeoisie*." The letter, together with a spirited rejoinder from the Government dated October 24, which reminded the Soviet Government that it had quite recently pledged itself not to spread discontent or foment rebellion in any part of the British Isles, was published by the Foreign Office in the middle of the election, apparently with the sanction of the Prime Minister, though in his public speeches he left it in doubt whether he considered it authentic or not. The public concluded that the Foreign Office would not have published it unless it was sure of its authenticity, and an excited cry arose against the Government which with this letter in its possession had continued to negotiate a treaty with the Russian Government, and had even promised to guarantee them a loan. Apart from these circumstances the atmosphere created by the letter was disastrous to Labour. Large numbers of men and women saw the country threatened by a Revolutionary conspiracy in which the Bolshevists were joining hands with internal enemies supposed to be in league with the Labour party. The Conservative party made skilful use of the opportunity thus offered them, and an immense number of voters concluded that the only safe thing to do was to vote Conservative.

The Conservatives Again in Power

Thus within twelve months the Conservative party retrieved their blunder of the previous year, and came back 415 strong to the new House, while both the other parties were shattered, Labour being reduced from 191 to 152, and Liberals from 155 to 42. The general run to shelter from Bolshevism had swept past the Liberal half-way house, and many electors vented their displeasure on the Liberal party for having helped to office and kept in office for even a short time a Socialist Goverment which was now said to be displayed in its true colours. Asquith, its greatly respected leader, lost his seat at Paisley, where he had to meet the concentrated attack of Labour, which rendered him no thanks for having helped it to office, and held him largely responsible for its eviction from office.

After a period of reflection he decided not to seek re-election and accepted the peerage which the King offered him immediately after the election. From now to the end of his life he was to be known as the Earl of Oxford and Asquith.

The formation of the new Conservative Government marked the end of the feud between Coalition and non-Coalition Conservatives. Mr. Austen Chamberlain came into the Government as Foreign Secretary, Lord Birkenhead as Secretary for India, and a little later, after Lord Curzon's death, Lord Balfour became Lord President of the Council. Mr. Winston Churchill, who by now had left the Liberal party and reverted to his Conservative allegiance, became Chancellor of the Exchequer. Having been brought back to power on a wave of emotion at a sudden election Mr. Baldwin was unpledged to any programme beyond a promise to act prudently and safely. He had dropped the all-round Protection for manufactured goods, which he had declared to be essential at the previous election, and limited himself to what was called " safeguarding " for industries which could make out a special case. But if Protection was for the time being off the boards, industrial and financial questions were more urgent than ever. Unemployment was increasing, great strikes threatened, Socialists were suggesting that what Labour had failed to win in Parliament might still be won by " direct action," as it was called, in the country. All the bitterness left over from an exceptionally bitter election was now to run into industrial channels.

The Locarno Treaties

In the meantime foreign affairs claimed attention. When he quitted office, the out-going Prime Minister and Foreign Secretary, Mr. Ramsay MacDonald, was still undecided whether Great Britain should subscribe to the " Protocol of Geneva," a plan drawn up at Geneva for " closing the gaps " in the Covenant of the League and improving the machinery of peace. This would have placed all the Powers under an obligation to take action against " aggressors " on any issue and made the Council of the League the judge of what constituted " aggression." The counterpart of this plan was to have been a general disarmament, and it was agreed that, if the nations disarmed, their liabilities under the Covenant would be diminished rather than increased. British opinion, however, saw in this proposal a possible entanglement in remote disputes—especially those about the " Polish Corridor " and other difficult questions in Eastern Europe—and was luke-warm if not hostile. Mr. Baldwin's Government rejected this plan, and the new Foreign Secretary, Sir Austen Chamber-lain, now devoted himself to working out the more limited guarantee of peace which, with the co-operation of M. Briand and Herr Stresemann, found expression in the Locarno Treaties signed on December 1, 1925.

This, instead of covering the whole field and dealing with all possible wars, endeavoured to make the wars which seemed most likely in the future—and especially a war between France and Germany—as difficult as possible. Britain, France, Germany, Italy and Belgium agreed " never to resort to war " with one another, and all undertook to come immediately to the help of any one of them which was attacked. Thus, if France attacked Germany, Britain would be bound to come to Germany's assistance, and if Germany attacked France, to her assistance. At the same time Germany made separate treaties with France, Belgium, Czechoslovakia and Poland to the same effect. Great Britain thus declined any special liability—apart from the Covenant—for affairs in Eastern Europe, but undertook to come immediately to the aid of any nation which was the victim of aggression in the course of quarrels between the Western nations.

On the conclusion of the Locarno Treaties Germany signi-fied her intention of entering the League of Nations. The graciousness of her reception was somewhat marred by a technical hitch which postponed it for several months, but this was overcome by the following September, and it then seemed that by the inclusion of the principal ex-enemy State the League was firmly on the road to becoming the complete international organization it was intended to be. Later events were unfor-tunately to cloud that prospect.

A difficult question which at one time threatened a renewal of trouble with the Turks was settled in June, 1926, when after long resistance they accepted the decision of the League of

Nations awarding Mosul to Iraq under British control. The importance of Mosul lay in its control both of the irrigation and of the vast oil supplies of Iraq, and there was a moment when it was thought possible that the Turks would defy the League and fight for its possession.

CHAPTER XXXI

THE GENERAL STRIKE

ON April 28, 1925, Mr. Churchill, the new Chancellor of the Exchequer, introduced his first Budget and announced a return to the gold standard which had been suspended during and since the war; that is to say, the Bank of England was again put under an obligation to pay gold at the price fixed by Parliament before the war for currency notes, and the free export of gold was again permitted. Sterling was thus anchored to gold, instead of being left to find its own value in the currency exchange market of the world. This had little or no immediate effect on the purchasing power of the pound in the domestic market, but it had an immediate and important effect on its value as a medium of exchange in international trade. Practically that effect was to raise the value of the pound sterling 10 per cent. in relation to the principal foreign currencies. From April 28 onwards either the foreigner buying British goods valued in sterling had to pay 10 per cent. more, or the British seller to accept 10 per cent. less, than the one had been paying and the other receiving up to that time. It was as if all British goods for sale in the foreign market had suddenly been marked up 10 per cent. Had the internal value of the pound been raised to the same extent as its foreign exchange value, the situation might have been met by reducing the price of the goods, but since that result did not follow, and the costs of production, including wages, remained unaltered, a reduction in price meant a net loss to the British seller. The latter was thus to choose between (1) maintaining his price and losing his market and (2) lowering his price and losing his profit or a large part of it.

Mr. Churchill argued that this move would be good for British credit, which suffered when its unit of exchange was liable to fluctuations, and that it would be easier to conduct business on a stable than on a fluctuating exchange. He also possibly had in mind that it would be more difficult for politicians to print paper money or to play other tricks on the currency if it were anchored to gold than if it were free. But desirable as these results might be in the long run, the immediate price which had to be paid for them was a heavy one. The general effect of British monetary policy had already been to force up the cost of British goods relatively to those of other countries and thus check the export trade, and now another 10 per cent. was added to their price. This increased the difficulties of trades specially dependent on exports and produced an immediate crisis in coal. The mine-owners declared that they had no chance of maintaining their foreign trade and working at a profit unless they could reduce their costs by lowering wages or increasing the hours of the miners; the miners replied that their wages were already too low, and refused to discuss either wages or hours. Negotiations and conferences failed to move either party from these positions and by the end of July the whole Trade Union movement and especially the Railway and Transport Unions, had lined up to support the miners in their struggle to maintain their wages and hours. A most serious situation affecting all industries seemed imminent, but at this point the Government intervened with the offer of a subvention in aid of wages on the basis of the *status quo*, and on these terms a truce was called.

The Coal Crisis and the General Strike

It proved only to be a truce, for ten months later when the country had spent more than £20,000,000 on subsidizing wages, miners and mine-owners were as far as ever from a settlement, both for different reasons rejecting the proposals of the Royal Commission, which had sat under the chairmanship of Sir Herbert Samuel, and reported in the interval. The crisis was reached in April, 1926, when the mine-owners issued notices to terminate their present contracts with a view to making new ones on a lower wage basis. Once more the Government tried to bring the parties together, the Prime Minister intervening personally with a plea for moderation on both sides, but again all efforts broke down against the refusal of the miners to accept either a reduction in wages, or an increase of hours and of the mine-owners to consent to anything else. The General Council of the Trade Union Congress now resolved to make the miners' case their own, and on May 1 announced that unless the mine-owners withdrew their notices and a settlement was reached in the meantime, they would call a general strike from midnight of May 3.

For a few hours the Government turned the blind eye to this threat, and continued negotiations, but on its being reported that the compositors on a certain newspaper had refused to set up an article which they considered "insulting to the workers," Mr. Baldwin, who had been much blamed by his own party for allowing the negotiations to continue after the threat of a general strike had been issued, decided that the breaking-point had been reached, and declined further parley. The strike-notices accordingly took effect, and on May 4 the country woke up to find its business at a standstill.

There is still some doubt as to the number of workers in the different trades who actually struck work, but the precise figure is of little importance. A railway and transport strike was alone sufficient to paralyse industry and suspend the ordinary operations of life; and if only this could have been made effective and continued for any length of time, it must have produced untold suffering and probably led in the end to violence and revolution. It was evident from the beginning that the workers had not thought out these inevitable consequences of their action. Their leaders protested that the last thing they contemplated was violence or revolution, and that they were only applying the legitimate weapon of refusing their work in defence of their standard of living, which they believed to be threatened all along the line by the attack on the miners' wage. From the point of view of law and order their conduct was exemplary. They adjured their followers to abstain from all violence, and they made exceptions for hard cases. But whatever their intentions, nothing could prevent the result of their action from being that which they disclaimed, and as the days went on and stocks became exhausted and the gradual cumulative results began to be felt in every household and especially the households of the poorest, they began to look for ways back from the precipice on which they were walking.

An Improvised Service

At the same time the emergency powers with which the Government had armed itself as soon as the threat of a general strike was made, proved much more effective than the strike-leaders had supposed. It was no longer railways or nothing. The country now had at its disposal a great fleet of motors and motor-lorries in private hands, and if the regular transport workers refused to handle them there was an abundance of capable amateurs to take their place. In a few days a sufficient service was improvised to remove the worst fears of starvation. At the same time amateurs developed a quite unexpected aptitude for all kinds of trade. Young men from the Universities ran goods trains through the night; others drove trams and buses, and private cars with their owners at the wheel took the place of taxis. Householders discovered that they could do their own repairs, and some continued to do them for a long time afterwards. The amateur " black-legs " were seldom or never molested; there was an almost complete absence of bitterness, and large numbers took positive pleasure in the novel tasks assigned to them.

Foreign journalists reported on the amazing spectacle of a country keeping this cheerful composure and good-nature in the throes of a crisis which almost anywhere else in the world would have brought rioting and bloodshed within a very short time. They said it was characteristically English, and could not have happened anywhere else in the world. But the English too learnt a good many things during the nine days that the strike lasted. They learnt for one thing what it was to do without newspapers and have to rely on an official newspaper. The *British Gazette*, the official newspaper, commanded all the talent of the journalistic and official world. Distinguished journalists edited it; Ministers and leaders of parties contributed to it; great lawyers expounded the law and the constitution in its columns. But its news was suspected and its views were discounted, and after a few days the public wearied of its exhortations. The strikers afterwards admitted that the worst of their mistakes had been the shutting down of the independent press, which would at least have given their side a hearing, and the public in general heaved a sigh of relief when the *British Gazette* published its last number, and they were free to return to their own newspapers.

The End of the Strike

The strike was called off on May 12, having lasted nine days. Sir Herbert Samuel, who had been chairman of the Royal Commission appointed earlier in the year, did notable service in building the bridge which offered the Trade Union Committee a way back without seeming to desert the miners, but there was no question that the strike had failed, and could only have been carried further if the leaders had been prepared to pursue it as a revolutionary movement, which was certainly not their intention or desire. But, though the other trades came in, the miners remained obdurate, and refused to accept the basis for renewing negotiations proposed by Sir Herbert Samuel and accepted by the Trade Union Council as good ground for calling off the General Strike. Under the uncompromising leadership of Mr. A. J. Cook, who refused all concessions and stood out to the last for a national agreement covering the whole trade and no extension of hours, they struggled on till the middle of November, when the exhaustion of their funds and their savings compelled them to accept the Government's terms providing for district settlements, and leaving the door open to an extension of hours. It was a disastrous and devastating struggle which not only played havoc with the coal trade but inflicted great injury on industry generally at a time when it was least able to bear it.

The Liberal Schism

The general strike created another schism in the Liberal party. Holding that it was a direct and most dangerous challenge to the authority of Government and Parliament, Lord Oxford and the great majority of the Liberal leaders rallied to the support of Ministers and took an active part in combating the strike movement. But Mr. Lloyd George was of a different mind, and notified his dissent by absenting himself from a meeting of ex-Ministers at a critical moment, and writing a letter in which he said he could not see his way " to join in declarations which condemned the General Strike, while refraining from criticism of the Government who are equally, if not more, responsible." A little later he contributed an article to the American press in which he painted a gloomy picture of the condition of Great Britain, and predicted that its present attitude would be worn down by " worry about its vanishing trade." Lord Oxford interpreted these signs as meaning that Mr. Lloyd George had definitely dissociated himself from his colleagues on a question of the highest import- ance, and a subsequent correspondence between the two men failed to heal the breach.

For the time being illness prevented Lord Oxford from pursuing the controversy, and four months later when he recovered he had decided to resign the leadership of the Liberal party. There were by this time more differences between the two men than the question of their attitude to the general strike, and Mr. Lloyd George was in the strong tactical position of being leader of the parliamentary party with a large fund of his own and a separate organization, which was to all intents and purposes a rival to the greatly impoverished official organization. This for several years past had been a cause of dissensions in the Liberal Party, and Lord Oxford now told his friends that, being faced with the alter- native of having " to lead a squalid faction fight against Mr. Lloyd George in which he would have all the sinews of war, or to accept his money and patch up a hollow and humiliating alliance," he was resolved to do neither; and in a speech at Greenock on October 15, 1926, he made his farewell to the party. Sixteen months later (February 15, 1928) he died, and the general verdict was that a great man and a great gentleman had gone from the scene.

Trade Union Legislation

When the general strike ended, the King and the Prime Minister made a strong appeal to the country to bury the past and make a fresh start in a spirit of peace and goodwill. There was a real inclination at that moment to give heed to this advice, but the long continuation of the miners' strike and the bitter war of tongue and pen which accompanied it kept the atmosphere heated, and when Parliament reassembled in 1927, the Government's supporters called loudly for legislation which would make a general strike impossible in the future, and curb what they believed to be the aggressive attitude of Labour. In response to this demand the Government introduced a Bill declaring any strike illegal which (1) had any object beyond the furtherance of a trade dispute within the trade concerned, or (2) which was calculated to coerce Government or intimidate the community or any substantial part of it. The same Bill also made picketing at the home of a worker criminal, forbade Trade Unions of civil servants to belong to any outside federation of Trade Unions, or to be associated directly or indirectly with a political party; and substituted "contracting in" for "contracting out" for the "political levy"; that is to say, the "trade-unionist was only to be required to subscribe to the fund which the Trade Unions collected for political purposes, if he signified his assent in writing and was not, as before, to be levied unless he signified his dissent."

There had been much debate during the general strike as to whether Sir John Simon had been justified in stigmatizing it as "illegal," but the point was really of little importance. A general strike presented the Government with an emergency in which it was obliged to use all its resources for the public safety, and the only question that could have arisen was whether it should or should not have occupied a few hours in obtaining special powers from Parliament or have sought an idemnity afterwards. But if it was thought desirable or necessary, there was no objection in placing it beyond doubt for the future that a strike of this nature was illegal. The Bill aroused fierce controversy, and was resisted to the last by the Labour party mainly because it went beyond this issue and was in effect a large revision of Trade Union law. It made the "sympathetic strike"—for example a strike of transport workers to support a coal strike—illegal; it forbade any strike for a political object, such as the strike which had been threatened to restrain the Government from assisting the Poles against the Russians; it severely limited picketing; and made it more difficult for workmen to raise the funds necessary to maintain their representatives in Parliament. There was a strong body of opinion that "direct action" intended to coerce Parliament ought to be checked, but Trade Unionists protested that the other objects were outside any issue that could fairly be said to have arisen out of the general strike, and denounced them as vindictive measures little likely to restore peace between Capital and Labour. Resentment on this subject undoubtedly accounted not a little for the defeat of Mr. Baldwin's Government in 1929.

De-rating and " Public Assistance "

The principal domestic measures of the remaining years of this Parliament were the great " de-rating " scheme introduced by Mr. Churchill in his Budget of 1928, by which agriculture was relieved wholly and industry to the extent of three-fourths of the the burden of rates, and local authorities compensated by grants from the Exchequer costing the taxpayer 22 million pounds per annum. This measure was criticized for its lack of discrimination between prosperous industries of a local character which could well afford to contribute to the rates from which they benefited, and others like railways of a national character which were called upon to pay for local objects, such as road-making, from which they drew little advantage, and even suffered disadvantage. The Government replied that discrimination was impossible in practice and that it was in the general interest to remove the incidence of rating from industry. Later in the year a Local Government Bill instituted the important reform whereby " Public Assistance Committees " of County and Borough Councils were substituted for Boards of Guardians. This was a useful step towards unifying administration and humanizing the Poor Law.

Peace and Disarmament

Peace and Disarmament had a chequered history after the conclusion of the Locarno Treaties. The Naval Conference at Geneva in June, 1927, broke down on a dispute between Great Britain and the United States about the allocation between big and small cruisers of an agreed amount of tonnage. Tempers ran high on both sides and American methods of propaganda outside the conference room caused some resentment. When the conference ended, Lord Cecil, who had represented the Government, resigned on the ground that he had " over and over again been compelled by his instructions to maintain points difficult to reconcile with a desire to reduce armaments." A subsequent attempt by Great Britain to reach a separate agreement with France on the basis of recognizing her view that reserves should not count in the computation of land forces caused much unrest among the other Powers and eventually broke down against the chorus of remonstrance and criticism.

On the other side must be placed the acceptance (July 18, 1928) of the American Kellogg Pact barring the use of war " as a legitimate instrument of policy." Somewhat prolonged negotiations, in which the Dominions were consulted, were necessary before the conclusion was reached and the impatient said that the Government was half-hearted. But British Ministers had thought it necessary to reserve British freedom of action in certain regions of which the welfare and integrity constituted a special British interest, and the Kellogg Pact had thus attached to it, so far as this country was concerned, what was called at the time a " British Monroe doctrine " parallel to the claim that events on the American continent constitute a special interest of the United States in which other nations are not concerned. That China was her special sphere of interest was subsequently pleaded by Japan as a reason for breaking the Kellogg Pact and defying the League of Nations.

With or without these reservations the Kellogg Pact, if sincerely accepted and acted upon, would be a daring innovation in the practice of the world. Up to the Great War, all the nations, including Great Britain, had considered war or the threat of war to be a legitimate instrument of policy, and not merely a last resort for national defence. All of them had made war or threatened war in furtherance of national interests and policies, and their diplomacy was governed by the belief that the most serious political deadlocks would result in war and could only be removed by war. Many doubts were expressed whether the mere acceptance of the Kellogg Pact would of itself revolutionize the practice of the world, but the fact that it was accepted is undoubtedly an important landmark in the history of opinion about war.

The Revised Prayer-Book

On two occasions, in 1927 and 1928, the House of Commons found itself suddenly converted into a forum of theological debate. Having completed their revision of the Book of Common Prayer, the bishops and clergy were now required to present the result for the sanction of Parliament. Here they came up against unexpected obstacles. The Revised Book proposed to legalize the practice of " reserving the Sacrament " nominally for the use of the sick, but in reality, as the Evangelical party asserted or suspected, to satisfy the Anglo-Catholic party, which practised adoration of the consecrated wafer. The debate reached high levels of theological and metaphysical argument, but it proved the Protestant feeling, which denies the possibility of a mystical change in the elements by the act of the priest, to be very much alive in the House of Commons and in the country. The Lords approved the Revised Book by a majority of 241 to 88, but the Commons rejected it by a majority of 238 to 205 in 1927, and rejected it again by an even larger majority when it was submitted a second time, after sundry changes, in 1928 (June 13). The bishops were urged to drop the controversial part of the proposed revision and obtain the sanction of Parliament, about which there would have been no difficulty, for the rest of their labours, but this they declined to do, and all further efforts to legalize the Revised Book were abandoned after the second rejection. It can scarcely be said that the controversy is exhausted, for large numbers of churchmen, including some bishops, were left saying that disestablishment was a necessary step to releasing the Church from control of its doctrine by the State.

The Election of 1929

The next appeal to the country was now coming in sight. Ministers remained sanguine that they would obtain a substantial majority, but the by-elections had for some time told a rather different tale. Unemployment was still increasing, Labour was in a state of resentment at the Trade Union legislation, the achievements of the Government, though solid, did not catch the public imagination, Mr. Baldwin's slogan " safety first " seemed uninspiring to large numbers who looked for a bold lead in difficult times. The Free Trade controversy was far from settled even in the Conservative party, and Mr. Churchill was engaged in a veiled dispute with the Home Secretary about which the Prime Minister could only say that their respective speeches were " examples of the many-sidedness of truth." When the election came at the end of May, 1929, the Government seemed to pass away by desuetude, and after the election found itself in a minority of 85 against the combined forces of Labour and Liberal.

From the world point of view the most important event of the year 1929 was the great American slump which not only caused widespread distress and ruin in the United States, but, through the consequent withdrawal of loans and credit, precipitated crises in many European countries. From this time onwards unemployment rapidly increased in nearly all countries, and the causes were set in motion which drove Great Britain off the gold standard and led her, in alarm for her trade balance, to abandon Free Trade.

CHAPTER XXXII

FROM LABOUR TO NATIONAL GOVERNMENT

IN the new House, Labour was once again the strongest party
with its 287 to 261 Conservatives. But it was again short of a
clear majority, and once more it depended on the support of
Liberals who, though only 59 in number, held the casting vote,
as in 1924. On the result of the election becoming known Mr.
Baldwin resigned, and Mr. MacDonald formed a Cabinet
of his old colleagues, with a few omissions and additions, and
left the Liberals to take their own course. They decided to
feel their way with an inclination to support the Government
as long as possible, and though there were critical moments as,
for example, on the Government's Coal Bill with its proposal
of export quotas for different mines, no positive causes for a
breach with the Government presented themselves for the
next two years. The legislation of this period was scanty.
The House of Lords rejected a Bill raising the age for leaving
school and making an allowance to parents of 5s. per child
remaining at school for a year longer; and though this Bill
would automatically have become law after two years, the
subsequent Government decided not to proceed with it, in
view of the financial situation. A Trade Union Bill, amending
and in some respects reversing the Act of the previous Government, raised differences between Liberals and Trade Unionists
and had to be withdrawn. Mr. Henderson, the Foreign
Secretary, won general approval by his conduct of foreign
affairs and especially by his efforts to reconcile French and
Italian views of naval power.

But during this period the financial situation was going
from bad to worse, and the position of Ministers being
undermined by their failure to deal with it. With unemployment increasing, revenue falling, and the new charges
laid on the Exchequer by Mr. Churchill's De-rating scheme,
Mr. Snowden, the Labour Chancellor of the Exchequer

had a prospective deficit of 47 millions to make good in his
first Budget (April, 1930). He contrived it for the time being
by adding to the beer-tax and increasing income-tax, super-
tax and death-duties by an aggregate of 31 millions. The
next year he was in a still worse plight, for while the declared
deficit was less by 10 millions, it was only kept down to this
figure by heavy borrowings to meet the deficiency on Unemployment insurance. On June 23, 1931, the Minister for
Labour, Miss Bondfield, came to Parliament for authority to
borrow £25,000,000 for this purpose, but she said frankly
that the deficit on the insurance fund was now at the rate of
£1,000,000 a week, and that the amount for which she asked
might easily be exhausted in three months. Already the
borrowing on this account had mounted up to £115,000,000,
and there was apparently no end to the process. By adding
to the petrol-tax, taking into the year's account a Treasury
balance of £20,000,000 left over from the " Dollar Exchange
account," and calling upon income-tax and super-tax payers
to pay three-quarters instead of a half of their dues in the
coming January, Mr. Snowden just managed to balance his
account, but these were desperate expedients which clearly
could not be repeated.

Mr. Snowden himself was full of warning, but the financial
problem opened a rift in the Government which was to become
a gulf in the weeks following his second Budget. While he
himself saw no way of meeting the situation except by
economies which would bring the national expenditure within
the limits of taxable capacity—now rapidly nearing exhaustion
—not a few of his colleagues believed it to be the duty of a
Labour and Socialist Government to increase the spending
capacity of the workers by extending and increasing unemployment pay, and were not greatly concerned if in so doing they
should break the established system of balanced Budgets and
carefully guarded credit. They believed the taxable capacity
of wealth to be far from exhausted, and claimed the backing
of economists who said that the process of deflation (i.e.
economy and the contraction of credit and new enterprise)
had been carried a great deal too far in recent years, and that
what the country needed was a dose of inflation through
" courageous borrowing." They therefore strongly resisted

the idea of either diminishing unemployment pay or contracting its area, or making any economies which conflicted with their view of social and Socialist policy.

But while this controversy was proceeding within the Government, the Chancellor of the Exchequer found the whole financial structure beginning to tumble about his head. On July 30 the May Committee—a committee on public economy under the chairmanship of Sir George May which had been appointed without much thought of its significance on a Liberal motion—presented its report. This expressed the view that at the present rate of expenditure the deficit in the next Budget would be £125,000,000, apart from the usual provision for debt redemption. This and the analysis of the situation which the report contained came as a thunderclap both at home and abroad. Foreigners, who had regarded British credit as impregnable and unassailable, took alarm, and in the next fortnight there were heavy withdrawals from the Bank of England, which had to seek assistance from the Bank of France and the Federal Reserve Bank of the United States. It was clear that the situation had to be faced without delay, and an Economy Committee of the Cabinet was appointed to deal with it as speedily as possible. But the divisions persisted, the Prime Minister and Mr. Snowden desiring to work with the bankers in restoring the situation, while other members of the Cabinet held the bankers responsible for the trouble and wished to seize the opportunity of bringing them under public control. Seeing no way of composing this quarrel, and judging the situation to be too dangerous for further delay, the Prime Minister tendered his resignation (August 24, 1931), and on the following day was commissioned by the King to form a Coalition National Government.

CHAPTER XXXIII

SOCIAL AND ECONOMIC

I

SOMETHING remains to be said about certain social and economic tendencies which were at work during these years, and which must be read between the lines of any record of the facts.

The period was as a whole one of advancing prosperity for all classes, accompanied by increasing unrest in the ranks of political and organized Labour. There is nothing surprising in the combination of these two things. Advancing education and a higher standard of living awakened a new sense of wants among the workers, and a livelier consciousness of the inequalities in the social scale.

In the last quarter of the nineteenth century the course of wages was almost continuously upwards, and that of prices continuously downwards. There was one considerable trade depression in 1885-6, but this was only a temporary check. On the whole all classes of labour gained, and in the great Dockers' Strike of 1889 unorganized Labour under the leadership of Mr. John Burns and Mr. Tom Mann won a victory which was of benefit not only to the London dockers but to casual and unorganized Labour everywhere. The next ten years were a time of industrial peace, and there was a widespread hope that methods of arbitration and conciliation had been found which would prevent serious conflict in the future. But Labour was now coming definitely into politics, and the formation of the Independent Labour Party in 1893 inaugurated a movement for the advance of the workers' cause, not merely by Trade Union action, but by obtaining control of the machine of government. The new Labour politicians urged that the method of working with the Liberal and Radical party should be abandoned, and an entirely new party formed which should stand for a Labour and Socialist policy independently of any middle-class progressive party.

The idea was only partly realized during the next twenty years, and at the election of 1906 there was a large measure of co-operation between Liberal and Labour which greatly contributed to the Liberal triumph of that year. But with a Liberal Government in power and Labour spokesmen in Parliament, organized Labour became more active, and during the next few years there were serious strikes in the railway, coal-mining, cotton, building and transport industries. Not all of these were successful, but several of them were on a scale which required Government intervention in the public interest. From this time onwards it was certain that the Government would be an active party in all great industrial disputes. The spread of trade-unionism from a local to a national form of organization entailed this consequence, but it was a wide departure from nineteenth-century practice, and required Governments to take an active and unremitting interest in industrial questions. There followed in due course the establishment of a Labour Department with a Labour Minister. Industrial and social questions now became of the highest importance.

The three Liberal Parliaments from 1906 to 1914 were much occupied with the House of Lords and Irish controversies, but the co-operation of Labour and Liberal was justified from the Labour point of view by the Trade Disputes Act, by the institution of old-age pensions, by the Trade Boards Bill, which greatly improved the position of sweated labour, by the sickness, accident and unemployment insurance established in these years, and sundry other social legislation. Some of these measures added substantially to the real wages of the workers and represented a considerable redistribution of wealth to their advantage.

The history of Labour during the war has still to be written, but in general it was a time of soaring prices with wages rather more than keeping pace. In fact the workers came out of the war with a substantial advantage compared with their previous position, but the very serious question remained whether they could keep this advantage when prices fell.

The struggle, open or veiled, on this question which has continued since the war ended has been one of the principal factors in the economic history of the country. The great strikes of this period—railway strikes, coal-strikes, general strikes—are all phases of the workers' resistance to the effort of employers to reduce wages to meet the continuous fall of world prices which has characterized these years. Employers complain that the "time-lag," as economists call it, between the fall of wages and the fall of prices, owing to the resistance of organized Labour, compels them to pay wages which are not earned by the proceeds of industry and places them at a disadvantage or supposed disadvantage with foreign competitors who pay lower wages.

This has had two principal results. It has accelerated the process of finding machine substitutes for Labour, and led to a rising demand for Protection, with the double object of sheltering the home manufacturer from the foreign competitor and giving back to him in increased prices some part of what he is paying in higher wages. This demand, though resisted to the last by its Liberal members, was conceded by the Cabinet of the National Government in 1932. It will only be possible to judge the result when the currency problems of the world have been solved, and the numerous other factors besides tariffs which now enter into world prices have been reduced to order. Whether for good or evil the departure is a momentous one for a country which depends so largely as Great Britain on its shipping and exports.

2

In spite of the severe unemployment of the years since the war, the general standard of living has sensibly improved as compared with the pre-war period. The family income has greatly increased; food and clothing are of better quality, more money is available for amusement and sport than ever before. Inadequate as it may be by any standard of prosperity, the allowance of the unemployed man is very often higher than the wage of the employed labourer twenty years ago. All this has been rendered possible by the increased productivity of industry, and, with whatever anomalies and shortcomings, unemployment insurance has greatly helped to carry the country through one of the most difficult periods of its history. In 1933 an investigator into unemployment stirred public feeling by stating that six million people were short of food. Thirty years earlier (1903) Campbell-Bannerman, on the authority of Charles Booth, declared that twelve millions were " underfed and on the verge of starvation."

On the other side must be reckoned the concentrated suffering of the coal, cotton, ship-building and heavy industries where continuous unemployment not only inflicts great poverty, but depresses the spirits and weakens the fibre of the continuously unemployed. The closing of the doors to emigration which before the war provided a natural outlet for a considerable part of the surplus labour of the country has aggravated this evil, and though migration to new trades and districts affords some mitigation, there remains what threatens to be a chronic problem of surplus labour for the future to solve.

The prediction of nineteenth-century economists that the introduction of machinery would create new demands which would more than absorb the labour temporarily displaced by it, has been largely thwarted by the restrictive trade policies which have prevented the free marketing and exchange of goods. When the war ended, the industrial nations found themselves with a capacity for production considerably in excess of demand, and the universal attempt to correct this by confining the home market to the home producer has aggravated the mischief. The process of speeding up production, while constantly contracting the areas of supply, which has been characteristic of these years, has led inevitably to the piling up of surplus goods for which no market can be found, and which continually depresses prices. Currency and exchange difficulties which have followed from the attempt to pay international debts and reparations in a world which is largely closed to the traffic of goods, have greatly complicated the issue for the time being, but the problem of modern machine industry is unlikely to be solved even when these are disposed of, unless the free flow of goods and services between the nations is restored.

Another serious factor on the debit side of this account has been the shortage of houses since the war. This has compelled large numbers to live in conditions of discomfort and overcrowding who could well afford decent accommodation, if it were available. Not the least serious part of this problem is that overcrowding rapidly makes new slums, and to that extent frustrates the effort to overtake the shortage of good houses. It would be untrue to say that Governments have shirked the problem, but the cost of labour and the high price of building material have made it extremely difficult to provide houses at rents which are within the means of the wage-earners or which do not absorb an excessive part of their earnings. The check to the solution of the housing problem, which was making rapid progress before the year 1914 must be counted among the greatest social disasters of the war. It can only be hoped that the re-awakening of the public conscience about the evil and disgrace of the slums will give a new impetus to the housing movement.

3

The individualist theory which prevailed for the greater part of the nineteenth century was being undermined in all directions before it ended. The structure of industry was changing; factories of a new type were growing up which required large and steady markets at fixed prices for successful and economic working. Trusts, Combines and Cartels sought to supply these by creating monopolies and extinguishing competition, and correspondingly consumers sought protection from the State, which in many countries endeavoured to stem the movement by anti-Trust laws, but generally with little success. When the war came the conversion of industry to the making of munitions greatly accelerated this movement, and led to an immense increase of steam power and electric power and factories equipped for mass production. At the same time both employers and workmen had become familiarized with the control and co-ordination of industry on a large scale, with the result that large numbers of employers came to believe that the same methods under private management would be profitable in peace, and large numbers of workmen were more than ever convinced that public ownership and control was the right solution in peace as in war.

The old issue of Individualism v. Socialism thus suffered a profound change. The free competition of individuals or small units had few advocates in either camp. The contending theories were now " nationalization " and " rationalization," both seeking monopolies, the one under public, the other under private control, the one contending that the elimination of private profit is the key to an efficient industry and a just distribution of the product, the other that it will lead to an inefficient and bureaucratized industry imposing immense losses on the State. In practice neither theory excludes the other. The employer who stands for private profit demands subsidies, tariffs and quotas from the State; the miner who wishes the coal-mines to be nationalized stands out for freedom to bargain with the State and even to strike against it in defence of his own wage. Great industries under private control, like agriculture or iron or steel, submit to have plans imposed upon them by the State. " Planning " is now the watch-word of all parties, planning on a scale which requires the individual to submit himself to a superior authority, whether the State or an organization of his own trade, or a mixture of both.

Great Britain being the land of compromise, it is probable that she will pick and choose and adjust her methods to circum-stances that are changing more rapidly than ever before in the world's history. The British Socialist is ill at ease with his continental comrade who insists on the last letter of the Marxian doctrine, and the idea of "the class war" has so far made little appeal to him. Whatever may be the arguments on one side or the other, the enormous hazards of sudden change in a highly developed society are brought home to every Government as soon as it gets into office, for just in proportion as it threatens credit, it deprives itself of the sinews of war. If there appeared in the world a Communistic State which provided greater happiness and prosperity for the mass of its people than other States basing their systems on private profit, Great Britain would no doubt be profoundly affected by its example, but if on the other hand deep poverty and chronic shortage of the necessaries and amenities of life are seen to attend these experi-ments, she is unlikely to be tempted by any theory to be lured into following them.

4

In the later years of this period party warfare has been greatly influenced by the change in the material which politicians have been required to handle. This in home affairs has been predominantly economic, and has tended to shape the issue as one between a Conservative party standing for the existing system of capital and credit and a Labour party demanding fundamental changes. The Liberal party, meanwhile, has found itself in the difficult position of being easily outbidden by the Labour party as an advocate of change, and having no desire to compete with the Conservative party as a champion of the existing order. It is quite possible that the reconciliation, for which Liberalism stands, between the two extremes is what the majority of English people most desire, but it is in danger of being without the organized expression necessary to make it practical politics. One possible remedy was suggested by the Speaker's Conference of 1916, which proposed that in a block of the larger constituencies elections should be held under proportional representation—a method which would give the electors an opportunity of returning candidates who are neither Conservatives nor Socialists. This has, so far, been rejected by the other parties, but the electioneering experience of the last few years suggests the need of some corrective to the violent swings of opinion which are encouraged by the present electoral system. The swollen majorities which accompany these swings have in recent years robbed Parliament of much of its interest in the public eye, and made it impossible for Opposition parties to perform their proper rôle of sustained criticism.

Great Britain is so far uninfected by the anti-Liberal and anti-parliamentary example set by Fascists and Communists in other countries, and her parliamentary institutions, having a far longer history and much deeper roots than those of most other countries, may be expected to resist them. But both the Labour and the Conservative parties have extreme groups which proclaim their hostility to parliamentary and constitutional methods, and it has become the fashion with some intellectuals like Mr. Bernard Shaw to speak derisively of Parliaments and Cabinets. To reform what is cumbrous, obsolete, or dilatory in the procedure of Parliament and make the technique of government conform to the rapidly changing material of politics is the proper answer to these assailants, and the British genius for developing institutions according to needs should be equal to this task.

Any precise forecast is impossible. Parties may divide and re-form under pressure of events in ways unthought of at the present time. Foreign affairs may rudely interrupt the course of domestic politics. Parliamentary institutions which are far from final in their present form, may be developed to meet the new economic conditions and to reflect a greater variety of opinion. The British genius for adaptation to circumstances without too much regard for political theory is unlikely to be exhausted. Indeed it may truly be said of these times that there never was so much awareness of political problems, or such serious and honest endeavour to find solutions. All our political parties have their " brain-trusts "; all are constantly engaged in producing plans, programmes, and constructive policies for the judgment of the public and instruction of Governments. To cure the confusion of politics by planning ahead is now the universal aspiration, and it is not likely to be quenched either by unexpected consequences, when plans are put into operation, or by the persistent habit of the public in thinking more of the sins of an outgoing Government than of the programmes of those who aspire to succeed it. This intense awareness of the problems lying ahead is a new fact of great promise for the future, but it needs to be corrected and fortified by some study of the past, and not least of the years which have specially contributed to the shaping of these problems.

INDEX

INDEX

Sonnino, Baron, 214
South Africa, 32-5, 77-8, 99-102
South Africa, Union of, 99, 124
South African Committee, 33-5
South African War, 40, 42 *et seq.*, 48-52, 114
South Pole, 134
South-West Africa, 19
Soviet Movement, 212, 258, 260, 262
Spa Conference, 222
Spain, 20, 84
Spartacists, 262
Speaker's Conference, 147, 308
Spee, Admiral von, 197
Spion Kop, 44
Stack, Sir Lee, 252
Standard, The, 41
Stead, W. T., 39-40
Stresemann, Gustav, 263, 286
Sturdee, Admiral, 197
Submarine Warfare, 192, 201-4, 229
Sudan, 14, 21, 36-8, 251-2
Suez Canal, 85, 175, 216, 251
" Supreme Council," 232, 240
" Supreme War Council," 217
" Suspensory Veto," 96, 122
Suvla Bay, 183
Switzerland, 212, 214
Syria, 232-3, 249

TALIEN-WAN, 38
Tangier, 65, 85
Tanks, Introduction of, 209
Tannenberg, battle of, 174
Tanta, 249
Tariff Reform, 120
Third International, 278
Thomas, J. H., 282
Thomson, Brigadier-General Birdwood, 282
Thrace, Eastern, 264-6
Three Emperors' League, 7-9, 11
Tigris, River, 175
Tirpitz, Admiral von, 51, 84, 116
Togoland, 19
Tonquin, 11
Townshend, General, 187
Toynbee, Arnold, 54
Trade Boards Bill, 303
Trade Union Bill, 294, 299
Trade Union Movement, 289-90, 292, 294-5, 303
Trades Disputes Bill, 93, 95, 303
Transvaal, 32-3, 42-3, 45, 78, 99-101, 124
Transylvania, 193
Trevelyan, Sir C. P., 282
Trialism, 155
Trianon, Treaty of, 231, 237

Trieste, 186
Triple Alliance, 9-11, 13, 17, 28, 55, 63, 151, 156, 159
Tripoli, 151
Trotsky, L. D., 267
Tunis, 9, 20, 151
Turkey, 2, 7-9, 13, 18, 85, 108, 110-12, 148, 150-2, 154, 174-5, 179, 181-3, 187, 216, 222, 228 *n.*, 229-30, 232, 242, 248, 255, 264-8, 286
Tyrol, 233

UGANDA, 20
Ukraine, 213, 258-9
Ulster, 139-45, 189, 243, 245
" Unauthorized Programme," 14
Unemployment, 299 300
Unemployment Insurance, 300, 303-4
United States, 31, 90, 201, 203, 209, 215, 222, 231 *n.*, 232-3, 236, 244, 246-7, 271-4, 295-6, 298
Upper Nile, 20, 29

VALERA, Eamon de, 243-6
Venezuela, 31
Venizelos, Eleutherios, 152, 265-6
Verdun, 172, 190, 192, 207
Vereeniging, Conference of, 47
Vereeniging, Treaty of, 99
Versailles, 217-18, 229
Versailles, Treaty of, 231, 234, 242, 262
Vesle, River, 172-3
Victoria, Queen, 21, 25, 35-6, 51-3
" Victory Parliament," 226
Vienna, 207
Vimy Ridge, 186, 208

WALFISH BAY, 19
" War-Guilt " Clause, 238-9
Warsaw, 261
Washington Conference, 246-7
Webb, Sidney, 282
Wedgwood, Josiah, 282
Wei-Hai-Wei, 39
Weimar, Republic, 262
Welsh Disestablishment, 27, 126
Westminster Gazette, 40
Westminster, Statute of, 274, 276
West-Ridgeway, Sir Joseph, 100
Wheatley, John, 282
" White " Russians, 260
William I, Emperor of Germany, 12
William II, Emperor of Germany, 12-13, 28, 33, 39, 51-2, 61, 64-7, 84-5, 90, 108-9, 113-16, 149, 155, 157-8,